To Floyd:
May you enjoy
this bit of town
history — as you
recover.

Bill + Doris

D1714636

the challenge of change

Edwin Collins

L. Russell Mayn

Eleanor S. Hines

Joseph A. Rarus

Mona Piotrowski

Ruth E. Bredge

Anthony A. Secondo

Mary B. O'Neil

the
challenge of
change

three centuries of
Enfield, Connecticut history

RUTH BRIDGE, *Editor*

published for the
ENFIELD HISTORICAL SOCIETY
by
 PHOENIX PUBLISHING
Canaan, New Hampshire

The Challenge of Change
  Bibliography: p. 297
  Includes index.
    1. Enfield, Conn.—History.   I. Bridge, Ruth E.,
1899-   II. Enfield Historical Society.
F104.E4C46   974.6'2   77-7148
ISBN 0-914016-43-1

Copyright 1977 by the Enfield Historical Society, Inc.

All rights reserved. No part of this publication may be
reproduced, stored in a retrieval system or transmitted in any
form or by any means without the prior written permission
of the publisher, except for brief quotations in a review.

Printed in the United States of America
by Courier Printing Company
Binding by New Hampshire Bindery
Design by A.L. Morris

Contents

Foreword

UP TO THE PRESENT TIME the only available history of the town of Enfield, Connecticut, has been the three volume history compiled by Francis Olcott Allen in 1900, of which only 250 copies were printed. This consists mainly of transcripts of the records of the town from the earliest days to about 1850. It is a valuable source of information but difficult to use for several reasons. It is not a chronological narrative that progresses through the years in an orderly fashion, and both diction and spelling differ from what is customary today. Spelling had not been standardized and every man spelled as seemed best to him. It is possible to find fourteen different ways of spelling Connecticut.

Consequently there has been need for a book easier to use and one that gives an account of the years from 1850 to the present. The Bicentennial Commission of the town initiated this project as a fitting way to commemorate the two hundred years of the independence of the United States.

At the request of the Bicentennial Commission a committee to undertake this work was formed as follows:

Ruth E. Bridge, Chairman	Mary E. Malley
Mary B. O'Neill, Co-Chairman	F. Russell Meyer
Edwin H. Collins	Mona M. Piotrowski
John M. DeBell	Joseph A. Rarus
Eleanor S. Hines	Clarissa H. Stow
Rev. Edward W. Johnson	Edward N. Thompson

Introduction

I T WOULD BE PRESUMPTUOUS to think that this story of a venerable town is a complete history. Hopefully it will serve as an introduction to the town for those who have not known its past, a refreshing summary for readers familiar with Enfield, and through the bibliography, a guide for those who may want to investigate further.

We acknowledge at the outset that there are many omissions of persons and events which can be part of a larger project. At the same time some trivia has been intentionally included to add flavor.

It was appropriate that the Bicentennial Commission should focus on the proud and fascinating history of Enfield during a time when our nation was celebrating its past and looking ahead to the future. The Bicentennial Commission is grateful to the following civic organizations which have assisted the Commission in sponsoring the project: the Enfield Historical Society, the Martha A. Parson's Memorial Trust, the Women's Club of Enfield, and the Enfield Rotary Club.

Special gratitude is due Ruth E. Bridge who agreed to serve as editor and enlisted the aid of those writers whose names appear opposite the chapters listed in the table of contents. This book would not have been made possible without their tireless assistance.

A Publications Committee consisting of Edward C. Allen, Anthony S. Secondo, and Robert L. Tanguay worked with Miss Bridge and the publishers, Phoenix Publishing of Canaan, New Hampshire. The Enfield Historical Society agreed to assume responsibility for handling the distribution of the history after publication.

The Commission wishes to express its gratitude to the many citizens of Enfield who helped in innumerable ways to make this book possible.

American Revolution Bicentennial
Commission of Enfield, Connecticut, Inc.

the
challenge of
change

the
early
years $\Big|$ **1**

Muster of the past . . . Enfield's
Bicentennial Celebration, 1976

CHAPTER 1

INDIANS

THEIR ARTIFACTS AND CUSTOMS

THE FIRST MENTION of the Indians of Connecticut is in the account of the discovery and exploration of the Connecticut River in 1614 by the Dutch explorer Adriaen Block. He found an Indian village, or fort, in the present town of South Windsor. According to some accounts he stopped and had a meal with the Indians. He reported that beyond this point the river became shallower and rocky and was not navigable more than two leagues farther. Some writers interpret this to mean that he sailed as far as the Enfield rapids where he was forced to turn back.

In 1631 a sachem of the Connecticut River Indians traveled to Boston and Plymouth to encourage white settlers to make their homes in the Connecticut valley which he represented as a fine, rich land. His invitation was declined. Afterward it was found that the Pequots were then harassing the River tribes so that it would have been a great advantage to have white settlers in their territory. Two years later

Boston people refused to join Plymouth in a trading venture in this region partly because of the large number of warlike Indians there.

A deadly smallpox epidemic struck the River Indians in 1633-1634 and very few escaped it. The chief sachem and most of his family and friends died and the Indian population was greatly reduced.

The Pequot War came to a head in 1637 after an Indian attack on Wethersfield. Captain John Mason, at the head of ninety men from Hartford, Windsor, and Wethersfield, and with seventy Mohegan Indians led by Uncas, set out to vanquish them and succeeded to such a degree that the Pequots were never again a problem.

Later, in King Philip's War (1675) when a desperate attempt was made by the Indians of the region to destroy the English settlements and to rid their lands of the white men who were everywhere pushing them out, it was Toto, a River Indian, who informed the people of Windsor about the intended attack on Springfield just in time to warn them. Although much of Springfield was burned the consequences would have been much worse without previous knowledge of the Indian plot.

Most of the Indians of the South Windsor area were Podunks who lived on the east bank of the Connecticut near the mouth of the Podunk, a small tributary of the Connecticut. This was the tribe from whom the land of Enfield and Somers was bought.

Before the coming of the white men, Enfield and the surrounding region east of the Connecticut River was once the home of a numerous Indian population. Evidences of this have been found along the streams—the Scantic, the Buckhorn, Freshwater, and the smaller brooks, at Crescent Lake and Shaker Pines Lake, at a quicksand spring on the Gowdy farm in Wallop, on King's Island in the Connecticut River, and along the ridges to the east from Wilbraham to Ellington, wherever spring water was available.

All this territory has been explored for Indian artifacts by Martin E. and Edward N. Thompson of Hazardville. As small boys they hunted for arrowheads, sometimes finding them in plowed fields which origi-nally were cleared by Indians and used by them for cornfields. As they grew up the Thompson boys never lost their interest in Indian lore and their collection of artifacts grew. In later years they made a serious study of the area with two important excavations carried on in the years 1938 to 1941, and 1940 to 1945.

Evidence of the largest concentration of Indians in Enfield was found on high ground at some distance from the Scantic River, in the area east of where Raffia Road is now located.

Here the Scantic Indians had their main fort. It covered many acres and was protected by a stockade made of heaped-up sand reinforced with fallen trees. Remnants of this can be seen back of some of the houses on the street called Indian Run. In the southerly part of the fort a mound of earth was built up to a height of about twelve feet which was used as a lookout.

More than one hundred fire pits were discovered here, each of which presumably served one family. Artifacts and chips were found in such quantity as to suggest that this was a permanent settlement. These artifacts consisted of a variety of arrowheads and many kinds of stone tools that tell the story of how these people lived. There were hoes for cultivating the crops they raised, sinkers for their fish nets, gouges for shaping dugout canoes, scrapers for working on animal hides, and axe heads to use in cutting saplings for the framework of their lodges. Shards of pottery came to light and some fragments of a soapstone bowl.

One seldom—or never—hears of a hurricane being of help to anyone, but the 1938 hurricane washed away the whole side of a hill at this site and in doing so exposed two elaborate burials, each with thirty-five spear heads arranged in a sunburst pattern. One stone dish was found nearby and one highly decorated clay pot. Until a few years ago this clay pot was regarded as the finest decorated piece of Indian pottery found in New England. At a more recent excavation in the Branford area another was found with similar decoration. These outstanding finds suggest that some Indian of great importance was buried here. Since this site was the headquarters of the Scantic Indians one possibility is that one of the graves is that of their chief, Scitico. The Scantics were a clan of the Podunk tribe whose main fort was in South Windsor on the Podunk River.

The same hurricane toppled some large trees behind the Methodist Church in Hazardville and brought to light a smaller site with twenty-two fire pits, perhaps a fishing camp. Martin and Edward Thompson, with other members of the Connecticut Archeological Society, carried on excavations at this site during the years 1940-1945. Many artifacts were found here, mostly of slate, quartz and quartzite, and basalt, better known as trap rock. This basalt probably came from the range that runs through Suffield and Granby. Glacial pebbles are thought to be the source of the quartz and quartzite but the source of the slate is not known. The collection of artifacts from this site, along with an account of the work, was turned over to the Peabody Museum at Yale University.

A study of these sites and the artifacts they yielded tells much about the lives of the Scantic Indians. There was good land for farming in this territory and corn was an important crop eaten in many ways. They also raised beans and squash. We still enjoy one of their dishes which even retains its Indian name—succotash. Like present-day farmers they used fertilizers on their fields but what they used were wood ashes and fish.

Tobacco was also grown and pipes for smoking it were found. Most of these were of clay but there were some of steatite, or soapstone.

The forests supplied the Indians chestnuts, walnuts, blueberries, apples, watercress, and other fruits. Deer, bear, moose, otter, beaver, mink, and muskrat were abundant so there was plenty of meat to be had and there were furs and skins for clothing. The rivers were full of fish and in the spring shad and salmon came up the larger rivers to spawn.

The forests also offered material for Indian lodges. These were made with a framework of saplings covered with sheets of bark. They were either round like an igloo or shaped like a quonset hut with two flat sides. Each lodge had a smoke vent.

The clay deposits on the banks of the Scantic River were utilized for making clay pots for cooking and for drinking water. Every camp or lodge kept a clay pot full of water close at hand so there was no need to go down to the spring every time they wanted water. They knew of the steatite, or soapstone, quarry on Soapstone Mountain in Somers and the outcropping of steatite in Wilbraham. From these came material for cooking vessels.

Since in this region birch trees do not often grow large enough for canoes the Indians sometimes shaped dugouts from logs with their stone axes and hollowed them out with fire and stone gouges. In a meadow near the Scantic the Thompsons once found such a dugout canoe. It was deep in mud. When they had dug it out it proved to be about ten feet long and thirty inches wide, made of cedar.

The Scantic Indians had two means of communication, by smoke signals or by the sound of a drum. Their fort in Enfield gave them a view of Mount Tom to the north, and of Rattlesnake Mountain in Hampden to the east, so they could get smoke signals that would warn them of enemies coming down the Connecticut River or down the Chicopee River above Hampden. They also used runners to carry messages. The Scantic Indians lived in constant fear of their great enemies, the Pequots and the Mohawks.

All of these Indians seem to have had their own religious beliefs and ceremonies. A large Indian burial ground was discovered at the mouth of the Scantic River in South Windsor. Since all the shallow burials seem to have been made at about the same time it is probable that these Indians died in some epidemic, perhaps that of smallpox in 1633-1634. Many of these burials were of young Indians, one of a child whose grave also contained a small and intact clay pot. The articles placed in Indian graves lead to the conclusion that there was a belief in some sort of after-life where these articles would again be needed.

Enfield records are almost devoid of any mention of Indians with the exception of the purchase of the land, and the only Enfield citizen who was present at the signing of the deed was John Pease, Sr. Now and then the name "wigwam meadow" crops up in reference to some piece of land near the Scantic. Early traders may have come across some Indians for one artifact not of Indian origin was found at the site of the Enfield fort, a Spanish coin of 1636. A hole had been bored through it so that it could be worn as a pendant. But as a tribe the Scantics must have disappeared before the settlers arrived and the settlers no doubt regarded this as a piece of great good luck.

CHAPTER 2

THE FIRST SETTLERS

THE FIRST SETTLERS of Enfield came from a group whose families had crossed the ocean to a life that they knew would be one of hardship and deprivation compared to what they had known in England. But the unsettled country offered them a chance to pursue their ideals and regulate their lives without the restrictions and possible persecution of a government that had no sympathy with their aspirations. Religion was a motivating force in their lives, the background of much of their thinking. Their beliefs determined the basis of Enfield's government and climate of life for many years.

To insure the success of their ideas, in Enfield's early days—as in many other towns—no grant of land would be made to a man who did not subscribe to their principles and share their ideas of right living. Also, any inhabitant who proved to be an undesirable citizen would be escorted to the town boundary and warned out of town.

Their concern that children should be taught to read at an early age stemmed from the importance they placed on the ability to understand the Bible and the laws of God. No other subject except writing is mentioned as having been taught in the first school and it was some years later that arithmetic and other subjects make their appearance. In some of the colonies colleges were founded very early—Harvard in 1639, William and Mary in 1693, Yale in 1701—in order to have educated preachers who could read the scriptures in the original Hebrew and Greek. Of Enfield's first five ministers, two were graduates of Harvard, two of Yale, and one of Williams.

The land upon which the Enfield settlement was made belonged to the town of Springfield, settled in 1636 under the leadership of William Pynchon. He had come to America in 1630, one of the group that accompanied Winthrop. He settled first at Dorchester, then moved to Roxbury where he engaged in the fur trade. From 1632 to 1634 he was treasurer of the Massachusetts Bay Colony, but he resigned in 1634 to go to the Connecticut Valley where conditions for carrying on the fur trade were better. He was very successful in this business, treated the Indians fairly, and was always on good terms with them. Eight families came with Pynchon and he bought land on both sides of the Connecticut River at Agawam for his new town, eventually settling on the east bank.

In 1647 the General Court of Massachusetts added a large territory to the Springfield settlement. This included the present towns of Westfield, Suffield, part of Southwick, West Springfield, Holyoke, Agawam, Chicopee, Enfield, Somers, Wilbraham, Ludlow, Longmeadow, and Hampden. Gradually the population spread out into this great empty tract of land that surrounded Springfield on all sides. In 1669 Westfield was settled, Hatfield followed in 1670, then Deerfield and Brookfield in 1673, Suffield in 1674, and Enfield in 1680.

So, with Windsor, Wethersfield, and Hartford already well established along the Connecticut River to the south when the first families arrived at Freshwater Plantation, as Enfield was then called, there were towns within reasonable distance in every direction except to the east. There lay an unknown wilderness with no habitations for many miles until in 1687 the town of Woodstock was founded by a group of pioneers from Roxbury. From then on the road to the east was known as the road to Woodstock.

Before 1680 there had already been some activity in the Freshwater Brook area. In 1653-1654 John Pynchon had been granted fifty acres of land between Freshwater Brook and Grape Brook. A number of grants of meadow land were made in the 1660s and one grant of land

"to keep swine." A little later Pynchon was granted an additional fifty acres provided he built a saw mill within three years. This is probably the saw mill on Freshwater Brook that was burned by Indians during King Philip's War. Through the years a few more men were given grants of meadow land until for August 4, 1679, this entry appears: "Arrangements made for settling lands at Freshwater Brook."

To carry out these arrangements Springfield appointed a committee of five men to undertake the business of granting land at Freshwater Plantation to new settlers. This news must soon have reached Salem for in the autumn of that year two young men who were living there, John Pease, Jr., and Robert Pease, came to look over this land. Tradition has it that they spent the winter in a hut dug into the side of a hill somewhere in the vicinity of the present Enfield cemetery. They must have been favorably impressed with the land offered, for the following summer they came back with their families and were the first to be granted land. They were followed in the next three years by about thirty other settlers mostly from Salem.

In December of 1680 the business of laying out the streets and highways of the new settlement was tackled. John Pease, Jr., who was a surveyor by profession, laid out the town plat and the highways. The main street which we know as Enfield Street was to be twelve rods wide. From the present South Road to Post Office Road the street was twenty rods wide to provide a parade ground for the militia. Three highways were provided to the east and two to the west. The latter two gave access to the river, one leading to the ferry crossing and the other to the Deep Hole where the fishing was especially good. Through the years other roads were added as more families moved in and the need arose. Each man was expected to clear the brush from the road in front of his lot as far as the middle of the road and to keep it clear. Trees growing along the streets were to be preserved "both for shade and comeliness."

In 1679 when plans were being formulated for laying out home lots, sixty or seventy acres were to be set apart for the use of the ministry and the church, and forty acres for the support of a school. There were also lots to be reserved for some useful persons. The useful person in one case was a blacksmith according to the following:

1699   The town for the encouragement of a smith do engage and grant to Andrew Miller a house lot lying by the middle highway which is a reserved lot, and also fifty acres of land belonging thereto, with a proportion of meadow, all is granted to said Miller upon condition he come and live on it and do the work of a smith for the town serving the town in the work seven years.

Genesis . . . the Enfield Street
Cemetery where history began in
the winter of 1680.

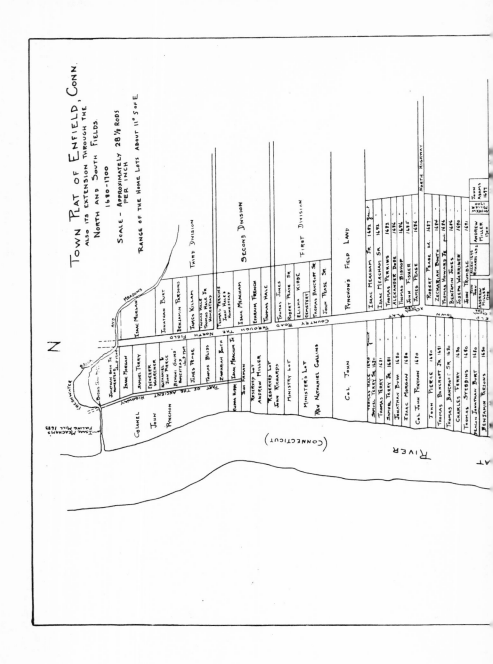

TOWN PLAT OF ENFIELD, CONN.
ALSO ITS EXTENSION THROUGH THE
NORTH AND SOUTH FIELDS
1680-1700
SCALE - APPROXIMATELY 28½ RODS
PER INCH
RANGE OF THE HOME LOTS ABOUT 11° S OF E.

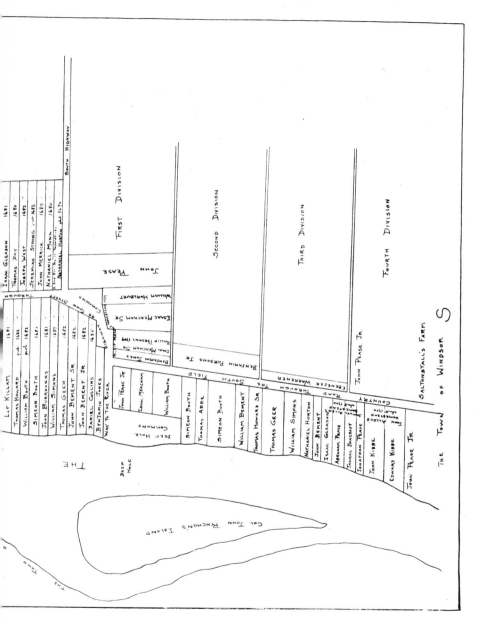

First known map of Enfield drawn in 1680

Parsons' House, built by John Meacham in 1782, from a photo taken about 1909 with sisters, Mary A. and Martha Parsons in foreground.

In 1712 a piece of land at the lower end of the town was granted to Philip Parsons on condition of his setting up a tan yard there. Thus men who could supply some service vital to the town were induced to settle.

As early as 1681 a plan was worked out for raising the money to pay the Indians for the land. It was decided that each settler should pay three pence an acre to Major Pynchon who would manage the business with the Podunk Indians.

The actual deed is dated March 16, 1688, and is signed by the Indian chief, Totaps, alias Notatuck, who made his mark, and by John Pynchon as well as three Indian witnesses and three Springfield men. The boundaries of the land were Asnuntuck (or Freshwater) Brook on the north, the Connecticut River on the west, and Poggotoffine or Saltonstall's Brook on the south. The land was to run from the river east to the mountains, a distance of about eight miles. The price paid was twenty-five pounds sterling. The Indians retained the right to hunt and fish on the land.

Totaps, alias Notatuck

his | □   L   mark

The land from Freshwater Brook north to Longmeadow Brook, which is also part of the town of Enfield, is not included in this deed as it already belonged to Springfield, having been bought from the Agawam Indians some years before.

In 1683 the population had reached a point where the settlement seemed large enough to be a town in its own right. Consequently, with the consent of Springfield, a petition was sent to the General Court of Massachusetts which was to meet in Boston on May 16 of that year asking that the Plantation at Freshwater Brook be made a township in its own right, to be called Enfield. This petition was granted.

In the same year, John Pease, Jr., was chosen constable, the first Enfield settler to hold office. The first Enfield Selectmen were John Pease, Sr., Isaac Meacham, Sr., and Isaac Morgan who were appointed by the Springfield Committee in 1684 to carry on the affairs of the town to the best of their judgment when members of the Springfield Committee were not available.

In 1692 the only two remaining members of the Springfield Committee turned over their book of records to the Town of Enfield which was now on its own.

After the main settlement of Enfield Street on the ridge just east of the river, the next section of the town to attract people was the mountainous land near the eastern boundary. Much of the land between Enfield Street and the mountains was low and swampy and covered with thick woods. This tract was regarded as an unhealthful place because of the danger of malaria, so people preferred to live up in the hills. Even now there are cellar holes scattered about this area which show where some of the early houses stood. Deep in the woods, as some of them are, it is difficult to imagine that the surrounding land once included plowed fields. The soil must have been poor and thin compared to that of the Connecticut Valley and in time erosion must have taken its toll. Perhaps that is one reason many of these hillside farms were abandoned.

The first man to venture out east was Benjamin Jones. He and his family spent several summers there in the early 1700s, returning to Enfield for the winter. Eventually they moved there permanently. Other settlers followed and that part of the town became known as the East Precinct, which in 1734 became the Town of Somers.

About 1713 people began to spread out into other parts of the town to the sections we know as Scitico, Wallop, and Jabbok or Shaker Pines. By 1720 the whole township was thinly settled. This was rapid progress for those days.

Although King Philip's War was over before the settlement at Enfield was begun, the memory of it must have remained. Later, off and on for many years, there were surprise raids on the small frontier towns to the north, the most notable being the attack on Deerfield in 1704. Frantic calls for help would sometimes be sent as far as Hartford. Against this background the Enfield citizens apparently did not feel entirely secure, for a place of refuge called a fort was constructed on land east of Enfield Street and north of Oliver Road. A stockade enclosing about an acre of land was erected. There was a small brook running through this tract and a well was dug for a water supply. But there is no evidence that the fort, so-called, was ever used.

For many years the boundary between Massachusetts and Connecticut was in dispute. Massachusetts based her claim upon the survey of Woodward and Saffery made in 1642. This survey Connecticut refused to accept, alleging that the boundary line was too far south, and in 1695 had another survey made. This, in turn, Massachusetts refused to accept. Enfield along with Suffield and most of Woodstock lay between the two lines. As early as 1704 the subject of breaking away from Massachusetts and joining Connecticut came up in town meeting.

The town by a clere voat doe yeld themselves to be under conettecoat thir goverment & furder voat that the select men with others shall signifie the Town's mind in that matter to conettecotts authority.

This met with no response and the matter dragged on for years. Finally in 1749 Enfield, Suffield, Somers, and Woodstock became part of Connecticut.

food and shelter

During the first hard years the settlers must have depended a great deal on food from hunting and fishing and the gathering of wild fruits and plants. The eastern part of the town was a favorite hunting ground. The records tell of deer, bear, wolves, and catamount in the mountains. Every spring the shad came up the Connecticut River and in those days there were also salmon to be had. Trout could be found in the smaller streams. In spring great flocks of passenger pigeons flew over the land. The pigeons and shad, coming as they did at the end of the winter when supplies were sometimes low, were a godsend. Wild berries and fruits must have been more than welcome in their season and many wild plants whose use is being revived today were probably well known.

Of necessity, every man—even the minister—was a farmer though he may also have had some other occupation. Grants of land to early settlers included fields and meadows as well as the home lot.

An idea of the crops raised in Enfield after the town was well established can be had from a list of 1738 showing the value of each item. It was customary, as money was scarce, to make payments in kind. This list is taken from town meeting records.

Voted to pay the town debts in the species following

in wheet	at 10s	pr bushel
Rie	at 7s 6d	pr bushel
Indian corn	at 5s	pr bushel
barly	at 7s 6d	pr bushel
oats	at 3s	pr bushel
flax	at 1s 6d	pr bushel
*Hemp	at 1s	pr bushel
Pease	at 10s	pr bushel
pork	at 0s 8d	pr pound
Iron	at 3 £	pr 100
Boards	at 3 £ 10s	pr 1000

* Hemp was raised for making candle wicks.

One of our most common foods, the potato, was unknown until about 1720. But to take its place there was corn whose culture and use had been learned from the Indians. It was eaten in a great variety of ways including hasty pudding (which is like a porridge), succotash, johnny cake, and other ways not familiar to us today. Another Indian plant that was found useful by the early settlers of New England was the pumpkin. This too was used in many different ways. It could be dried and would keep a long time.

For fruit, apple and peach orchards were set out and many quinces were raised.

Farm animals were a valuable possession. Oxen and horses were work animals, while cattle, sheep, and swine provided meat and milk, as well as leather and wool for clothing.

The town had enclosed fields called commons where farmers in the neighborhood could keep their animals. Fence viewers were appointed to see that the commons were well fenced since any animal at large could do great damage to crops. Each farmer had a distinctive ear mark or brand, registered with the town, to identify his stock. Stray animals were taken to the nearest pound and kept there until claimed by the owner. Every section of the town had a pound with some nearby farmer as the pound keeper.

No trace of these pounds remains but the road in Hazardville whose name was changed to Park Street some few years ago is still known to old inhabitants by its former name of Pound Road. An old map shows this pound at the corner of what is now called Park Street and Hazard Avenue. Another pound was located on Town Farm Road somewhere between Abbe Road and Broad Brook Road, but no one knows exactly where.

Of the earliest houses in Enfield there is no record. It is only tradition that tells of the Pease brothers' dugout. There may have been other habitations of this general type as these dugouts or cave homes were not uncommon in early settlements. There could also have been some log houses but, of whatever kind, these places were very crude by our standards.

A typical pioneer home of those days had one room with a loft above reached by a ladder. It would have had a dirt floor or one of split logs laid flat side up, called a puncheon floor. Oiled paper was sometimes used in the small windows instead of glass, which was expensive and hard to come by. Sometimes there were wooden shutters in the windows. There would have been no running water—just a well outside or perhaps a nearby spring; no sink, just a bench or table to hold the basin and pails for washing; no stove, only a fireplace for cooking and heat. There were few articles of furniture in the first homes and most of these were home made—a bench, a stool or two, a chest, perhaps a bed that folded up against the wall when not in use.

As time went on, larger and better homes were constructed but with all the mechanical aids we have today it is difficult to realize the immense amount of hard labor that went into the building of a house of the Revolutionary era. An article written in 1925 has this to say:

It was no easy matter in those early days to get together the material for a house. The great timbers, mostly of oak, were all prepared by hand, likewise the clapboards and shingles. The frames were held together by wooden pegs or pins and even the nails were hand made.

It is interesting to note in this connection that for several years an inspector of nails was elected along with the usual town officials.

The larger homes built when people were more prosperous were of course better furnished. Usually there was a large fireplace with an oven built into it at one side.

In some homes meals were served on a table board laid on trestles. This could be taken apart when the meal was over and put aside. A salt dish would have been in the center of the table. Some families may have had a pewter platter or two for serving dishes. For everyday cooking there were iron kettles to hang on the crane in the fireplace and a bake kettle, which was an iron pan on legs with a cover and a long handle, to use on the hearth. Meat could be roasted on a spit. Once or twice a week there would be a baking day when the oven was used. First a fire had to be built in the oven and kept going until the oven was thoroughly heated. Then the ashes were raked out. Foods that took the longest time to bake, like a pot of beans, were put at the back with use of a long-handled wooden shovel called a peel. Then other foods were put in and the oven closed.

At night the fireplace furnished some light. Other ways of providing light were with pine knots called candlewood, Betty lamps which were shallow receptacles with wicks that burned grease or oil, and candles. Making candles and soap were essential tasks of the housewife.

The spinning wheel was always going, for the housewife was responsible for clothing her family. She could not solve the problem by going to a store and buying cloth. She started with a fleece sheared from a sheep, which had to be cleaned of bits of leaves, sticks, etc., then thoroughly washed. The next step was dyeing it, but the housewife first had to make the dye. Next it was carded—which meant pulling it smooth between two paddles with wire teeth. It was finally ready to spin into yarn. The yarn was woven into cloth and whatever garment was needed could then be cut out and sewed together.

If linen cloth was needed, one started with flax plants, and there were many more steps in preparing the flax for spinning. Some of them which required more strength than most women possessed were done by men.

Little girls were taught to knit at about five years of age and could then help to make stockings for the family. A little later they were taught spinning and when they were tall enough they learned to weave.

church and school

As aforementioned, when the town plot was laid out a tract was reserved as ministry land to be used for the benefit of a church. Settlers who accepted grants of land were under obligation to establish a church and support a minister. In 1683 it was decided to erect a small building twenty-by-twenty that could be used as a meeting place on the Sabbath. There the people planned to assemble both morning and afternoon for services led by one of the prominent men of the settlement since they had no minister. This meetinghouse was somewhere in the vicinity of the present Enfield Street Cemetery.

In 1684 the town was taken to court in Springfield because it had no minister. When it was explained that efforts were being made to find one the town was excused.

Not until five years later was Enfield successful in finding a young man who agreed to fill this position—the Reverend Nathaniel Welch of Charleston—but before he could be installed or move his family to Enfield he died, at the age of twenty-three years.

Four years later, with the town still lacking a preacher, plans were made to encourage some young man to come here to settle for his lifetime, as the custom was then. He would be given a home lot with dwelling house, field and meadow land of which six acres would be cleared for him, and an orchard would be planted. Also he would be supplied with firewood.

No one was found to take advantage of these provisions until 1699 when the Reverend Nathaniel Collins of Middletown came to Enfield as the first minister. His salary was to be seventy pounds yearly. Every man sixteen years and older was to give him one day's work each year for four years. To this last provision all agreed except four or five persons. Enfield always had its dissenters. Mr. Collins served as minister until 1724 when he resigned. From 1729 to 1735 he was the town clerk. He died in 1756 and is buried in the Enfield Cemetery. He had a large family and some of his descendants are living in Enfield at the present time.

On part of the house lot granted to Mr. Collins the Martha Parsons House now stands, and there the first parsonage was built. It is thought that when the present structure was built in 1782 the first parsonage was used as an ell. When the present ell was built, probably some time in the 1860s, the old one was demolished.

The church and what it stood for played a large part in the lives of Enfield's early citizens. The Sabbath began at sundown on Saturday and from then until sundown on Sunday no unnecessary work was done. There was a long preaching service in the morning and another in the afternoon with an hour or so at midday for lunch. Sermons were at least two hours long, the time measured by an hour glass on the pulpit. No churches were heated in those days and in winter it must have been an ordeal to sit through those long services. But no one who was physically able stayed away.

Many had to walk or ride horseback long distances. The settlers living in the East Precinct, as Somers was called, found it so difficult to get to the meeting house in winter that in 1721 they were allowed to have their own services during the winter months. Later, in 1727, the Somers Congregational Church was organized. It was located on land now part of the North Cemetery on Springfield Road.

If you can imagine what it would be like to walk from Somers to Enfield and back in the dead of winter with only a trail to follow through the snow, or to ride horseback, you have some idea of what these people endured to get to a church service.

Jonathan Edwards' sermon, "Sinners in the Hands of an Angry God," preached at Enfield in 1741, is an extreme expression of the harsh religion of his day. But because the ideas he expressed so vividly were generally accepted it is no wonder that people were preoccupied with religion and their own salvation. Then too, the importance of religion must have been brought home to them by the great uncertainty of life and the recurring presence of death in their midst. So little was known in the fields of medicine and sanitation that to fall seriously ill was almost a death warrant. The ordinary childhood diseases which in our time have practically disappeared were a real scourge then. Statistics record many deaths of babies and little children, and old graveyards have many small stones with pathetic epitaphs carved on them:

Lie still sweet babe
And take your rest,
God called thee home,
He thought it best.

****

O what is life! tis like a flower
That blossoms and is gone;
It flourishes its little hour
With all its beauty on.
Death came, and like a wintry day
It cut the lovely flower away.

Next in importance after providing for a meeting house and a preacher was the matter of a school. In 1647 Massachusetts had passed a law that every town of fifty families should provide a schoolmaster to teach the children to read and write. This would have applied to Enfield as part of Massachusetts but it was probably some years after the establishment of the town before there were fifty families in Enfield. Meanwhile parents were supposed to see that their children were taught reading and writing.

It was not until 1702 that Enfield voted "that the town have a schoolmaster," and the next year John Richards was invited to keep school and teach the children five to nine years old. His salary was to be fourteen pounds yearly and he was to have twenty acres of land if he came. There was no school building at that time so if he actually did come to Enfield he must have kept school in some house.

The town voted to build a schoolhouse in 1708 and "to set it in the most convenient place in the street." It was sixteen-by-eighteen feet and must have been the only such building for some years though there are indications that the outlying districts were not forgotten. Now and then records mention the school being moved to some other location for a limited time so that no part of the town would be deprived. This probably means that the schoolmaster moved around. Such an arrangement was called a moving school.

In 1754 it was voted to build five schoolhouses and 500 pounds was voted to take care of this building program. They were located in—
Wallop—upon a hill called College Hill
Scitico—near James Ferman's, in the most convenient place
South End—near Joseph Hall's barn
Middle of the town—place where it has always stood

North End—near John French's, in the most convenient place

There was nothing compulsory about children attending school in those days. The town provided a schoolmaster and a building and it was up to the parents whether their children took advantage of this opportunity. As to school supplies, so essential today, nothing of the kind is mentioned simply because there were none. The family geese provided the quill pens for writing and it was part of a teacher's job to sharpen these pens as needed. Ink was home made, paper scarce. What they wrote on is a question. In some towns we hear of birch bark having been used. Slates did not come into use until later and blackboards were unheard of. Lessons were taught mostly by rote. The schoolmaster may have had a primer and some of the children may have had a hornbook. This latter was not really a book but consisted of a single sheet of paper fastened to a thin piece of wood and covered with a bit of horn. On the paper was printed the alphabet, some syllables for practice, and the Lord's Prayer. Books of any kind were rare and precious but every family had a Bible and many children learned to read from that. It was not until after the Revolution that textbooks began to make their appearance. One of the first was Noah Webster's famous Spelling Book published in 1783.

The following description of an Enfield school of the 1770s is taken from a paper written for the Centennial of 1876:

Each school, there were five in town at that time, contained one room, with desks fastened to one side of the room for writers, who sat upon benches made of heavy planks supported on legs. The small children sat upon low benches of planks laid upon blocks. The rooms were warmed by fireplaces supplied with wood furnished by the parents of the children.

(The desks fastened to one side of the room were like a long slanting shelf. The children using them faced away from the center of the room.)

slaves, travel, and customs

Now and then when reading the Enfield records of years long past one comes upon mention of a Negro, or "a man of color," as these people were often called. These items are mostly found in the town and church lists of baptisms, marriages, and deaths. Usually not much information can be gleaned from these terse, matter-of-fact statements but they do show that Enfield had a small number of colored inhabitants from early years.

In 1680 it was estimated there were about thirty slaves in all Connecticut. These had come from Barbados, sometimes three or four a year. The slave trade must have increased as the years went by for Sanford in his *History of Connecticut* tells of a cargo of slaves being brought up the river to Middletown and lodged in the jail to be sold at auction. By 1774 when the white population of Connecticut numbered 191,392 there were 5,085 Negroes and 1,363 Indians.

Also in 1774, Connecticut forbade further importation of slaves and provided that Negroes born after March 1, 1784, were to be free at the age of twenty-five. Six years later Enfield appointed a committee to go to the next Assembly with a petition that "the Negrows in the State be released from their Slavary and Bondage." This thinking was ahead of its time and nothing came of it. The census of 1790 showed that Connecticut had 2,759 slaves and 2,801 free Negroes.

A few of the Enfield Negroes are designated as "my negro Coffee," "Flora a black woman belonging to Mr. Prudden," "Caesar a negro belonging to Capt. Pease," leading one to conclude that these were slaves. On the other hand there was apparently a whole family of colored people by the name of Freeman, one of whom was a blacksmith, evidently free Negroes.

One item of special interest is an 1848 record that tells of the death of John Buke (or Buker), a colored man and a Revolutionary pensioner, age ninety-five.

The Connecticut River offered early settlers a ready-made highway and an easy method of travel. The rapids at Enfield prevented large boats from going farther up the river but small boats could be poled over the rapids. William Pynchon of Springfield, who was engaged in the fur trade, early built a warehouse on the east side of the river below the rapids. There goods could be changed either to carts or to small boats and continue to Springfield, hence the name Warehouse Point.

On the original map of the town plot one of the roads leading west to the Connecticut River is designated as Ferry Lane. Until the first bridge was built across the river in 1808 this ferry provided a way of reaching Suffield and other towns to the west. The land south of Ferry Lane was the home lot granted to Lot Killam in 1681. In recent years this land belonged to the Edgar family and is at present owned by Mrs. Tart. A small brick building facing south some yards west of Enfield Street (once a blacksmith shop) is the only indication of the old road to the ferry.

Another ferry near the mouth of Freshwater Brook must have been started prior to 1778 because in that year the town sent two men to the

General Assembly "to try to get the ferry now in Isaac Kibbe's hands to be established for the town of Enfield." This ferry was north of Freshwater.

Until the close of the Revolution the most common ways of getting from one place to another were walking and by horseback. With a pillion, which was a sort of cushion attached to the back of a saddle, a horse could carry two persons. Carriages were rare in Enfield though a few persons owned chaises which were two-wheeled carriages. Not many farmers owned even a farm wagon or a cart. Roads were very poor, more like trails, full of brush and anything but smooth. "Working on the road" simply meant cutting the brush, not at the sides of the road as today, but clearing the road itself.

An interesting sidelight on early travel is the fact that when the third meeting house was built in 1775 (our Old Town Hall) the agreement specified that it should be "complete with stepstones." These stepstones were what we know as horse blocks, and churches in those days commonly had a row of them in front of the building for the convenience of those who arrived on horseback.

When the present Congregational Church was built in 1848 roads were better and carriages more common. So instead of horse blocks, sheds were provided at the rear where horse and carriage could be left during services. This was the custom with most churches and these rows of sheds existed until the automobile came in, when they were adapted for other uses or taken down.

Though the life of the early Enfielders may seem hard and grim to us they had their holidays and social affairs just as we do. Many of their holidays grew out of the need for neighborly help. Clearing the trees from a piece of land or putting up the frame of a house or barn were impossible tasks for one worker alone. With no machinery the only practical way to accomplish these tasks was for all the neighborhood to help. Men, women, and children turned out for these occasions and at noon or after the work was done there was a feast of good food and an opportunity to chat with friends and catch up with the news (no newspapers, magazines, radio, or TV in those days), and the children had their games.

Election Day was one of their holidays. The minister preached an election sermon and the women baked special election cakes. An old recipe that probably goes back to the early 1800s starts with four pounds of flour, two pounds of butter, and other ingredients in proportion, with two gills of yeast instead of the baking powder which would be used today. It was evidently meant to feed a goodly number. Recipes for election cake in modern terms can be found in some standard cookbooks today.

Training Day involved a military review when the militia gathered at the training ground and were put through their paces and displayed their marksmanship. Everyone attended to enjoy the show.

Whenever a new house or barn was built there was a raising, which meant a break in the regular routine. House frames were made of much heavier timbers than is now the case and raising was hard and dangerous work that required the combined manpower of the town.

The frame of a building was held together by mortise and tenon, and the beams and posts and the sills were prepared and numbered before the raising started. One group of men worked on the front part of the frame. After the posts had been fitted into the top beam, or girt—working on the ground—the real raising started. When the men could reach no higher, long poles were used to finish pushing the frame into an upright position. Another group of men standing inside the foundation, also with long poles, prevented the frame from going too far. The tenons were slipped into the mortises in the sill, and fastened with wooden pegs called treenails. This process was then repeated by a third group working at the back.

Another use of manpower in place of one of today's mechanical devices occurred when the church built in 1775 was converted to a town hall. There was no use for the steeple and the method proposed for getting rid of it was to attach a rope and pull it down. It was a good enough plan, but the first try resulted in the rope breaking and the men going down instead of the steeple.

The raising of a new meeting house was a very special occasion and a day for rejoicing. This entry occurs in the town meeting records for June 24, 1706: "The town agree and voat all to meett all with one consent on day when mr Right the carpenter shal apoint to raise the meeting house and the hole town shal atend the work the first day and then those men shall atend the work afterwards which mr Right shal chuse and the town engage to pay them.

"The town furder ingag to satisfie for all the Provision and drink the select men shall see case to provid for the asd worke."

Many kinds of working "bees" were held, the best known probably the quilting bee and the spelling bee. But any work could be made a social occasion in this way with some kind of competition—such as spinning, or clearing the rocks from a field, for example.

Two of our holidays are conspicuously absent from the list, Fourth of

July and Christmas, but Thanksgiving was probably observed in much the same way as today.

Holidays also suggest the subject of children's games. Like children everywhere, they skated, flew kites, and played tag, ring-around-the-roses and London Bridge is falling down. Other games were hopscotch, blind man's buff, and for indoor amusement cat's cradle, checkers, and backgammon—games familiar to most of us.

Just as the children handed down their games to today's children, so we are heirs to the town their fathers started and guided through its early years as best they could according to their lights.

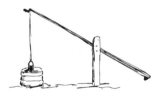

CHAPTER 3

THE ENFIELD SHAKERS

SHAKERISM EVOLVED in the early eighteenth century from a small religious group who fled from persecution in Southern France to London, England, where they gained converts from the Quakers and Methodists. Under the leadership of James and Jane Wardley they formed a small society known as the United Society of Believers. They held that there was direct communication between man and God, and allowed themselves to be guided by the spirit and visions from Him. During religious meetings the group would sit silently and meditate until suddenly they would receive a sign—"vision"—from God and would start to tremble, shout, sing, and shake. Because of these gyrations, skeptics nicknamed them shaking Quakers, soon shortened to Shakers. This name the Society accepted and adopted as their official name.

influence of Ann Lee

Among this small group was a young woman, Ann Lee. Born one of eight children in a poor family in Manchester, England, she was bright and active as a child. While still a young girl, financial conditions demanded that Ann earn her own living. Her first employment was in a cotton factory; later she worked as a cook. Married at a young age to Abraham Stanley, a blacksmith, she bore him four children, all of whom died in infancy, each death leaving its mark of depression on her. However, she gained friends easily and her capacity for leadership was apparent even at her young age. Strong in body and mind, throughout her life she had many heavenly visions, often spending entire nights praying to God to show her the way to salvation. Within the United Society of Believers Ann found solace and became an aggressive participant.

Because of her "popularity" and following, Ann was often shamefully and cruelly abused and was imprisoned several times. Upon her last imprisonment in England, she envisioned the sin of Adam and Eve in the Garden of Eden and from that time on believed and testified that no one living in the sin of gratification of lust of the flesh could be a follower of Christ. This principle was to become the basic tenet of Shakerism. It was her belief that God commissioned her to preach the gospel of a pure and virgin life. Upon her release from prison, she accepted the title of "Mother" and formally assumed the leadership of the Society. Ann preached the revelation that the Godhead was equally male and female, the second coming of Christ being in female form, through her. Shortly after her release from prison, Ann had a vision bidding her to take a few choice followers on a voyage across the sea.

On May 19, 1774, Ann Lee, her husband Abraham Stanley, her brother William Lee, with James Whittaker, John and Richard Hocknell, James Shepherd, Mary Partington, and her niece Nancy Lee left England aboard the ship Mariah, bound for America. On August 6, after a stormy three-month trip across the Atlantic, they landed in New York harbor, whereupon the group separated to find work as blacksmiths, weavers, and shoemakers—the first trades that enabled these eight believers to improve their lot. Ann and her husband found employment with a family in New York City; William Lee and John Hocknell settled near Albany, and the others found employment in the surrounding area. John Hocknell had supplied financing for their trip to America and it was he who purchased the land at Niskeyuna in upper New York near Albany and arranged for the rest of the group to join him there.

Abraham Stanley did not share his wife's belief in Shakerism and she could not convince him that the celibate life was the way to God and salvation. Shortly after coming to America, they separated and Ann joined the others at Niskeyuna, from then on devoting the rest of her life to God and spreading the gospel of Shakerism. Though times were lean and the small society was not gaining in numbers, Ann never lost her faith. She anticipated the great religious revival and predicted many new converts would join the Shaker fold.

During the eighteenth century a great religious revival created much excitement throughout the Eastern colonies. People felt that the established religions did not meet their needs; many believed the second coming of Christ was imminent, convinced of this by their own religious leaders. In June of 1779 a religious revival in the New Lebanon area proclaimed the second coming of Christ was imminent. This excitement lasted until late fall when many people became discouraged and disillusioned. Traveling west in 1780, Talmadge Bishop and Reuben Wight, two men disappointed by the seemingly unfruitful revival, came upon Ann Lee's small group at Niskeyuna. They became so convinced of what they heard and saw that they hurried back to relate their experiences to Joseph Meacham, a lay preacher, originally from Enfield, Connecticut, but then practicing in the New Lebanon area of New York and a member of the New Light Baptists. Meacham sent a very trusted associate, Calvin Harlow, to verify what the two men had encountered. Harlow firmly believed in the second coming of Christ and was convinced of Ann's authenticity. After hearing this testimony, Joseph Meacham decided to visit this small group of Shakers to see for himself. Mother Ann had a "timely vision" of the visit of Joseph Meacham and made special preparation for his coming. When he arrived at the log cabin where Ann and her followers were living, he was given breakfast. Immediately thereafter he started to question Ann and the others. By the end of that day, May 10, 1780, after many hours of interrogating Ann and James Whittaker, he was totally convinced that Ann was truly one with God in the second coming of Christ.

Throughout the eighteenth century the church was very powerful. Even though many people were dissatisfied with their religion, they were reluctant to change; human beings have always feared what is different and not easily understood. Church leaders were fearful of losing their congregations and spoke from the pulpit of the dangers of Satan leading them astray. The emergence of Ann Lee upon the scene with her completely foreign concepts was very difficult for the lay person to understand. Her concept of Christ and the Trinity was so far removed from the Christian doctrine that only the sheer simplicity of these devout Shakers could have enabled their rise in numbers.

Ann Lee comes
to Enfield

Between 1781 and 1783 Ann traveled extensively throughout New England making new converts. Her first trip to Enfield in 1781 was met with much opposition by fearful townspeople, among whom were men of influence in the town and in the church. In the midst of a religious service Ann and her followers were dragged from their meeting into the streets where they were threatened with tar and feathering. In passing through the town, the noisy mob drew the attention of a young Revolutionary War officer, Elija Jones. Seeing that Ann and her small group were peacable and inoffensive, he accompanied them to the Connecticut River at Lovejoy's Ferry, assuring them of safe passage to their next destination.

While traveling from Stafford on her second trip to Enfield in the fall of 1782, Mother Ann and some of her followers were pursued by Captain Charles Kibbee of Somers and a group of twenty to thirty men. They followed Mother Ann and her group to the home of David Meacham, brother of Joseph Meacham, broke into his home and caused much destruction and violence. John Booth, a constable from town, was summoned and was successful in halting this disturbance, but not before David Meacham had sustained injuries. The rioters were summoned to County Court in Hartford, where they were required to settle the matter with David Meacham or stand trial. A confession of their conduct before their own church was David Meacham's only request for punishment, but the rioters refused and stood trial. They were found guilty and fined. This event marked the end of mobbing and rioting against the Shakers in Connecticut. When Mother Ann made her final appearance in Enfield in 1783 she was allowed to enter peaceably and without harassment. The few men who had opposed her no longer had any influence with the townspeople or with the church.

While on her many tours to gain converts and spread the Shaker beliefs, Ann encountered numerous hardships and, though successful in her goal, her health was ruined. On September 8, 1784, shortly after her return to New Lebanon from a strenuous crusade she died at the early age of forty-eight. James Whittaker inherited the task of carrying on in her stead and when he died three years later in 1787 Joseph Meacham became the leading minister of the Society of Believers. Ann had envisioned that he would be the one to increase in great numbers the members of her faith. Her vision was to be proven.

role of Joseph Meacham

Born in Enfield, Connecticut, February 22, 1741, Joseph Meacham became one of Ann's first American converts. Joseph's father had founded the Baptist church in Enfield, inspired by the famous sermon of Jonathan Edwards, "Sinners in the Hands of an Angry God." This tall, slim man with a pale complexion and hazel eyes numbered many among his congregation.

On Christmas Day in 1787 the small group of believers gathered at their first meal under the communal form of the Society. Joseph Meacham realized that living a celibate life in a communal form of society would need a segregation of the sexes. He determined that this would require a female leader so that equality of rights would be adhered to in each and every community. Only in this way could he see that the devotion and obedience of present and future Shakers would be assured. Joseph Meacham named Lucy Wright to stand alongside himself as an equal in the leadership of the Shakers. Lucy Wright was born in Pittsfield, Massachusetts, in 1760 of parents who had long been prominent in their town. She received a good education, was intelligent, strong willed, and quite womanly. Both Lucy and her husband Elizur Goodrich became very loyal to Mother Ann. Ann had recognized and encouraged the leadership and capabilities of Lucy. The highest authority of the Church, "The United Society of Believers, Shakers," was established in New Lebanon in 1792 under the ministration of Joseph Meacham and Lucy Wright.

Though many converts were made in Enfield beginning in 1781, it was not until 1792 that a formal Shaker community was established. While Mother Ann is credited with spreading the Shaker doctrine, it was Joseph Meacham who brought growth and order to the sect.

Joseph Meacham and Lucy Wright were invested with the power of appointing the ministry for each of the different societies. Chosen to lead the first Enfield community in 1792 from the head ministry in

New Lebanon were Calvin Harlow and Sarah Harrison. It became their special duty to bring the Enfield community into order, guide and supervise the spiritual concerns of the Society, and to counsel, advise, and judge in all matters of importance. Calvin Harlow and Sarah Harrison also had the authority to appoint elders, eldresses, deacons, deaconnesses, and trustees for each family.

The first qualifications listed for becoming a Shaker were that all debts must be paid, a person must be free of all legal obligations, and must make restitution by confession for all wrongs committed against any man and against God. Although one could become a member of the United Society by simply adopting its moral code, membership into the Church Order required an economic commitment and the complete surrender of one's worldly goods to the Shakers.

Members were also obliged to sign a covenant agreeing to the rules and regulations of the Society. It stated that they agreed to the principles of Christ's second appearance in one, Mother Ann; to obey the appointed ministry, deacons, deaconesses, elders, and eldresses, and not bring any charge of debt against the Believers for property that was given of free will. The rules and regulations were read to each prospective member so all knew exactly the terms being agreed upon. The covenant was then recorded and made available as public record with each person's donations being written as part of this covenant.

Shaker beliefs

The Enfield community grew and prospered to a total of five families situated so that they formed a cross with the Church Family in the center. Each family was supervised by two elders and eldresses, two deacons and deaconesses, and two trustees. The elders and eldresses were appointed by the ministry who presided at the Church Family. Deacons, deaconesses, and trustees were selected by the elders and eldresses of each family. Members numbered between thirty-five and forty per family when the Shaker community was at its prime in 1855.

The ministry both set down all the rules and regulations for the families and assumed the exclusive right to make alterations or changes in the orders for the protection of the members. Any member wishing to make a visit to another family or community had first to request and receive permission from the ministry. All gifts were directed to the ministry for acceptance or rejection and all donations were directed by them. They were also separated from the other members, living in their own quarters and dining alone.

The elders and eldresses derived their strength and guidance from the ministry. Periodically, they reported the state of affairs of their families to the ministry. It was their duty to oversee the family; they were entrusted to teach and guide them to work for the general good health, and the spiritual and physical well being of each and every member. A Shaker was required to confess any sins immediately to the elders and eldresses, who would then pass judgment upon them.

The deacons and deaconesses and trustees handled all domestic responsibilities of each family. All business transactions of any nature were handled by the trustees. Since women were not allowed to make monetary transactions of any kind, only men were appointed trustees. They were required to keep accurate and detailed records of all business dealings and to keep the books solvent. In making a journey for the buying and selling of goods, they were instructed to avoid dealings with anyone who had shunned God, and upon returning were required to give full account of their time and business to the elders.

Since the Shakers did not volunteer for military duty, they were mistrusted and not tolerated kindly for their unwillingness to join the colonists in the fight for independence. It was a natural reaction of the colonists since the Shakers were Englishmen and disinterested in what was happening between the colonies and England at this time; perhaps they were not even aware of the reasons for the conflict.

In 1815 a declaration published in Enfield expressed the views of the Shakers on bearing arms, paying fines, and hiring substitutes to take their place in military service. They concurred in God's insistence that contributions to and incurring acts of violence against another human being were sinful and alien to everything Christ preached. Since they did not participate in government, they refused to pay fines for refusing to bear arms, but they paid their taxes and donated food, clothing, and equipment for both the War of 1812 and the Civil War. Shaker food and lodging sustained many of the soldiers and the newly freed slaves and the Shakers kept abreast of all that was happening during those times.

In 1792 when the Shakers began their communal style of living in Enfield, they were fortunate to receive a large donation of land located at the northeastern corner of Enfield from David Meacham, brother of Joseph. The early nineteenth century found the Shakers flourishing and an important asset to the town of Enfield and surrounding communities. The rolling hills reached out to the borders of Somers and

East Longmeadow, Massachusetts. As the Shakers grew in numbers, more land, nearly 3,000 acres, was acquired.

expansion

The Church Family or First Family was the first to be formed in 1792 with the North, South, East, and West Families following thereafter. Each family excelled in different areas. The Church Family, of course, was always the center of activity with the ministers being housed there. Since each family was accountable to the ministry, some form of business was always being attended to and solutions to problems being sought. Throughout the 137 years the Church Family was in existence, many different ministers presided including, Nathaniel Deming, 1796; Daniel Goodrich, 1812; Sarah Harrison, 1792; Thomas Damon, 1846; George Wilcox, 1895. Jefferson White founded the seed business in 1802 and ran it until his death in 1859. Each brought his own ideas and talents to bear. The last large dwelling house was built in 1876 with steam heat and good ventilation, the latest modern conveniences of the times, with the kitchen containing running water and improved appliances for cooking and baking. Part of it was later converted to a completely equipped hospital.

The ministry of each community made frequent visits to New Lebanon where the highest order of Shakers presided. On their way to and from New Lebanon, they would visit the various Shaker communities. These short visits of one or two days were warmly welcomed as news of sister communities was always of special interest. If the visitors found their hosts to be in need, they would extend their stay to help complete the work.

Though the Church Family was best known, the North Family was noted for its fine hospitality. Sister Emily Copley, 1895, always gave everyone who visited the North Family a hearty welcome. Elder Gilbert Avery was also a resident with the North Family at that time and was loved by all. It was Omar Pease who built the big dwelling house and large stock barn found on the North Family property. He was instrumental in having the public highway moved about ten rods to the east. His most precious hobby was forestry and to him credit is given for the 150 acres of pine forest in Enfield. Most of these pines were lost, however, during the hurricane of 1938. Elder Omar Pease had lived with the Shakers since the age of two. He died in 1883. After his death, Richard Van Deusen was placed in charge of the North Family, coming from the Church Family. Born in Tyringham, Massachusetts, he had lived with the Shakers since the age of seven. Credit is due him for the fine fruit orchards and the training and breeding of fine horses. His death on August 6, 1893, was a great loss not only to the Shakers but also the Town of Enfield. During the early 1900s the leadership of the North Family was in the hands of Elder George Clark and Eldress Miriam Offord. In 1913 the North Family was disbanded.

In 1810 Elders James Slate and Enoch Pease, Eldresses Judith Emerson and Clarisa Eley moved from the Church Family and started the South Family. A most avid Shaker of the South Family in the mid-nineteenth century was Elder Robert Aitken. His life was dedicated to gaining converts for the Shakers and he traveled extensively to do so. The South Family was also noted for its excellent farms. Elder Thomas Stroud, 1897, is credited with keeping model greenhouses and poultry pens, with the cultivation of small fruits and nuts of special interest to him. He made a science of his farming and in his leisure time studied much on the subject. The dehorning of his well bred Jersey cows set a precedent that was followed immediately by the rest of the Shaker community, and today by dairymen throughout the world. Eldress Marion Patrick, also a member of the South Family, shared Elder Stroud's interest in fruit culture. In 1853 the South Family moved into its new dwelling house which still stands today.

In 1818, Elders Nathaniel Deming, Daniel Goodrich, Eldresses Dana Goodrich and Sarah Markham moved from the South Family and began the establishment of the West Family in the area of Bacon Road to Shaker Pines Lake. About forty members from the Harmonist sect of Rhode Island joined the West Family of Shakers in 1825. In 1854, the West Family and the South Family were united under one leadership.

The East Family was established in the early 1800s with farming their main source of income until they disbanded in 1874.

With the excellent drainage for water, and fertile land free of stones, all of the early Shakers soon became prosperous agricultural farmers but they also excelled in animal husbandry. Judicious breeding of dairy cows, horses, and other farm animals aroused the envy of all who visited the area. Fruit orchards were given special care and the apples picked from their trees were the basic ingredient of many long cherished Shaker recipes. All Shaker fare was of the finest with most of the food being grown on their own farms. Blackberries, currants, and dandelions were used to make delicious wines and extracts. Cranberries and blueberries were in abundance, as were chestnuts, butternuts, and walnuts.

the buildings

As the Shakers prospered, many buildings were erected to accommodate their growing numbers. Most smaller structures were made of wood with the larger family dwellings constructed of brick, the roofs covered with slate, and the walls plastered. Walls and woodwork were painted in various colors, with blue woodwork and white walls predominating, all cleaned daily to keep them clean and neat. Whenever a large building was being framed or raised, all the families and people from the surrounding villages participated. Some of the smaller buildings were moved from one place to another whenever it was determined that they would serve a more useful and practical purpose elsewhere.

All buildings to be occupied by both brethren and sisters were built with separate entrances, men entering on the left, women on the right. Long narrow boards with pegs jutting out were hung on almost every wall and along the hallways for hanging clothes and chairs when not in use. Rooms were furnished with the bare essentials and drawers were built into the walls to take care of those articles that could not be hung. Provision was made for adequate ventilation with room temperature not exceeding 60 degrees.

The upper floors of the family dwellings were divided into rooms which could lodge four to eight persons. Each room contained a bed for each occupant, the necessary toilet equipment, a mirror, a stove for heat in winter, a writing table, and an abundance of chairs which, when not in use, were hung on the pegs on the walls. A wide hallway separated the men's dormitory from the women's. The floors were covered with soft colored mats made by the Shakers.

On the ground floor were the kitchens, pantries, storerooms, and a large dining hall. The Church Family dwelling had an extra, separate, dining hall which served as an inn for visitors to the Shaker community.

Shaker customs

A multitude of rules and regulations guided all Shakers in their daily routine. Shaker clothing was plain and practical. Brethren wore drab colored suits, shirts that were buttoned to the throat, and white or gray stiff-brimmed hats. Sisters' dresses were of various colors, close fitted at the waist, with long flowing skirts over which long narrow aprons were worn. Around the shoulders each sister draped a scarf to hide the shape of the bust. Long hooded capes were worn in winter with close fitted bonnets to hide the hair and profile. Shoes were high heeled until the mid 1800s when the low heel was adopted. All clothing was made and cared for by the Shaker sisters. Shaker brethren made the shoes and sometimes helped in making hats.

Mother Ann's motto, "Give your hands to work and your hearts to God," was instilled very deeply into their lives. In the summer months they arose at dawn, started each day with prayer, with the sounding of bells to tell them when meals would be served. Each member had specific chores which were rotated periodically. After the winter season arrived, the Shakers made good use of their time. Candles were dipped and bonnets and clothing were sewn. It was also winter when most of the furniture was made, the icehouse filled, seed bags were cut and filled for sale, catalogs and almanacs were printed to advertise Shaker products. Winter was also the time for school, when young people were taught to read and write.

the Shakers
as craftsmen

Work was regarded as an important form of worship with "a place for everything and everything in its place." The Shakers were skillful inventors and each invention was created to increase comfort for the community, to enhance productivity, and to ease the work of the members. If any individual possessed special knowledge and skills, he would travel to other Shaker communities to share his talents. Though they did not patent their inventions, the Enfield Shakers are credited with the invention of the one-horse carriage, rotary harrow, circular saw, cut nails, clothespins, packaging and selling of garden seeds, and the first dried breakfast cereal made from corn that was split and dried.

Shaker furniture was first and foremost functional. Pine, birch, maple, and butternut were plentiful and used for all items. The most popular pieces were the chairs and rockers. They were light and strong, differing in size and design, with every component of their structure carefully measured and fitted to suit the human body. Dining room chairs were built with low backs to enable them to slide under the table when not in use. Tables were built in many styles and sizes. Shakers' desks were almost as varied as their tables. Although personal writing was not encouraged among the sisters and brethren, they were avid record keepers and it is probable that most of the early desks— neatly lined and constructed with compartments for ink wells, pens, and other writing equipment—were made exclusively for the elders and eldresses of the ministry. Order and neatness were a religious principle and the Shakers lived up to this by building ample storage facilities. From wall to wall, floor to ceiling, the Shaker craftsmen patiently built their complex of drawers, closets, compartments, and cupboards.

Shaker beds were so short and narrow that one wonders how grown adults could sleep on them. Narrow mattresses filled with feathers and cornhusks covered the rope springs. Beautifully crafted cradles were made for those Shakers who were sick and also for the very young orphans.

Many Shaker craftsmen served their apprenticeships as children in the Shaker community. They were trained in many talents by the time they reached legal age so that any who chose to leave the community were skilled in a trade that would ensure their future.

It is interesting to observe that Shaker craftsmen seldom limited their endeavors to the construction of furniture alone. Their boxes were fine examples of Shaker perfection and many were sold to the outside world in graduated sets. Careful attention to design was also given to the workshops, which were spacious, light, and airy. The work benches were indeed functionally constructed with long rows of drawers underneath and the walls behind them lined with tool cupboards. Before breakfast the craftsmen kindled fires in their shop stoves and laid out materials for the day's work. This varied each day with a Shaker brother perhaps spending a day at the sawmill on Shaker Pines Lake (which was constructed by the Shakers for their industries in the nineteenth century) roughing out lumber for future needs, or perhaps a day at the lathe in the workshop turning pegs or chair legs or whatever was needed to complete his project. During the early years each Shaker craftsman made every piece, start to finish, but as the demand for their fine articles increased, it was necessary to employ production procedures. Mortising, dovetailing, and other joinery operations were performed on a production level at this later date to furnish all craftsmen with supplies. Still, they labored at a leisurely pace and were not oppressed with time schedules and progress reports.

Shaker ingenuity was evident in all of their machinery, with most being powered by water turbines. Sawmills came first among the project priorities of most Shaker settlements and Enfield was no exception. In the early nineteenth century a dam was constructed to form Crescent Lake, which borders Enfield and East Longmeadow, Massachusetts. Dams, waterwheels, and turbines conveyed power from these streams to the mills where wood was prepared for use. It was then cured and dried to eliminate splitting and warping. Glues were made from the hoofs of horses and other animals and prepared in glasslike sheets. When needed, it was broken off and boiled and applied hot to join the pieces together. Many ways of joining were used, including doweling and dovetailing. Paint was applied to finished pieces and homemade stains were used extensively.

Food was plain, wholesome, and plentiful. The superior garden seeds, first packaged in 1802, led to a very profitable industry for the Shakers. Herbs were cultivated and their purported remedial qualities for illnesses were well known all over the Northeast.

The Shakers also raised superior breeds of cattle and sheep. Housed in large, spacious barns, such stock were cared for with love and kindness. Townspeople came often to the Shaker community to buy milk, butter, and cheese—all of the highest quality. Turkeys, chickens, pigeons, and guinea hens were raised and sold to the outside world.

the Mount of Olives

Every Shaker settlement was required to set apart a piece of land as a sacred worshipping ground known as the Holy Mount, so in 1842 a search was made to establish a plot. It was called the Mount of Olives, locally known as Holy Hill; Shaker legend claimed it to have been named by the Lord and Savior through a vision of one of the brethern. About one half acre in size and situated on a high hill one mile northeast of the Church Family, it was encircled with a high stone wall while inside a wooden fence enclosed the marble stone or fountainhead. It was forbidden for anyone to touch or enter the sacred enclosure. The Shakers believed that Christ would appear for the third time at the sacred spot. Each spring and fall a great celebration was held at this site. Fasting, confession, and prayer preceded the festivities and then a great feast was prepared for all to enjoy.

Each day in the life of a Shaker began and ended with prayers. Their hymns, revealed to them by a divine spirit, were practiced during the week to be sung on the Sabbath. On Saturday evening at 7:30 the Shaker Sabbath began and all gathered at their family meetinghouses for a short service. Early Sunday morning the main Church Family meetinghouse would find all Shaker families together. Sermons or merely informal addresses would be given by the elders, interspersed with hymns, prayers, singing, and dancing. At all times sisters stayed on one side of the room and brethren on the other. Sunday school followed with adults studying the Bible as interpreted by Mother Ann Lee and children using small cards made especially for their instruction. In the evening the Sabbath day ended with a short prayer meeting. Except for a short period of time in the early nineteenth century, all prayer meetings were public. Then in 1884 with decreasing numbers the large main meetinghouse was closed, and a small chapel was used.

Throughout the nineteenth century various religious groups visited the Shakers to observe and study their habits. A kind of ecumenical council was arranged with each group sharing the other's views. It was during this time that the Shakers gained many converts from the Adventists, Christian Scientists, Church of the Perfectionists, and others.

During the winter months many strangers came to the Shakers professing their faith, only to leave when Spring came. These were known as Winter Shakers, but there were many others from all over the world who visited and paid for their food and lodging and they would come again and again, with some eventually joining the Shakers.

The hard working Shakers did find time for some recreation. It is known that on occasion a group would travel to New London and other Connecticut beaches to enjoy some fishing and swimming for two or three days. Warm weather was also the time to find them exchanging visits with the other Shaker communities. In winter they took sleigh rides and went ice fishing.

concern for the community-at-large

Though the Shakers kept to themselves for the most part, the surrounding townspeople were always well aware of them. They were respected everywhere for their kindness and generosity because they often traveled many miles to help someone who was sick or in need. On New Year's Day, poor and needy citizens from the outside world were invited to come to the Shaker community. They were given a nourishing meal and were encouraged to take along all the food and clothing they could carry home with them. The Shaker community served as one of the first and finest orphanages in the United States, raising abandoned and parentless children until they were of legal age to choose for themselves the outside world or the life of a Shaker. They gave money to those who lost their homes or barns by fire, they gave cash donations to the Connecticut Asylum for the education of the deaf and dumb, they helped financially to build roads, and they helped parents of Shakers who were in need.

On many a fine autumn day Enfield citizens were able to buy or trade for a Shaker brother's produce. Depending upon the season, one might buy or barter for such varied items as cider, potatoes, peas, brooms, mops, or baskets.

The Shakers were not without their share of hardships and bad luck, but their faith and charity helped them through such hard times. In 1822 the young and aspiring Enfield community suffered a fever epidemic which brought death to many of the sect. When a member of the Shaker Society died, his body was laid to rest in the cemetery, the gravestone marked only with the person's initials and age at the time of death.

decline of the movement

Many reasons and theories have been expressed relating to the Shaker decline. Certainly the Industrial Revolution's improved communications were among the primary reasons. The coming of the railroad through the Shaker community after the Civil War made travel and further knowledge of the outside world inevitable. The halt of sales in packaged garden seeds to the South during the Civil War crippled the Enfield Shakers' prime source of income. This, with the dwindling number of believers and unreliability of outside help, made it impossible for them to continue maintaining their large farms. Little by little the Shaker property was sold off as small individual farms. In 1917, the eight remaining Shakers in Enfield sold the largest portion of the Shaker property to John Phillips and went to live at Hancock and New Lebanon. John Phillips grew tobacco on the property and in 1931 it was sold to the State of Connecticut. It is now the site of the two state prisons. Though most of the Shaker buildings have been demolished, a few still remain, with only the South Family property being privately owned.

The Shaker legacy is one of rich and interesting value. Buried in the cemetery which is marked today by only one stone are the remains of many who helped shape the progress of Enfield and the surrounding communities. Their immortality attested to on this stone can be found in homes and museums throughout the United States. Their furniture and wares are still much sought after and their spiritual simplicity and human generosity live in the few Shaker sisters who remain at Canterbury, New Hampshire, and Sabbath Day Lake, Maine.

the Enfield Shakers

. . . a photographic portfolio

"Give your hands to work and your hearts to God."
ANN LEE

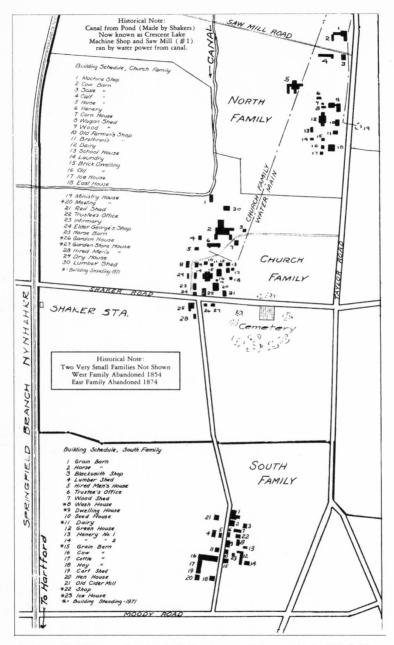

Section of 1896 map showing building layout of three principal Enfield Shaker Families.

View of North Family buildings along Taylor Road.

Church Family buildings across Shaker Road from building #25.

South Family buildings, looking Northwest from field.

"The Enfield community grew and prospered to a total of five families with the Church family in the center."

portfolio / 49

A South Family group.

Church Family dining room.

"Shaker clothing was plain and practical and cared for by the Shaker sisters . . . food was plentiful and wholesome . . . order and neatness a religious principle."

South Family wash house.

Typical Enfield Shaker small barn.

Shaker Station and Post Office, Enfield.

"Shaker furniture was first and foremost functional. It is interesting to observe that Shaker craftsmen seldom limited their endeavors to the construction of furniture alone."

Above: Enfield Shaker rocker of maple. The original rush seat is protected by a handmade woolen cover.

Left: Enfield Shaker chest made of butternut is 96" high, 39" wide and 17½" deep. The left cupboard has two shelves and the one on the right an unusual cutout shelf for storage of taller articles.

Right: Pincushion, spoolholders and needle and pin book made by the Enfield Shakers. The pincushion in the center has a blue glass base, and is covered in red fabric with black fringe and a black velvet band covering the join.

Bottom right: Enfield Shaker Deaconess desk and chair. The butternut and maple desk was probably made by John W. Copley (1841-1908) who joined the Enfield Society in 1852 and left in 1865. The chair is of curley maple.

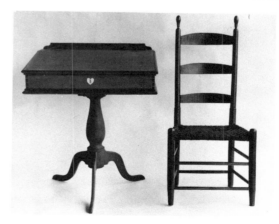

"Their boxes were fine examples of Shaker perfection and many were sold to the outside world. Their furniture and work are still much sought after . . ."

Above: Enfield Shaker sewing box is 8" in diameter and contains 17 spindles for spools in addition to the inner box. The date 1815 is inscribed on the bottom.

Left: Enfield Shaker sewing desk made of several kinds of maple. It is 41½" high, 31¼" wide and 26½" deep, and has a total of twelve drawers, a small cupboard and a pull-out shelf of pine.

Right: Varied sewing equipment made by the Enfield Shakers. The pincushion at the left is designed to be clamped to a table, the small items are acorn emery needle sharpeners and small pincushions, and the pincushion on the right is fastened to an oval maple box with a "finger" closing.

the
years of | **2**
growth

Family pastoral . . . in a period of
dynamic industrial growth

CHAPTER 4

AGRICULTURE IN ENFIELD

IT IS NOT HARD to imagine some of the attractions for the first settlers to Enfield—the Great River, offering transportation and a connection with the rest of the world, the pleasant fertile meadows along the river, used by the Indians for growing their corn and pumpkins and vegetables, the high ridge running parallel with the river, a great place to build their homes. They must have looked at this land with the eye of the farmer, for in 1679 the settlers were, for the most part, farmers. They had to be, for about the only way to subsist was to raise or grow most of the items needed for food and clothing. The forests were everywhere to provide the materials for their houses and barns. The land, while not the deep and rich soil which was later to be discovered on the Western plains, was fine and sandy, free from stones for the most part, and sufficiently fertile to support a good agriculture, particularly grazing.

59

So the agriculture of Enfield began, first along the Great River, then spreading eastward until it embraced all of the town to the mountains. It was destined to become the major livelihood for most of the residents until well into the nineteenth century, when the burgeoning industrial revolution began to make its effect felt here as well as elsewhere in Connecticut and the Northeast. Then for agriculture in Enfield, which had struggled through its growing pains and reached its heyday, began a period of decline which has continued to the present time. Industry has gradually replaced agriculture over the last century both as a way of living and in terms of actual land use. Where for centuries lay fields and forests and fine farming land now stand factories, businesses, malls. Much fertile soil is buried beneath the concrete and asphalt of highways and streets. The needs of a bedroom town, for homes as well as industry, have preempted much land which for years produced food and fiber, crops that fed many people or supported animals which in turn produced meat and milk for our own use.

While agriculture can no longer be called one of the major occupations here it still fills an important place in the life of the town. Farming itself has changed to such an extent that, even without the industrialization that has taken place in our town, the land would no longer support the number of farmers who were once in Enfield. Farms today are of necessity much larger, and the type of agriculture is much more intensive than that of the 1700s, for instance. In addition, the fact that farm land and farming still exist here provides the non-farmer a welcome relief from factory walls in the form of green fields, growing crops, and open space. It also enables many who work mainly in industry an opportunity to supplement their income with some part-time farming, where the land and the time available do not warrant a full-time farming enterprise. So it is quite probable that agriculture in some form will continue to be an important part of the Enfield scene for a long time to come.

in the beginning

Enfield had its beginning as an agricultural community in 1679, when Colonel John Pynchon and his Freshwater Committee, acting upon the authority of the town of Springfield, Massachusetts, made grants of land to nineteen Springfield residents on condition that they settle and improve it within three years. Only three of the original nineteen ever settled in

Enfield. However, that same year John Pease, Sr., Elisha Kibbe, John Pease, Jr., and Robert Pease, all of Salem, Massachusetts, erected a hut against a hill near the Great River and spent the winter in Enfield. The following year they were granted land here and brought their families from Salem, Massachusetts. It might therefore be said that Enfield was really a colony of Salem.

The first business in getting the settlement started was the division of the land, a duty which was handled by the Freshwater Plantation Committee. The original town plot was divided into 64 home lots, each containing between 10 and 14 acres of land. They were 10 to 14 rods broad and extended 160 rods on a side, either toward the river or easterly from the main street. Besides this each settler was granted from 30 to 60 acres of field land, the size depending on which allotment he was eligible for. These original grants were made with the stipulation that the grantee settle on the land and improve it within three years, or the claim would be forfeited and returned to the Committee to be regranted to another. Later meadow land was added to the original grant. Those with 30 and 40 acres received 4 acres of meadow. Those with 50 acres received 5 additional acres, and the 60-acre grants received 6 acres. This need for meadow land seems to indicate that cattle and sheep were particularly important to the early inhabitants, as well they might be, for from the cows they obtained the milk, cream, butter, and cheese—dairy products which they depended on so much for food. Their cattle also furnished meat and hides for leather, and they were the prime source of power, as well. Their oxen plowed and tilled the land, did the heavy jobs in clearing the land, and were generally indispensable to this early type of agriculture. Sheep were equally important, for meat, wool, and hides.

During the early years of the settlement all of these animals were allowed to run on the town common—cattle, sheep, even hogs if they were yoked and ringed, and geese. All animals using the commons had to be properly identified, usually with a brand or a certain combination of notches in the ears. It soon became apparent that "good fences make good neighbors," and accordingly the Committee ordered every lot owner to:

1. Clear the brush on the side of his lot which bordered the highway (Enfield Street), with a penalty for non-compliance of five shillings for public use.
2. Make ditches and drains to carry the water off the property with as little damage to their neighbors as possible, and also to clean these ditches and drains at least once a year.

3. Put up forty yards of good substantial fence between him and his neighbor's lot, each neighbor responsible for twenty yards. Penalty for failure to do so was forfeiture of twelve rods to his neighbor for every rod undone. Pretty stiff penalties by today's standards.

Although each resident had the right to pasture his cattle and sheep on the commons this was not exactly "free" pasture, for in 1684 the Committee ordered each owner of an allotment to work two days each year cutting brush and underwood on the commons so that the cattle and sheep could have a better field. This was, of course, in addition to the brush cutting required along the highway in front of each lot.

By 1683 the need for meadow land was increasing so meadow lots were laid out to the east along the "Scantuck" River. All the lots were to be seven acres and ran from hill to hill across the river, taking all of the lowland on either side of it. There was also to be a passage for carts and teams across all the meadows, and for going up the hill and across the river wherever it was most convenient. History does not tell us where on the "Scantuck" these first meadows were laid out. However, there are still meadows on the Scantic in the Wallop section of the town which, although they do not conform to the original specifications, quite likely trace back to this original division.

With exception of the open meadows along the Connecticut River, Enfield as the settlers found it was covered with forest. On the ridge just east of the river were deciduous trees, oaks, maples, birches, and the like but to the east on the swamps and the sandy plains, clear to the mountains, the original growth was white pine. These great forests began to be cut down and destroyed to make more grazing land for cattle and fields for crops. The questionable practice of annual burning over pasture land to improve the grazing also destroyed much timber and eventually made the land less productive rather than improving it.

There are conflicting accounts of the capabilities of Enfield's first farmers. One account says, "Enfield settlers prospered in the pursuit of husbandry during the first 40 years, (1680-1720), converting the wilderness into fruitful fields and erecting buildings," while another source comments that "the original settlers were not especially good farmers," and that "they merely subsisted, in fact hardly that, for they had to rely on neighboring towns for provisions and supplies. Two annual blessings which they received helped to keep them from actual famine—the arrival of shad and pigeons." Regardless of which account is correct (and there may be some truth in each of them), the town was practically settled by 1720.

Certainly much of the land in Enfield was not of the finest quality for farming as the early settlers found it. In fact, when the Freshwater Committee petitioned the General Court of Massachusetts to be confirmed as a separate township in 1683, they described the land thus:

That the best of the land, which is not above a mile and a half from the Great River, is woody and swampy land and must by hard labor be won for improvement, and then at the end of that mile and a half, and in some places not half a mile, the rest for about five miles eastward from the Great River is generally piney and barren sandy land capable of no improvement, so that much of the land that must be improved will be six or seven miles from the Great River to the mountains.

No wonder that agriculture "languished" during those first forty years. Farmers also suffered by having so little to improve the land. Manure from their animals and wood ashes were about the only fertilizer materials available. Phosphates and lime were unknown, of course, as well as the need for them. Still they persisted. Their first cash crop came from the forest trees which surrounded them. From the pines they took turpentine and tar then sawed the trees into boards or hewed them into beams and timbers for their buildings. Trees not used for lumber were burned to get the wood ashes from which was obtained potash for fertilizer. Charcoal was also made in small amounts.

Corn (Indian) was the staple crop from the very first. It was invaluable for feeding about every farm animal raised at that time. The whole plant could be utilized, as the fodder and the ears stored well through the long New England winters, and the grain could be ground into meal to feed the hungry farmer and his family—or his livestock. In fact, corn was so universally grown and used that it very often became a medium of exchange, especially as money was a very scarce commodity. On many occasions the town allowed payment of taxes in corn as well as in wheat, oats, rye, flax, and boards. The records of the Freshwater Committee of 1686 note: "Ordered that those behind in their rates (taxes) be called in and payment demanded in corn."

Besides corn, wheat, rye, and barley were also grown, but with less success, as these (particularly wheat) were subject to diseases which cut down their yields and made them less reliable as crops. In spite of these shortcomings they continued to be grown. In fact, the Colony encouraged farmers to grow English "grane." Some flax must have been grown early in Enfield's history, as there is mention of linen among the items exported at that time. A 1737 town meeting mentions that Christopher Parsons was chosen surveyor of hemp and flax. This job was quite likely the result of action by the Connecticut legislature, which attempted to stop the steady drain of money from the Colony to pay for manufactured goods from Britain. Since two of the products which were commonly purchased were cordage and linens, they reasoned that if the Colony were to make itself self-sufficient in these items the money drain would be much less. It was therefore decreed that each family should plant at least one spoonful of hemp or flax seed the first year. The second year each family with a plow team must plant a minimum of one quarter acre of hemp or flax. The surveyor's job was to see that each family complied with the rule.

One of the first things the early inhabitants did as they started to improve their property was to set out an orchard, as indicated by an entry from a 1693 town meeting encouraging a minister to settle here. It says, "We do also engage to fence in and close, and bring into a way of improvement, six acres of land, some for plowing and some for pasture, and to plant an orchard." We know very little about those old orchards. What were they like? Presumably they contained the scions of many an English, Dutch, or French tree, but what were the varieties? Were they Pippins or Summer Rambos, or Gilliflower, or some other kind now long forgotten? Most of the old varieties have now disappeared. We do know, however, that regardless of variety they made good cider. So, of course, there had to be a cider mill and, while it may not have been the first, there is a record that in 1739 liberty was granted Ephraim Terry and Joseph Pease to "sot up a cyder mill and house—" and to enjoy it as long as said house shall stand—except that ye town shall have liberty to hang horses there except at cyder time." At the same town meeting Thomas Abbe was granted liberty to set up a similar mill, so it would seem that by this time there were plenty of orchards bearing and plenty of "cyder" to press—and enjoy.

farming in the eighteenth century

After the turn of the eighteenth century the town began to fill with settlers, and their cattle, horses, pigs, and sheep also became more numerous and more troublesome. Where earlier had been forest and pasture land there were now crops which could be trampled or eaten, and roaming animals began to wreak much damage to them. The town therefore began to build pounds to contain the animals allowed to roam at large, and to enforce the rules regarding them. In 1719 eight men were chosen as Hogg Reeves or constables, and in the same year the inhabitants at the east end of the town were given the liberty of building a pound in that section—at their own expense. The next year, however, swine running at large were still a problem, so much so that a committee was formed to enforce the law relating to it. After that, hogs were allowed on the common only if they were yoked and ringed.

About the same time the town maintained ownership of its own bulls which were used by the residents to breed their cows, thus saving citizens the expense of buying their own. Town meetings records of the period often contain references to this, as in 1714 when the townspeople voted to "leave it with the selectmen to dispose of the town bulls—either to kill them as they think most convenient," or later in 1719 "voted the selectmen buy a bull or two if they can get them, and to assess the town for so much money as may be needful to defray the charge."

The Town of Enfield was once in the sheep business, too. Yes indeed! By voting to hire a shepherd in 1718 and to pay the cost by tax receipts, the town was to have all the advantage of folding the sheep and the income from them. A committee was chosen as sheepmasters—Captain Terry, Isaac Pease, Sr., and Sam Parsons to hire the shepherd and dispose of the sheep from time to time to the town's best advantage. This flyer into sheep raising must not have been too successful, however, for the next year it was voted that owners hire a shepherd to keep sheep at their own expense—and that was that. The burgeoning of sheep raising brought other troubles, too. Rams were being allowed to run and mate with the ewes from August through November, bringing much loss to the owners of the ewes from lambing in the cold winter months. A penalty of two shillings for every ram found on the commons was put into effect, but a dozen or so years later the problem still persisted. The penalty was then increased to:

Whomsoever shall observe any ram or rams go upon the common with the ewes from the first of August until the middle of November from year to year–such rams shall be forfeited to the person or persons so observing them.

This must have solved the problem, as it was never mentioned again. During 1737-1765 it was possible for each settler to record an "ear mark" with the town by which his animals could be identified in case they strayed, which happened quite often. These marks consisted of crops (a piece of the ear cut off) in various parts of the ear, half crops,

Plough made in Enfield during the 1812 to 1860 period.

slits, swallows tails, half-pennies, holes, and cuts made in the ear in distinctive shapes, such as staples. Since each animal had two ears, of course, many combinations of "marks" were available and it made a very effective identification system. Following is an example of such an entry by the town clerk: "May 22nd. 1738, John Abbe entered the mark of his cretures, which is a crop on ye right ear and a slit in ye crop, and a half crop in ye upper side of the left ear." Or a simple one: "March 21, 1748 Isaac Kibbe entered ye mark of his cretures, which is a hold cut with an iron tool in ye near ear." A little rough on the animal momentarily, but effective identification. If an animal did stray and was picked up by others, this fact was also recorded in the town records. In fact, not only stray animals but also stray logs found floating in the river were recorded, and presumably the information was publicized on the town sign post. Logs were marked with their owner's mark, in this case a brand. Some of these entries are interesting and give us some idea of the agriculture of those days, for instance this one: "Taken up by John Pease Oct. 20th, 1772 a red steer year old past, marked with a halfpenny underside of right ear." Or another: "Taken up by Ebenezer Terry Jr. Oct. 27th. 1779 one mare."

It is difficult to reconstruct a picture of the agriculture of Enfield during the eighteenth century from the records as there are so few of them available, but the minutes of the town meetings give many hints about what was being raised. From the many references to "Merchantable boards" and grain and livestock, it is quite evident that these products were high on the list of those being produced by farmers. Horses too had become numerous and important enough to add a new town official—Brander of Horses. In fact, several town officers affecting farmers were elected. A Hayward was chosen to see that fences were kept in repair for keeping cattle out of cropland. Another title, Packer of Tobacco, is self-explanatory but indicated that Enfield was then raising enough tobacco to be able to export some; also that this important product needed inspection to insure customers of quality. Another officer, the Gager of Casks, had some interesting duties. It was his job to see that the buyer got *what* he paid for and *all* that he paid for. For even back in those days there were some unscrupulous characters who would add sand or chips to the barrel before filling it, or would use an oversize bung to take up some room in the cask. Then there was the Sealer of Leather, whose task was to inspect hides and leather before it was sold to make sure it was fully tanned and not over-limed. Hides could not even be tanned unless they were stamped by this official. Field Drivers were much like our dog wardens of today, but were responsible for impounding cattle, swine, sheep, and horses found where they didn't belong. These men must have been busy as the town had several pounds and complaints about stray animals were very numerous. Key Keepers held the keys to the town pounds, which were locked to keep people from letting their own animals out and reclaiming them without paying the fee.

In the year 1800 great changes were made in the rules concerning restraint of cattle and other farm animals, for the town was growing in population (then about 2,000) and these creatures were making a nuisance of themselves and damaging crops. After several attempts had failed to correct the situation the following law was voted upon with much stiffer penalties than previous regulations:

No horses, cattle, asses, mules, swine, or sheep shall by their owners be suffered to go at large without a keeper in any of the highways at any time, and in any part of the Town of Enfield, and if at any time any or either of the aforesaid creatures be found going at large without a keeper in any of the highways of the town, it shall be lawful for any person, and it shall be the duty of the Hayward appointed by the town, to take up the aforesaid and confine them in any of the town pounds, and the fee to be paid by the owner or owners shall be seventeen cents for each or either of the horses, cattle, asses, mules, and swine, and two cents for each sheep, whereof three quarters shall belong to the impounder and one quarter to the keeper of the keys.

It was also to be unlawful for the owner of such animals to allow them to feed on any unenclosed land, the penalties being the same as above. Then just to make sure that these animals would not be rescued by their owners, the law further stated that:

If any owner or person shall rescue any of such animals from the person or the official impounding them or from the pound, they shall pay a fine of two dollars and fifty cents plus *the sum of three dollars for pound breach.*

They handled the problem of the wandering goose a little differently, enacting this regulation:

Geese found at large without a keeper on unenclosed land shall be taken up by the person finding them or by the Hayward, and confined by them, notifying the owner if known, or posting a notice nearest the corner of the road where the geese were taken up. If the owner shall not appear within ten days and pay the possessor 4 cents for each goose and 2 cents per day for the keep of each goose, the geese shall be forfeited to the possessor, and he may convert them to his own use.

Rescue of each goose without paying the fees brought a fine of two dollars plus damages.

At a later town meeting the townspeople evidently thought their action a little harsh in regard to the impounding of geese running at large, for they changed the law to read:

Geese may go at large on the commons and unenclosed land in the Town of Enfield being well yoked with a yoke of not less than 12 inches in length—from the rising to the setting of the sun each day, any law or vote of the town to the contrary notwithstanding.

Shortly after the Revolution a strange religion sprang up in the northeastern part of the town. The wild and stormy faith included "speaking in tongues," and "Shakings," thus winning for them the name of Shakers. While their religion with its contributions to the industry of the town is treated elsewhere in this volume it is important to include them here also, for they were to make a tremendous addition to the agriculture of Enfield for the next one hundred and twenty-five years.

Accounts vary as to the land they owned, but it was at least two thousand acres—perhaps more—of some of the best farmland in Enfield. Thrift and an abhorrence of idleness were a part of their faith so it is little wonder that they thrived for well over a hundred years. Among the five "families" they owned many large farm buildings, herds, and flocks. Their cattle and horses were noted for miles around for always being fat and in good health. All their operations were carried out systematically and with strict economy. In a sense, they practiced subsistence farming, for they grew nearly everything they needed for food, clothing, and shelter. They raised their own grain, horses, cattle and sheep, tanned their own leather to make their own boots and shoes for the members of the families numbering in the hundreds, spun their own wool, and wove their own cloth. They even made some of their own farming tools, judged by outsiders to be some of the best; they sawed their own lumber and ground their own grain.

The Shakers' chief source of income over the years was from the sale of seeds and herbs. They grew them, dried them, sorted and packaged them, and then shipped them to every state, as well as to many foreign countries. It was a large and profitable business. During the year 1856, for instance, they shipped fourteen thousand pounds of herbs alone, "powdered, papered, and labeled." They made extracts, too, using the pure soft water from a mountain spring. Three of the most popular were Dandelion, Thoroughwort, and Butternut.

The pig was one farm animal not grown by the Shakers. In their religion the spirit proclaimed swine as unclean, and not to be eaten or kept on the Shaker premises. They obeyed this edict almost literally using tallow, butter, or goose oil as substitutes for lard when they prepared food. Well, *almost* literally, because there were a few occasions when one of the Shakers couldn't say no to an invitation to a roast pork dinner from one of the neighbors. One elder at the North Family Shakers was Omar Pease, a descendant of the first settlers and quite an

Devon oxen in Enfield early in the nineteenth century.

experimenter. He had the idea that he could sow a pine forest and tried it on the hilltop known as "Holy Hill," where the minimum security section of the Connecticut State Prison now stands. The resulting magnificent stand of white pine was a monument to him for many years.

After the Revolutionary War, economic conditions began to improve though for many years the improvement was almost imperceptible. The eastern part of the town was still for the most part covered with forest. Land prices were low, with woodland selling usually under two shillings per acre, and even good farm land bringing little more. Allen's *Enfield* described the situation as follows:

The fences used in the east part of the town were chiefly hedges of brush and ditches and those on the main street were in very bad condition. The pastures and streets were covered with bushes and scrub oak and the hay that was used was of an inferior quality mostly obtained from the meadows. The dwelling houses were miserable huts built without regard /to/ convenience or comfort, badly calculated /to/ protect the people from the cold of winter, or the heat of summer. The few exceptions to /this/ class were some unfinished wood houses generally destitute of back buildings except barns, or much convenience. Carriages were almost unknown at this time. Four or five chaises as they were called, and as many two-horse farm wagons constituted all the means of conveyance /or/ passage /?/ except the horse, the saddle, and the pillion. There was little or no cash in the town at that time, and the farmers generally /were/ badly in debt, and found great difficulty /in/ paying their taxes.

From 1790 to 1800 conditions improved greatly for farmers, as increased demand for farm products occasioned by the European wars then in progress resulted in higher prices. This in turn advanced real estate prices, both trends encouraging greatly increased production of farm products. At the same time, there began a trend of emigration which continued until after 1810. Most of the emigrants were headed for the frontier and the cheap lands of the West. Those leaving, however, failed to slow the incipient boom in farming, and quite possibly may even have hastened it. Farms of the period were much improved by cultivation and produced great quantities of grain for market.

into the
nineteenth century

As Enfield rounded the turn into the nineteenth century events and economic conditions were to exert a profound and happy effect on her agriculture. The growth of the nearby cities increased demand for our farm products. As the industrial revolution began to affect agriculture subsistence farming began to disappear. Farmers, enjoying more income, began to buy some of their clothing and domestic items instead of making them.

A look at a farm account book of this period is interesting and enlightening. Here, for instance, are some selected items from the farm accounts of Isaac Pease of Enfield in the year 1829:

5 lbs. pork @ 4c lb.	$ .20
8 bu. oats	3.00
1 qt. of gin	.11
½ bu. potatoes	.25
½ days work dreysing flax	.33
2 loads manure on your garden	.75
Hors & wagon to Wallop & Forge	.50
to reping 3 acres, bound & shook	3.00
to oxen to drawing 2 lodes hay &	
3 hands to help.	.50
8 gallons sidor	.20
6 eggs	.06
2 qts. milk	.08
2 lbs. butter	.24

—and these were good times!

A year later, at the end of the year, the same account book contained this interesting observation: "The end of the year 1 of January. It was a very pleasant day for the time. 2 day January plesant—people plowing."

Mother Nature was smiling that January, no doubt, but she could—and did—frown on other occasions, as we shall see in a moment.

Enfield farmers along with farmers everywhere have traditionally fought the weather. Sometimes they have won and sometimes lost but their loss in 1816 was truly a disaster. That was the year known as "the year without a summer" and as a recent issue of the *Hartford Courant* observed: "April and May were cold. Connecticut farmers noted that the fruit trees did not blossom until the end of May."

Then a hard frost destroyed the budding leaves and blossoms, killing fruit, corn, and some vegetables as well. Warm weather finally arrived in the first few days of June. Farmers began replanting their crops. At noon on June 5 the temperature in Williamstown, Massachusetts, where records were kept was a balmy eighty-three degrees. But by seven o'clock the next morning it had dropped to forty-five degrees— and that was the highest temperature recorded that day! A severe frost occurred every night from June 6 to June 9 from Canada to Virginia, killing newly-planted corn and vegetables.

The ice was an inch thick in northern Vermont and icicles a foot long hung from eaves.

In northern New England towns, newly shorn sheep, although sheltered, perished and thousands of migratory birds froze to death.

The weather stayed very cool all summer and on August 20 another cold wave arrived. Frost was reported as far south as East Windsor and most of the staple corn crop was destroyed.

By the next spring famine stalked New England and the first general migration from New England to the Middle West began, spurred by the dismal weather of the summer before.

The cold-weather culprit was volcanic dust thrown up by three great eruptions which took place between 1812 and 1817. The dust kept the sun's rays from penetrating the atmosphere as much as usual, while heat continued to radiate from the earth. Whatever the reason for this "unnatural" phenomenon it was an event which would be long remembered by Enfield farmers and people all over New England as one of the worst weather years in their memory.

Better times lay ahead, however, for with the opening of distilleries in Agawam and Warehouse Point and later in Enfield there was created a whole new market for the farmers' rye. Thus began a truly golden age for local farmers. Rye became their most important cash crop, but in addition they also fatted their cattle on "still swill" or distillers' grains, a by-product of the distilling process. Farmers of the period became quite prosperous as the substantial farmhouses built around 1800 and shortly thereafter will attest. Some farmers even became money lenders.

More evidence of the agricultural reform which was beginning to spread over the country was the founding of what we now know as the Union Agricultural Society, or Four Town Fair, in 1838. Although

Enfield is one of the participating towns, actually it all began in Somers as the result of an exhibit by Somers farmers. Interested to see which school district could show the largest number of cattle, they rounded up 210 yokes of oxen and showed them on Somers streets in that year.

So much interest was aroused that it was later agreed to form an organization to promote such exhibits: the Cultural and Mechanics Arts Society. The membership at that time was limited to Somers, Enfield, and Ellington with the first regular show held in Somersville in 1839. The next meeting convened at the inn of Henry A. Abbe in the Wallop district in Enfield, and the society was enlarged to include the town of East Windsor, although no attempt was made to hold the fair there until 1845. For many years the annual fair was primarily a cattle show with eighty yoke of oxen and steers exhibited as late as 1883 and over half of them from Enfield. Over the years other classes were added: sheep, swine, poultry, pet stock, horticultural produce and flowers, plus domestic manufactures, fine arts, and fancy work.

The name of the organization was changed to the Union Agricultural Society of Enfield, Somers, Ellington, and East Windsor at a meeting held in Enfield in 1861. The 1870 session of the legislature granted the group a charter which was gradually forgotten over many years until a vote was finally passed to reactivate it in 1934. A tobacco fair was proposed in 1874 to be held in Hazardville but apparently it never was held. An experimental two-day fair was held in Enfield in 1898 to introduce a European-type fair with produce being sold similar to an auction. This idea was apparently unsuccessful and was discarded.

Although over the years the fair has rotated around the member towns there have been several attempts to make a permanent home for it. The first was in 1850 when it was proposed to hold the fair in a fixed place. This was dropped but the question was again discussed in 1874, 1882, and in 1889 when a special effort was made toward centralization but it was voted down by a large margin. Finally, in 1960, the Society bought a piece of land in Somers consisting of fifty-five acres and made its permanent home there.

With permanent facilities currently consisting of an exhibit hall, rest rooms, electric service, and water supply the fair now operates as an annual three-day show furnishing entertainment and educational exhibits to people from a large area.

This history now returns to the area's dawning distillery era. It was to be of short duration, however, as following the Civil War the Internal

Revenue Department placed a federal tax on spirits. This plus the opening of distilleries near the western grain fields sealed the doom of the gin industry in Enfield. With the closing of the region's distilleries went the market for rye, a mighty blow to the agriculture of Enfield. There was still more trouble on the way, however, for with the coming of the railroads also came cheap beef from the western plains. Buffalo beef there for the taking began to compete with ours raised on highly taxed land and costing much more to produce. It was too much for our farmers to take and beef raising gradually died out. Many farmers changed from cattle to dairying and from rye to tobacco. Our sheep industry also succumbed to western competition about the same time.

the tobacco story

Tobacco has been a part of Enfield agriculture almost since the town was settled. It was apparently considered an important crop here even during the eighteenth century. Each year at the town meetings a Packer of Tobacco was chosen as a result of an attempt by the General Assembly to prevent fraud and dishonest practices by regulating the curing and packing of tobacco. For the most part, however, the acreage grown by individual farmers was quite small, two acres being considered a large crop until the invention of the tobacco setter early in the 1900s.

The first tobacco raised by the settlers was the same as that raised by the Indians. This variety, quite small with a bitter taste, was later replaced by other improved strains from the West Indies. In the acute economic readjustment following the Civil War farmers everywhere came out as losers, ours being no exception. From the 1870s to 1900 were heartbreaking years. Beaten by Western competition for their products, hampered by high taxes, and finally in the depression years of the 1890s beset by ruinous prices for their products, it is no wonder that agriculture began its slow decline during the period. Fortunately, for some Enfield farmers at least, the powder mills nearby and other rising industries in the town provided employment with which to supplement their meager income.

Though dairy farming had taken over where beef raising had left off and our farms had become more specialized, there was a need for a good cash crop. Tobacco began to supply that need. In 1890 a duty of two dollars per pound imposed by the government on the imported Sumatra wrappers which were competing seriously with our product had the effect of boosting production and increased the profit potential of the crop. Add to this the fact that the tobacco setter came into use about 1900, making it possible to plant many more acres than could be planted by hand. So it was no wonder that Enfield experienced such a boom in tobacco growing. From 1900 to 1921 the acres of tobacco grown in Enfield increased tremendously—peaking at 1,500 acres on 200 farms, and many tobacco barns or "sheds" were built. Tobacco shed "raisings," as they were called, became quite common and were quite a social event, looked forward to by young and old alike. They offered men the chance to show off their strength, the women an opportunity to advertise what good cooks they were, and for the kids it was an exciting occasion—with plenty of good things to eat. The farmer having the raising did all the preliminary work, or had it done. The ground was graded, the piers poured, the frame was spiked together in sections or "bents," and laid horizontally in readiness to be raised into position. Plates, rafters, girts, and braces were made ready and stacked nearby to be handy when needed. When everything was arranged the day was set, the neighbors called, the farmer's wife with her helpers, usually some of the neighbors' wives, prepared the food—cakes, doughnuts, pies, sweets of all kinds, and the drinks—cases of soda for some, beer for others, and even some "hard stuff."

On the day of the raising, neighbors and friends converged on the site from all directions and, after much friendly banter and kidding, the men gathered around the frame of the new shed. Each man armed himself with a pike pole, usually supplied by the carpenter, and the gang got in position to raise the first section of the frame. The sharpened ends of the pikes bit into the frame members and at the command of "heave" every one lifted and the heavy frame section began to rise into place. After many "heaves" the section was finally lifted into a

Setting tobacco on June 8, 1914. Henry Abbe drives and Linden Abbe and hired man set.

Suckering broadleaf tobacco before harvest in years gone by.

vertical position and braced in place. The whole process was then repeated with section after section until the whole frame was up, connected by the plates, and braced. Next the rafters were put on and at that point the raising was over with the carpenter left to finish the shed.

Raisings could be dangerous. The frame could and sometimes did slip, or a sudden gust of wind could topple it before it was finally secured, so it was mighty important that every man do his job, and do it well. Sometimes there were hitches—as on one occasion when the carpenter had made a mistake in the height of a concrete pier, and the frame did not fit on it. One of the men promptly solved the problem by grabbing an axe that was handy and chopping off the top of the pier—a rather back door approach. Another time one of the raisers, who had been imbibing a little too freely before the raising, decided to dance a jig on the plate of the new barn, a slender beam at least sixteen feet from the ground and only eight inches wide. Luckily, he didn't fall, and of course he provided great entertainment for the crowd which yelled its encouragement. When each raising was completed everyone headed for the refreshments, which in amazingly short time disappeared, but still not before any exciting moments of the event had been

76 / *the challenge of change*

The shaded fields of a typical tobacco farm.

relived and the status of the crops, the weather, or the chances of the next political candidate had been discussed. Finally, one by one the neighbors left for their own farms. This event was repeated many times during the tobacco boom years in Enfield. No one section of the town has a monopoly of the type of soil which will grow tobacco well, so its production was spread pretty much over the whole area.

Between 1900 and 1910 there was a new development in the tobacco industry here. Experiments in Windsor had proven that it was possible to grow Cuban tobacco in Connecticut by reproducing the tropical climate of Cuba and Sumatra artificially. This was done by enclosing the tobacco field in a "tent" of very loosely woven cloth. The resulting tobacco had a thinner leaf which made superior wrappers for cigars and could compete with the Cuban tobacco which had previously been imported. Several of these "shade grown" plantations were established in Enfield soon after 1910, and have been successful enough to survive to the present time. L.B. Haas Co. began its operation in 1911 on Maple Street in Hazardville. I.H. Woodworth set up on the John McNamarra farm on Raffia Road and expanded later to land on Pound Road. William and Henry Hunting established shade tobacco production in 1920 in the East Wallop section of town and were later bought out by the present owner, the Consolidated Tobacco Corporation. Other growers from out of town have also rented land in Enfield to raise shade grown tobacco from time to time.

Since Enfield farmers began to specialize in tobacco, growers have

Broadleaf harvest of the past . . .

experienced wide fluctuation in their fortunes. Tobacco is a high cost, high risk crop, very vulnerable to the vagaries of the weather, easily damaged by wind or frost or ruined in a few minutes by a summer hailstorm. Field diseases can lower the quality of the crop or ruin it altogether. No one who has raised tobacco here will soon forget the devastating effect of the "Wildfire" disease. Fortunately that blight has been controlled, but there are others like the "Blue Mould," which gave the shade growers so much trouble. More recently another problem called "Fleck" has appeared as a result of the pollution of the atmosphere. The crop is not even safe after it is harvested and in the shed, for then it is subject to the rotting and moulding known as "pole sweat" which can cause much damage, particularly in damp, muggy weather. There have also been years when hail practically wiped out the crop in Enfield, but usually the damage is more spotty. In 1938 a hurricane which struck while tobacco was curing in the sheds demolished many barns and damaged others as well as much tobacco. Many of these sheds were never rebuilt—in fact it has been reported that at least 170 tobacco sheds were taken off the assessor's list in that one year. Tobacco acreage here peaked around 1921 and remained high until the stock market crash in 1929. In 1931 with the depression in full swing the price of broadleaf binder tobacco dropped to fourteen cents per pound, about half of what it had brought the previous year. In 1932 it hit a low of twelve cents. The discouraged growers cut back their production as the government came in with acreage controls. Paid by the government if they did not grow tobacco over their allotments,

. . . and more modern style.

most growers signed up for the program. As a result, production was brought more in line with demand. Prices began to improve slowly but the tobacco boom was over for Enfield and acreage has remained low ever since.

In 1952 another development further depressed demand for broadleaf tobacco of the type being grown in Enfield. This was introduction of a new process for making a "manufactured leaf " to be used for cigar binders (the layer just under the wrapper): the whole tobacco leaf is ground up, stems and all, with other scrap tobacco, and rolled out into a paper-like sheet for use by the cigar makers. At first it was thought (hopefully, by the growers) that this innovation would not be accepted by the cigar makers—and particularly by the smoking public. Unhappily for the growers, however, it was accepted eagerly by the cigar makers, and because of its cheapness had a great effect on the demand for natural binders. Enfield and all other growers of broadleaf tobacco in the Connecticut Valley have been adversely affected by this development.

Tobacco growing still depends for the most part on hand labor. While there have been many attempts to mechanize at least a part of the process, most of these have been unsuccessful. The invention of the tobacco setter was an exception. It did speed planting tremendously. There are a few farmers living today who can remember what a slow and laborious job it was when done by hand. First the readied ground had to be marked out and hilled with a horse-drawn hiller. The locations of the plants in the row were then marked with a hand-pushed

Broadleaf hung for drying in one of Enfield farmer Joe Kaleda's tobacco barns.

device resembling a wheel, with projections on the rim which stuck into the ground and left an impression where each plant was to be placed. The planting team, one man with a basket of plants, the other with a bucket of water and a ladle just large enough to contain the water needed for one plant, started down the row. One man planted while the other watered, and so it went till the job was done—back breaking work to say the least. There have been some improvements in the harvesting process too, although much hand labor is still used. Most of the outdoor tobacco raised here today is placed on hook lath before being hung in the sheds; however, it was not always so for back in 1890 or thereabouts it was done a little differently. First the plants were cut down and wilted well, then loaded into carts and taken to the shed. The carts were driven into the shed and the plants were tied directly to the poles one at a time by the "hanger," a man who took a string and as each plant came to him placed the butt of the plant against the pole, took a turn around it with the string, then crossed the string to the other side of the pole ready for the next plant, which was placed diagonally opposite the first. While this could be done much faster than it could be described, it was still slower than later methods of "spearing" or "hooking." One method, which was never used to any great extent, was called "spearing on the ground," so-called because the spearer thrust one end of the lath into the ground until it supported itself, placed the spear on top, picked up a plant from the ground and speared it onto the lath, continuing until the lath was full. It was a dangerous method (you could get the spear in the neck), hard on the tobacco too, but one man could do it—probably why it was used. Although most attempts to mechanize tobacco growing have failed, the shade tobacco growers do have a machine to sew the leaves in the sheds. Broadleaf growers also have used a machine to pull the plants off the spear laths; however, most growers now use hook lath so these machines are used very little any more.

Although reduced demand and overproduction have been the most compelling factors in the reduction of tobacco acreage in Enfield, there are other reasons for the decline. After World War I the increase in cigarette smoking prompted a corresponding decrease in the demand for cigars. As the pace of American life quickened there seemed to be less time for leisurely cigar smoking, while a quick "drag" on a cigarette could be managed more easily. More women also began to smoke, and of course they preferred the cigarette as a more feminine practice. As cigarettes and cigars use entirely different types of tobacco there was less demand for the pipe smoking type of tobacco grown in Enfield. Later, with the start of hostilities in World War II, came a tremendous increase in the aircraft and other defense industries close by. The relatively high wages paid by these new industries competed directly with farm labor, so that some small growers gave up tobacco entirely to work in the shops or perhaps continued to grow a small amount, relying entirely on family labor to care for the crop.

The latest blow to tobacco growers in Enfield, as elsewhere, has been the evidence that smokers are more likely to suffer from lung cancer than people who do not smoke. The Surgeon General's warning, "Smoking may be injurious to your health," required on packages of cigarettes has not affected cigar smoking except by inference, but the fact remains that many people have given up smoking altogether. Tobacco production in Enfield has remained fairly stable for the last few years at about 300 acres, all of it under federal acreage control.

Although the first cigar factories were established in East Windsor and Suffield about 1810, to Enfield goes the distinction of having the last of the old time cigar makers in New England. At this date John M. Ward still plies his craft at his little shop in Thompsonville, turning out about 300 stogies a day. Using tools, many of which are 100 years old, he bunches, molds, presses, books, and wraps—producing cigars from purest tobacco, most of it Connecticut grown, without using additives or "homogenized" leaf. He is the last of a class of skilled artisans. When he dies or quits, the process of cigar making around here will have been just about completely mechanized. As he says, "There's no use in any young feller trying to learn this up against machines."

potatoes replace tobacco

As tobacco began to be phased out in the depression years of the 1930s, potatoes began to be grown by some farmers as a substitute cash crop. They fitted in quite well on land suitable for tobacco, thriving on the fertile, well drained soils here and producing yields and a quality of product which compared favorably with the famed Maine "spuds." Potatoes had been grown in Enfield from the early days, but only in small quantities and mostly for the local trade. By the 1930s, however, great advances had been made in mechanizing the handling of the crop. Tractors had developed to the point where they could be used in place of horses on row crops, and were cheap enough for the moderate sized farm to afford one. The potato planter, potato digger, and field sprayer had all been invented so it was possible to handle many acres quickly and easily. Insect pests and soil and seed-borne diseases could be controlled quite well by spraying, while heavy use of commercial fertilizer produced bumper crops. Many farmers built large storage units for potatoes during the years just prior to World War II to keep their crop through the winter and thus take advantage of the higher prices usually in effect then. Potato production reached its peak in 1955 with about four hundred acres grown on ten farms. It has since declined, with approximately one hundred acres at present, on three farms.

While many of the potato growing operations had become mechanized during the 1930s, the actual picking of the potato at harvest time was done by hand for a long time. As local labor for this back-breaking job became scarce during the war years of 1941 and thereafter, laborers were imported from Puerto Rico and Jamaica. For several years they were the primary source of such labor here, until about 1960 when the potato combine was developed. It mechanized the potato harvest to a point where these workers were no longer needed.

Potato growers in Enfield have witnessed a wide swing in their fortunes over the years that they have grown the crop commercially. For the most part the ups and downs have been the result of widely fluctuating market prices. These were caused in turn by conditions in other growing areas such as Maine and Long Island, which also supply the market Enfield growers depend on. Some of the unprofitable years have also been due to wet weather encouraging crop rot diseases that sometimes cause almost a total loss. There have been good years too, when prices soared to fantastic heights and the business was highly profitable, but the uncertainties of potato farming, the growing demand for housing land, and better opportunities in other occupations have all conspired to reduce potato acreage in Enfield.

commercial dairying
in Enfield

When the distilleries disappeared, beef cattle raising left too since it depended to a certain extent on the by-product of the stills for an economical fattening feed. Beef raisers switched to dairy cows as the growth of our own town and that of the nearby cities of Hartford and Springfield began to improve the demand for milk. Dairy herds were quite small for a long time, usually numbering about ten to fifteen cows. There was a good reason for this. Fifteen cows were about all one man cared to milk by hand himself, hence the herds were limited in most cases to that number and farmers who generally hired helpers for the cropping season would let them go in the fall.

One of the interesting and changing aspects of dairying and cattle raising in general was the varying method of moving the animals. Railroads were used for long distances after about 1840, but for shorter moves cattle were driven over the road until after 1910, or until trucks came into use. There are at least two men in Enfield who recall taking part in such a drive in their youth. Howard Pierce, a Wallop farmer and lifelong resident, remembers driving cattle from Northampton, Massachusetts, to the Wallop district of Enfield starting at five o'clock in the morning. Mortimer Granger, Jr., well known auctioneer

The Olin Olmsted house and barns . . . a typical Enfield farm . . . from a photo taken in 1932.

here, recalls driving beef cattle many times as a boy from Melrose to the slaughter houses in Hartford and comments that it was quite a chore at times to keep them out of people's gardens along the way. Before the days of the motor truck cattle dealers would start out with a herd of cattle in the morning and drive them over the road from farm to farm, trading as they went—selling a cow here, buying another there, returning with an entirely different herd than the ones they started with.

At first most of the milk produced was skimmed for the cream (usually by the farmer's wife), the cream then being churned into butter and sold locally. The skim milk was usually fed to the pigs. Some farmers retailed their milk, ladling it out of the can with a tin dipper. No bottles were used. Later the Ellington Creamery picked up the cream from farms in the eastern part of town. Milk for this purpose was stored in ice water in what was known as a Cooley Creamer. Cans with a graduated glass panel in the side, through which the amount of cream present could be read, were attached to a specially designed rack and lowered into the tank. When the pick-up man came he drained off the skim milk, read the amount of cream on the gauge, and credited the farmer with that amount. Michael Maloney collected cream for the Ellington Creamery for many years. In 1888 the Somers Creamery was organized by a group of Somers businessmen and became the milk market for many of the diary farmers in the eastern part of town. Most of this milk was then shipped by trolley to Springfield to be sold as fluid milk.

Milk was collected daily from each farm and during most of the year was hauled to the Somers plant in a wagon except when winter storms made bobsleds necessary to get the milk through. The hauling job was done usually by a farmer who had a spare team and some spare time. The first hauler, Richard Sunderland, was followed by Marshall Collins, Barnard Turner, and finally John Lynch. In 1916 this creamery moved to Springfield but Enfield farmers continued to ship to it.

By 1921 dairy farmers became discouraged by the chaotic conditions in their markets, almost totally controlled by the milk dealers, and began to form cooperatives to improve their bargaining power. The New England Milk Producers Association was the first of these, followed by the Connecticut Milk Producers Association a few years later. Both of these organizations enabled Enfield farmers to obtain better prices for their milk. While the dairy farmers of eastern Enfield have produced mostly for the wholesale market, others have become retailers.

In 1861 Amos D. Bridge decided to go into business for himself. He erected a house on what is now School Street in Hazardville and, as he had a large family and also boarded some help, soon found it necessary to have a few cows for milk. He built a barn and started a small dairy herd about 1865, along with his many other enterprises, and found himself in the dairy business. By 1910 Bridges' Sons had developed a fine herd of Registered Holstein cattle and a dairy in which they bottled and delivered their milk, supplying most of the village of Hazardville. Their cows were from some of the best breeding stock of that day, setting many production marks—including one of over 26,000 pounds of milk in one year, a great record in those days. Some of their highest producing cows were milked four times a day. The herd also included many show winners at the Eastern States Exposition and national breed shows. Like many other fine herds in Connecticut this one suffered a tremendous set-back when compulsory tuberculosis testing started and many fine cows were ordered slaughtered after discovery of this disease. These cows were replaced with tuberculosis-free stock, however, and the herd made a great comeback, continuing until 1940 when it was dispersed.

On Elm Street George Poole maintained a large modern dairy conducted by his son-in-law George Rutherford. Mr. Poole was not only very influential in development of the carpet industry in Enfield and elsewhere but was also locally famous for his work in transforming the old Town Farm—which contained a large swamp and pond—into a fine home and farm. Nearby on Elm Street Lucius Allen also had a sizable herd and dairy, bottling and delivering milk throughout most of Thompsonville. More recently there have been others, notably Smyth's Dairy and Cimino Bros. on Enfield Street. All of these were of great importance in their day in supplying the entire town with milk and dairy products. Although some survived longer than others, all eventually succumbed for a variety of reasons. The rising cost of labor made home deliveries so expensive that dairies were not able to meet the competition from supermarkets and dairy stores where the customer picked up the milk. Smyth's Dairy, the largest and the last to go, was finally forced out by the recent tremendous population growth and industrial expansion requiring much land formerly farmed.

While dairying has been important in Enfield Agriculture, dairy herds here have never attained the great size they have in other areas, possibly because of the competition of tobacco for the use of the land. Some of the largest herds have also been the best producing. Raymond Abbe in the Wallop section developed a high producing herd of thirty milking Holsteins in Enfield which attained a yearly average of 16,174 pounds of milk and 630 pounds of butter fat per cow.

Olin Olmsted, also in the Wallop section of town, kept a fine herd of Guernseys which was well known and highly regarded in this area. He farmed on land close by the Buckhorn falls, purchased in 1819 by his father who had been a strong-willed temperance advocate refusing to sell his rye to the distilleries or his apples for cider, nor would he raise tobacco. Olin eased the family temperance a bit for he did raise some tobacco.

Olin also gained a reputation as a horticulturalist. He was always interested in improving his varieties of apples and corn, as he was dissatisfied with many of them. He made many crosses of both corn and apples on his own farm and it was while inspecting the corn in one of his fields that he discovered a variety known as Opaque 2, which contains much more protein than normal. He brought it to the attention of the Connecticut Experiment Station in New Haven. As a result he was honored posthumously in 1971, more than fifty years later, in a letter to his daughter from the Indian Agricultural Research Institute of New Delhi expressing an appreciation of the great value that this strain of corn has been to the people of India in combating protein malnutrition, and gratitude for this important discovery. They found that children fed on a diet containing Opaque 2 corn responded as well as children fed protein from milk.

Before moving to his father's farm in Enfield Mr. Olmsted had raised dairy cattle in Springfield at the "X," peddling the milk in Springfield and supplementing the supply with that shipped to him

The Smyth dairy farm as it looked in the early 1940s.

daily by rail from the farm in Enfield. After Mr. Olmsted's death, the herd was maintained for a while by his son-in-law Fred Pyck but was later dispersed. The farm tract has since become the site of a housing development.

There have been several other prominent dairymen in Enfield. Richard Smyth on Hazard Avenue built up a large herd of Holstein cattle which supplied much of the milk for his dairy. This highly productive herd unfortunately had to be dispersed after a disastrous fire leveled the great barn which housed them. His brother George Smyth also kept a herd of dairy cattle on his Enfield Street farm. The northern-most dairy farmer in Enfield was Bernard Shea whose farm straddled the state line between Massachusetts and Connecticut. He kept a large herd of predominantly Jersey cows and sold milk wholesale. When the I-91 throughway was built, it appropriated a large chunk of his farm, but he relocated on Brainard Road and continued dairying until about 1970 when the herd was dispersed. Cimino Brothers operated as another producer-retailer on Enfield Street and maintained a good-sized herd for many years. They conducted extensive retail routes throughout the town.

Until 1912 all milking here was done by hand, but in that year Linden Abbe purchased the first milking machine used in Enfield. It was quite crude compared with present day equipment but worked very well nevertheless—it used foot power and was capable of milking two cows at once. The operator sat on a seat and peddled to produce the vacuum needed for the milking. It was the first but certainly not the last of many inventions which would have a great effect on the dairy industry here. By no means the least of these was the field baler which made it possible to store twice as much hay in the same space as before while also cutting the time and labor needed for haymaking. Other major improvements followed, including mechanical refrigeration— which did away with the need to cut and store ice—and tractors which began to replace horses about this time. Once in motion the wheel of mechanical improvement turned swiftly, bringing into use a whole generation of haying, planting, and tillage tools all capable of doing their jobs much more quickly and efficiently than work previously done by hand.

There was just one drawback to all the new equipment, however: it cost a lot of money. The investment in farming began to rise sharply. Shortly after World War II one major investment was forced on our dairymen after the Cooperatives handling their milk decided to eliminate the pick-up of cans from the members, so it became necessary to install stainless steel storage tanks on each farm. Some dairymen with larger herds made the change but for older men with only a few cows and no one to carry on the business it was the end of the line. They refused to make the investment, and sold their cows instead. Thus the number of dairy herds in Enfield was reduced drastically at that point. Also, during these post-war years, feed prices rose considerably along with higher taxes, rising costs of labor, and inflation all adding their burdens to an industry never known for its high profits and practically squeezing it out of the town. Today there remains only one commercial dairy farm in Enfield plus the institutional herd at the Osborn Prison Farm.

poultry keeping
in Enfield

It is difficult to say when poultry keeping began in Enfield but it must have been soon after the first settlers arrived. Eggs are such an important ingredient in cooking that it is natural to suspect colonial women would have insisted on having some poultry to provide them. While many references are made to geese in the early history of the town, there is no mention of chickens, though the early inhabitants surely must have kept them. They remained, however, as backyard and barnyard flocks, sufficient in size only to fill their owners' needs for meat and eggs, with any surplus of eggs, particularly in the spring months, probably traded for groceries at the neighborhood store. This was generally the situation until the end of the nineteenth century. By that time demand had risen for poultry meat and eggs in the nearby cities where people could no longer raise their own chickens. So, at that time, from the somnolent barnyard beginnings there arose in Enfield a type of agriculture which would last for about fifty years, occupy the lives of several farmers, and become an important part of the local agricultural scene, but eventually disappear and leave little but sagging barns and rotting coops to remind us of it.

Although George Poole kept a large hennery as one of his many farm enterprises on Elm Street before 1900, perhaps Enfield's first real commercial poultryman was Ralph Moody, a practical and ingenious sort of man, far ahead of his time in poultry raising. He began in 1922, hatching his chickens in kerosene incubators, converted some of his existing buildings to laying houses, and expanded his flock by building new houses. Though he preferred Leghorns, he also kept some other breeds, raised some capons, and retailed many of his eggs. His farm contained many home-built mechanical aids to cut down on labor. He pioneered in raising battery broilers, and used a "back to nature" method of raising pullets in the woods to save the cost of building shelters for them. He even hoisted feed to the top of his laying houses to let it fall through chutes to the chickens below. While this method of handling feed became very common in later years when "bulk" feed and automatic feeders came into use, it was an innovation in those days.

Other townsmen built their flocks at about the same time. Lyman Norris on Maple Street in Hazardville began in a small way in 1919 with sixty pullets, half of which were hatched and raised with hens. That same year he started a retail egg route, getting $1.10 per dozen—a powerful incentive to go into the poultry business. Over the next few years he increased his flock until finally he had several thousand birds producing market eggs. In 1921 an adult poultry club was organized with the help of the Connecticut Agricultural College Extension Service. It was a great help to farmers who were just beginning as commercial poultrymen, supplying them with useful information for their

Feeding time at the Norris poultry farm in 1922.

business and encouraging record keeping and business methods which would help them succeed. Many of the men who later had large commercial flocks belonged to this club. Marshall Collins was another convert to poultry keeping about this time. In 1920, discouraged by the low price for milk from his cows and the great risk and unpredictability of the tobacco business, and amazed by the profits his children were making from their little 4-H poultry project, he decided to try raising chickens himself. During the next twenty years he gradually increased his flock, retailing most of the production; produced hatching eggs for several years, ran a small hatchery for a time, then returned to marketing eggs again. The flock of about 10,000 birds was continued by his sons after his death until 1969 when it was sold. There were also several poultrymen in the Thompsonville area. Charles Button on Elm Street, a Mr. Sharapan on King Street, Joseph Pasini on Shaker Road. These men had flocks totaling several thousand layers. A later arrival in the business was Raymond Rutherford, of Elm Street, with a flock of about 5,000 birds producing hatching eggs. He started with Leghorns then switched to New Hampshire Reds. After his death in 1952 the business was sold to Joseph Grace who continued hatching-egg production for a few years until the farm was sold for building development.

Of all the poultrymen in Enfield the Pilches were the most widely known. They were also the largest and their contribution to poultry raising—particularly the growing of broilers—was the greatest. The business was run by two brothers with Chester, the elder, in charge of sales and Francis handling production. Chester's entry into the business began with a 4-H poultry project when he took over his family's fifty hen-brooded chicks on a two-acre backyard in Feeding Hills, Massachusetts. In 1929 he enrolled in an Extension course to learn the art of sexing day-old chicks. The demand for this service was so great that on completion of the course, and after two years' practice to develop his skill, he was so much in demand as a chick sexor that he had to hire a chauffeur to drive him between hatcheries so that he could rest his eyes. In 1937 the brothers bought the Ralph Moody farm, built a large laying house in 1939 and a brooder house in 1940. This was soon to become the largest breeding establishment in the area. After World War II the Pilch School of Chick Sexing was established and more than 400 students were taught in a three-week G.I.-approved course. The school is no longer in operation.

Primarily the Pilches were breeders of meat-type chickens. They were so successful at producing a superior bird for this purpose that they won the Maine Broiler Breeding Test Award in 1964 with an entry which produced 3.09 pounds of meat in six weeks on 1.76 pounds of feed per pound of grain, a phenomenal achievement, making it possible to market broilers commercially two weeks earlier than previously. With this sound genetic base, the Pilch brothers expanded their plant and business until they had 150,000 breeders which supplied them with one-third of the thirty million meat-type breeder females used by the broiler hatching-egg producers who supply the nation's two billion chicks for broilers. Besides their Enfield plant, which was the international headquarters for nine subsidiary corporations, they operated six plants in the United States, Canada, and in overseas market areas. At the peak of their operations their employees numbered 260; they did over $1,000,000 business per year, and Pilch meat-type breeding stock was known in all the major countries of the world. In 1969 the business was sold to the Dekalb Corporation, which operated in Enfield for only a short time before moving the business elsewhere.

Enfield's poultry industry has gone now, a casualty of our everchanging economy. Barely fifty years have passed since it all began with a few chickens, some good prices, and the lure of profits to be made, yet today not one commercial poultryman remains.

The reasons for its demise are many, among them the surging growth of the town that posed environmental problems for large poultry establishments, the soaring capital investment required, the competition of housing and industry for the same land, and the economic uncertainty of the business—a cycle of years of depressed prices followed by a short boom then another bust. Modern poultry keeping has become a complex, highly mechanized, and automated business, and not suited to heavily populated areas. Enfield farmers have not had the means or the inclination to follow it further.

vegetable ventures

Before 1900 there was very little specialized vegetable production here, mostly general farms with a mixture of animal and crop enterprises. Vegetables were raised primarily for home consumption with perhaps an acre or so of turnips to sell in the fall or a patch of squash or pumpkins to sell or store for the winter; root crops were raised to some extent as they stored well and could be sold or used a few at a time throughout the winter. The local markets and grocers used some but could not absorb all the local supply. The growth of Hartford and Springfield, however, created a demand for fresh vegetables which reached out to the surrounding towns, and it began to be profitable for Enfield farmers to take their produce to either of these cities. In 1890 Addison Brainard, who raised several acres of vegetables, hauled a load into the produce market in Springfield every morning during the summer and fall with a horse and wagon, leaving at 3:30 A.M. and returning about noon. Many other farmers here have made similar early morning trips to the produce markets to sell their vegetables.

When the depression hit in 1929 tobacco prices plummeted and farmers began to cast about for crops to take its place. Some began to plant potatoes, while others were attracted to cucumbers as there was a good demand for pickles at the time. Most of these pickle producers signed contracts with the Silver Lane Pickle Company of East Hartford. The crop was a poor substitute for tobacco, but it was better than no income at all. For a summer of fighting bees, backaches, and boredom the farmer received about three dollars per thousand for #1, or perfect pickles, and a dollar per thousand for #2, or slightly imperfect ones. It was no get-rich-quick scheme by any means, at least not for the farmer.

Sweet corn has been a popular garden crop with much of it being grown for the local market, though some is also shipped out to nearby cities. Until effective sprays and dusts were developed, corn ear-worms were very destructive, lowering the quality of the corn considerably, but today insecticides control this problem very well.

Every bit as popular as sweet corn, tomatoes have accounted for many acres for years. Usually they have been field grown, but to take advantage of the higher prices available in the off season, at least one market gardener in Enfield has gone into the production of greenhouse tomatoes, a very specialized business.

Strawberries, though of some importance here, have not been raised very extensively in the past, probably because they are rather risky, easily damaged or destroyed by frost. They also require much hand labor to harvest. In recent years, however, development of the "Pick Your Own" idea has revived much interest in this crop, with the result that there are now several acres under cultivation.

As the population of our town has increased, and particularly since the post World War II influx, the opportunities for marketing produce at the farm have increased markedly. Many roadside stands or farm markets have sprung up as a result. These supply fresh vegetables daily from the farmer's own fields, supplemented usually with some items that are not locally available, brought in from the city produce markets. This type of marketing enables the farmer to realize a better return for his product and supplies the consumer with really fresh vegetables.

Over the past twenty years, from 1955 to 1975, the number of acres of vegetables grown in Enfield has decreased less than that of any other farm crop. It now stands at about 400 acres.

So here we are three quarters of the way through the twentieth century and the changes and adjustments continue—some call it progress but others are not so sure. In agriculture's long history in Enfield there have been many changes, some slight, some slow, some sudden, some stupendous, some good and some bad. From bare survival and meager subsistence for all, to modest income and a frugal life for many, on to prosperity and a good life for some, and for others—failure—the changes have been never-ending. Even so, our agriculture has come a long way and has served the town and its citizens well.

Our farmers have seen agriculture change from an extensive type using many acres to intensive, with land being used sparingly, and from general farming to highly specialized enterprises. Horses have replaced oxen, tractors have replaced horses, electricity has brought a host of machines and equipment to end the drudgery of many farm tasks. Machinery of all kinds has come upon the scene.

Yet there is still the weather to fight. Nothing has changed that, and the competition is always there—just waiting. There still don't seem to be enough hours in the day to get everything done.

CHAPTER 5

ENFIELD CHURCHES

Organized Congregations

THE ENFIELD CONGREGATIONAL CHURCH
1295 Enfield Street / Organized: 1680

   The story of the Enfield churches is largely an account of the growth of the town as one ethnic group after another came to Enfield. Shortly thereafter a church of the denomination they had known and attended in their native land was established.

   The Congregational Church was the first. It was the church of a group of Puritans most of whom came from Salem, one of the early Massachusetts towns whose people had been denied the privilege of freedom of worship in England.

   The Enfield Congregational Church was authorized in 1680 by the Springfield committee in charge of the Freshwater settlement. One of the requirements for those accepting a home lot was to form and build a church at the earliest opportunity. The first building was not erected until 1683. It stood near the present Enfield Street Cemetery and the area behind it was used as a burying ground. The oldest gravestone to be seen reads: "1690—Isaac Morgan, son of Isaac Morgan." Little is known of this early church and community. For about seventeen years there was no minister and services in this 20 feet by 20 feet log church were conducted by its members. As was the custom of those early days, it was mandatory to attend church or suffer a fine.

When it became apparent that this little building could no longer serve the town's needs it was replaced by a larger one located across the street from Post Office Road. A large engraved boulder now marks the location. It is thought that the stone foundation is still in the ground. It is interesting to note that the people were called to church by a drummer. He beat his drum in the "town street" and when all were ready, beat it again for the minister. The drummer also beat his drum for funerals, on lecture days, and for town meetings. In 1742 the drummer was paid twenty-five shillings for the year. The town operated this way until 1784 when a bell was donated and mounted in the third building, now the old town hall.

A long service was customary in the morning and another in the afternoon, with an intermission at noon for lunch. The sermons were at least two hours long. Since early churches were unheated, in winter people brought heated stones to rest their feet on for a little warmth and during the noon lunch hour these stones would be reheated at the fireplace of some nearby house. Later footstoves were used.

During the time of this second church it was the practice to assign pews to the members on the basis of each man's importance according to age, wealth and rank. This was called "seating the meeting house" and was done by a committee. Needless to say this often led to trouble. However, the custom lasted until 1835 at which time money for church expenses, including the pastor's salary, was raised by an annual sale of pews. This change gave members the opportunity to have any pew they wished by renting it for the year and did away with the chore of seating the meeting house. There is a trust fund in the Enfield Congregational Church today which establishes a particular pew rent free. The custom of renting pews was dropped long ago but some churches in town still have a box in the vestibule for pew donations.

About 1749 a group of members broke away from the original church and organized a second church. They were dissatisfied with the direction the religious teachings were taking and wished to have a more strict interpretation. They were called Separatists or Strict Congregationalists. A church building was erected about 1764 but there was no legal existence until 1770 when the General Assembly granted their petition for establishment as an independent church, the Second

Ecclesiastical Society of Enfield. The existence of this church was comparatively brief and many members eventually returned to the First Churches as was to be the case in a later division.

This same situation occurred again about 100 years later, in 1855. Another group, who believed in strict Calvinistic doctrines, left the First Church and established the North Congregational Church, but they too had a short existence. Their church building stood on the west side of Enfield Street in the middle of what is now the driveway to the Enfield High School.

The single most important event that took place in this second meeting house was the sermon, "Sinners in the Hands of an Angry God," delivered by Jonathan Edwards of Northampton on July 8, 1741. The people were terrified by his vivid description of what would happen to sinners in the hereafter.

About 1772 the church members felt that this church had to be replaced with a larger one for the growing town. This was a difficult time in our country but plans were drawn up, the building erected, and finished in January, 1775. It was a plain rectangular building with a steeple and was built by Isaac Kibbe.

On Thursday, April 20, 1775, an event took place that awakened Enfield to the Revolutionary War. As was the custom in those days, there was a lecture every Thursday afternoon at the meetinghouse. Sometime during this lecture a rider on horseback raced into town, stopped at the tavern across the street and announced that war had started in a little town near Boston. Upon hearing this news the town drummer, Thomas Abbey, got his drum and walked around the meeting house beating it loudly. This broke up the lecture and everyone came outside to find out what had happened. The next day, he, with about seventy-five other Enfield men, marched off to war. At the end of the war he came home with the rank of captain. It is his statue that stands on the lawn in front of the Congregational Church today.

By 1844 the third meeting house was showing signs of wear. It was voted to put up a new building instead of repairing it, and a committee was appointed to solicit subscriptions.

It was at this time that the third church building was sold to the town for a town house. It was moved across the road, the steeple pulled down and the portico added. We know it now as The Old Town Hall. Several sites were suggested for the new church. The members could not agree on this point and it was moved that a committee of disinterested persons from adjacent towns be asked to decide on the best location. So

The present Enfield
Congregational Church, built in
1849, as it looked at the turn of
the century.

in January, 1848, Judge Morris of Springfield, Herleheigh Haskell of Windsor, and Oliver Chapin of Somers duly visited Enfield and gave it as their opinion that the best site for the new church was the Miner Place, so called. However, at the next meeting of the Ecclesiastical Society it was unanimously voted, thirty-nine to zero, to build the new church on the Jane Pease property immediately east of the site where the third building was situated.

The present church building was dedicated on February 14, 1849. The plan for it was drawn by F. M. Stone of New Haven, the builder was Newton Moses, also of New Haven, and the interior decoration, in fresco, was done by Molini and Allegri of New York City in "an elegant and tasteful manner." This was changed in 1912 to the present style.

Over the years there have been other changes. In 1874 a chapel was built in the rear, the gift of Dr. Harry Allen Grant. It was replaced in 1962 by the present parish house which provides Sunday School rooms, kitchen facilities, and an auditorium.

HAZARDVILLE UNITED METHODIST CHURCH
330 Hazard Avenue / Organized: 1835

The two Methodist churches, Hazardville United Methodist and Enfield United Methodist, do not owe their origin to any ethnic group. They were inspired by a camp meeting held on Job's Hill in Somers in 1829. Following this, groups met in private homes in different parts of the town for religious services, in Scitico, Jabbok, Wallop, and a section later known as Thompsonville. Every two weeks there was a preaching service at the Scitico schoolhouse which was located approximately at the east corner of Hazard Avenue and Holiday Lane.

When the congregation outgrew the schoolhouse and a church building was needed, a site was chosen farther west on the road between Scitico and Enfield. This road was probably only a cart path and there were only three or four houses within half a mile of the site, but there in the woods the church was built in 1835. It was about equally distant from Scitico, Wallop, Jabbok and West Enfield, as the Thompsonville section was then called, and convenient for the farm people who would attend. There were seventy-six members of this early church.

At first the church was supplied by circuit preachers with the first established minister coming in 1838. The building itself was thirty-two feet by forty feet and cost $1200. It was very plain with uncushioned seats and plain glass windows. There were stoves in the corners under the gallery. This building is still in existence but is now a four family apartment house across from the Old Cemetery in Hazardville which was there before the church.

Like the Congregational Church there were services both morning and afternoon on Sunday, and moreover Sunday School came in between. About the same time that the church was built the manufacture of gunpowder was started in what we know as Powder Hollow. As this enterprise grew and attracted more people to the area the church grew and flourished also.

The present brick church was built in 1872. Many additions and improvements since then have made the building more suitable for current needs. In 1923 a new organ and pictorial windows were given to the church. The latest addition—1961—provided class rooms, new kitchen facilities, a church office, pastor's study and an auditorium.

All this nearly went up in smoke in 1970 when lightning struck the steeple. Before any great damage was done the fire department arrived and by quick and careful work the fire never reached beyond the steeple where it had started.

A bell which had been bought for the first church in 1844 now hangs in the steeple of the present church. That bell was once responsible for catching a robber. Across the street there was a tin shop. In the middle of the night a wagon was stealthily driven up to it, but before the would-be robber could load up with tin ware there was a loud peal of the bell. All the neighborhood was awakened and the thief was caught. The bell had evidently been left in an unstable position which it changed of its own accord at the time of the attempted theft.

FIRST PRESBYTERIAN CHURCH
Organized: 1839

The First Presbyterian Church in Enfield was formed by Scottish immigrants brought here by company agents to work in the carpet mills. Orrin Thompson had built a factory for weaving carpets near the mouth of Freshwater Brook in 1828. He knew that in Scotland there were qualified weavers and through his efforts many came here to live and work.

When the first Scottish weavers arrived here in the fall of 1828 there were no houses ready for them and they were boarded in some of the taverns used by the river boatmen. Houses were soon put up near the river and the street was called Scotch Row. Later more houses were built at Cottage Green which was the pride and joy of the early Scottish settlers with its green lawns and flowers.

At first many of these newcomers attended the Congregational Church but its teachings were not close enough to Scottish beliefs and it was too far to walk in bad weather. They wanted their own church so in 1838 they approached the Presbytery in New York to establish a church in Thompsonville and the next year, 1839, the First Presbyterian Church was formed. This church had the unique honor of being the first Presbyterian organization in Connecticut.

Orrin Thompson, although never a member, was instrumental in the growth of this church. Seeing that they did not have a place of worship, he built a church for them on the corner of Church and North Main Streets and gave it to the members rent free. His gifts included a church bell, communion table, silver service, and generous amounts of money. That was in 1840. Times changed and difficulties beset the Thompsonville Carpet Manufacturing Company which failed and caused great unemployment. The church property and building had never been deeded to the church as the members had thought was Mr. Thompson's intention, and in 1854, along with the carpet business, it was taken over by the Hartford Carpet Co.

In spite of hard times the members wanted to save their church. With a great amount of sacrifice and some outside help they were able to separate themselves forever from any carpet company control.

The original building saw its first expansion in 1845, and to take care of their ever-increasing numbers, it expanded again in 1859 and in 1875. Except for minor improvements it remained the same until 1971.

By that time the years had taken their toll of Thompsonville. Buildings were falling into disrepair, and large businesses which once flourished because of the carpet company, moved elsewhere when the carpet mill closed. The church building needed major repairs and modernization, however, space was not immediately available. This was the original Presbyterian church in Connecticut, it was well financed, and had more than 350 members. In the end the "Old First" decided to move.

Property was acquired below Enfield Street between King Street and Old King Street and a large modern building was erected. The church was designed by Galliher and Schoenhardt of Simsbury. There was no attempt by the building committee or the architects to maintain the colonial appearance of Enfield Street. The desire was for a good modern building and to make the best use of the property where it is situated. Although some consider the structure too radical for Enfield it serves the needs of the congregation well.

ENFIELD UNITED METHODIST CHURCH
41 Brainard Road / Organized: 1841

Like the Hazardville United Methodist Church, the Enfield United Methodist Church was an outgrowth of the camp meeting of 1829 held on Job's Hill. Thompsonville, or West Enfield as it was called then, had its groups of people who held meetings in private homes.

There were very few people living in this section when the Thompsonville Manufacturing Company was started in 1828. This enterprise attracted workers including many immigrants.

Through the efforts of Rev. John Howson, an Englishman who had come over to work in the carpet mill, the Thompsonville Methodist Church was organized in 1841. There were seventy members. Their first meeting place was the Bell School on what is now Elm Street, still in existence as a dwelling house. Later a church was built on High Street east of Pearl Street.

In 1884 a large brick church was erected, again on High Street, but this time west of Pearl Street. This was used until 1964. By this time Thompsonville was no longer a small village. Many homes in the center had given way to business establishments and there were parking problems for churchgoers. The downtown area had also become quite run-down. A new modern church was built on Brainard Road in a residential area, and the High Street building was sold to the Amvets.

About this time the name was changed to the Enfield United Methodist Church.

UNITED PRESBYTERIAN CHURCH
Organized: 1845

Until 1845 the First Presbyterian Church was the only church of that denomination in Enfield. In 1841 the church choir wanted to use an organ in the services but the ruling body said "NO." Four years later three elders favorable to the idea consented. The opposing side vehemently objected and stated that instrumental additions to a church service was nothing short of sin. "No fiddle in the Kirk" soon became a common phrase among the dissenters. So a division took place in 1845 and a new church was formed in brotherhood with the Associate Reformed Church of North America which evolved into the United Presbyterian Church of North America.

This new group immediately started to build a church and within a year succeeded in putting up an unpretentious building on the southeast corner of Pleasant and School Streets. The property was purchased for $1.00 from Orrin Thompson's carpet company with the stipulation in the deed that the building and property be returned to the company when they asked for it. It was fifty-five years before they called for the return of this property. Although the church had recently been enlarged by the addition of a chapel, the members gave it up gladly when they learned that the carpet company was planning a huge expansion which was to include the property.

A new church building was erected on High Street in 1901 at a cost of only $7,000 more than the price paid for the old one by the carpet company. It was larger, lighter, and more modern than the old one, in a better section of town and closer to its members. There was a new organ. The original reason for the separation had disappeared some years before.

In 1943 this building was nearly destroyed by a fire that raced through the church from cellar to attic. It took eleven months to repair the damage.

It was felt as far back as the 1950s that there was small need for two Presbyterian churches. Also Thompsonville had changed and High Street was not as suitable a place for a church as it had been in 1900. After careful consideration the decision to merge with the First Presbyterian Church was made in 1972 and in time was carried through successfully. The United Presbyterian Church left its old home on High Street and became part of the Calvary Presbyterian Church on King Street in 1973.

ST. ANDREW'S EPISCOPAL CHURCH
28 Prospect Street / Organized: 1854

St. Andrew's Episcopal Church in Thompsonville and St. Mary's Episcopal Church in Hazardville both started in 1851 as missions of St. John's Church in Warehouse Point.

The Thompsonville congregation met first at Mechanic's Hall and later at Odd Fellow's Hall. The membership was expanding and a church building was greatly needed. Plans were made on St. Andrew's Day in 1854 to make a parish out of the mission. By 1858 enough money had been collected to lay the cornerstone of the present church. It was ideally situated as it was near the carpet mill and the homes of the people who worked there. As the carpet business flourished or faced hard times, so did the church, since many of the members were employed in the mill. In 1867 the Tariffville plant of the carpet company burned and the workers were transferred to Thompsonville. This gave the church an extra boost.

In 1902 a parish house was built for church and community functions. An organ fund was started which resulted in a pipe organ being installed in 1935 with pipes which were originally in Carnegie Hall. An electric organ is now in use although the front pipes of the old unit have been retained. Other more recent changes are Hargrave Hall in the lower section, the undercroft has been refitted as a nursery, the belfry replaced, and memorial windows installed.

ST. PATRICK'S ROMAN CATHOLIC CHURCH
64 High Street / Organized: about 1827

Like nearly all the early churches the record of the first Roman Catholic church to be established in Enfield is somewhat vague. The first mass known to have been conducted in Enfield occurred in October, 1827. There were at that time many laborers of Irish descent working on the Thompsonville-Windsor Locks Canal. There was no Catholic church anywhere in the area for them to attend, and very few priests in Connecticut at that time. In 1829 another priest traveled here, stayed several days, and accomplished great things among the workers. Communion was given and children were baptized. However in 1831 only ten Roman Catholics could be counted. Mass was not said again for three years. Three more years passed before there was a priest in the area again.

There were few Roman Catholics anywhere in the New England area, so few in fact that one priest was assigned to Hartford, Middlesex and Litchfield Counties in Connecticut, plus Hampden and Berkshire Counties in Massachusetts.

In 1840 a priest was assigned to Hartford and monthly services were held in Thompsonville for six or seven years. As the Catholic population gradually increased a priest in Windsor Locks ministered to the needs of Enfield. In 1860 land was purchased on the west side of Pearl Street for the first Roman Catholic church building. This was not far from where the present church stands.

The church was finished rapidly, served well, and was expanded in 1863 to accommodate many carpet workers from Tariffville where the plant had burned down. Other buildings followed. A rectory was completed in 1873 but was given over to the Sisters of Mercy who used it for a convent. A school also was built about 1873. Such rapid expansion makes for large debts but before long the need for a larger church became apparent.

Fortunately a large building lot was available on the corner of Pearl and High Streets. The building was finished in 1890 and immediately occupied. The interior was truly beautiful from the stately columns to the lofty dome, marble altar, gold trimming, and colored windows. Arranged throughout the sanctuary were numerous religious paintings. In every way the attempt was made to reflect the true Roman effect. With a great deal of effort and sacrifice the large debt incurred at this time was completely cleared in 1921.

In the early 1900s masses in Italian were added for the benefit of the many immigrants from Italy who did not understand English. From then on there has always been one Italian speaking priest at St. Patrick's.

On January 5, 1949, a disastrous and devastating fire occurred. At 1 P.M. fire was discovered in the rear of the church. As it spread it became obvious that the building could not be saved and it was a complete and total loss save for the walls. Every pillar was gone as was every window, the altar, the floor, the paintings. Those watching, Roman Catholic and Protestant, priest and minister alike, shed tears. It was a terrible loss. Only St. Anthony's statue was spared and that is now in a prominent place in the new church.

Masses were held in the old Enfield High School after the fire. Plans were formulated to rebuild within the burned and blackened walls. The first service was held in the basement on November 1, 1949. On November 19 of the next year the present building was finished and dedicated with the interior more beautiful than before.

ST. BERNARD'S ROMAN CATHOLIC CHURCH
426 Hazard Avenue / Organized: about 1863

As the gunpowder works in the east part of Enfield developed the population grew and it became obvious that a church was needed for both the Irish and French Canadian workers employed in the mills and on the farms. This led to the division of the first Roman Catholic church, St. Patrick's, and St. Bernard's parish was organized. A four room brick school had been built in Hazardville in 1862 and the old wooden school building was acquired by the Roman Catholics in 1863 and was, as far as is known, their first meeting place. This building is now a two family home on Hazard Avenue.

By 1870 a search was begun for suitable land for a new church building. A Mr. Sylvester Charter came forward and donated some land which is part of the present church property. The church was immediately started and was finished in 1880. The construction costs were offset by pledges of about $8,000. Of this amount Colonel Augustus Hazard contributed $500 plus "other considerations." Much of the early excavation was done by volunteer help. Stories persist that the foundation hole was dug by powder and farm workers returning home at the end of the day. They would stop by the church property and dig and scrape with their teams until a foundation could be laid. They would then return and backfill until the property was graded. The foundation stones were quarried in East Longmeadow and drawn to the site by horses. As the village of Hazardville grew so did the church and its influence. With the closing of the powder mills times were not so prosperous. But the original building stood until 1955— approximately seventy-five years.

During the 1950s the entire town was expanding more than two fold. St. Bernard's was one of the first churches that recognized the need to expand and modernize, to look ahead and sense the needs and wants of the future. In 1955 it seemed in the best interest to tear down the old church and build anew. Under the strong leadership of its priest adjoining property was purchased, the old sanctuary was torn down and the present attractive building erected. The rectory, however, is the original rectory though much changed.

At present 1,600 active families call St. Bernard's their church.

ST. MARY'S EPISCOPAL CHURCH
383 Hazard Avenue / Organized: 1863

Just as Orrin Thompson had sent to Scotland for expert weavers to work in his carpet mill, Colonel Hazard sent to England for experienced powder makers to work in his gunpowder mills.

As his business began to prosper more and more English powder makers arrived and it soon became obvious that these Englishmen did not have a home church. The only church in Hazardville, the Methodist, was not quite suited to their needs, nor was the Congregational Church in Enfield which was several miles away.

St. Mary's started in a small way in 1851 as a mission of St. John's Church in Warehouse Point. In 1863, due to the interest and help of Colonel Hazard they were able to lay the cornerstone of the present church. There was (and still is) a large home on the main street which was occupied by the powder company superintendent. This imposing home had a huge front lawn landscaped with beautiful trees and shrubs. Colonel Hazard donated property to the east of this home for a church, plus a $5,000 trust for its maintenance, to the Episcopal people of Hazardville.

After the Civil War there came a time when the village was not so prosperous and hard times came to St. Mary's. There was great concern that the church would once again become a mission. After the great powder mill explosion of January, 1913, the company closed for good and this had great impact on the church. No full-time priest was hired, but St. Andrew's in Thompsonville provided a priest part time. Through World War I, the Depression, and World War II the church continued the struggle to exist as best it could.

With the growth of population in the 1950s and 1960s church membership increased and finances improved. A rectory was bought at the rear of the church property in 1958. An annex and a parish house were built later. However, the sanctuary is little changed since 1863.

ST. ADALBERT'S ROMAN CATHOLIC CHURCH
90 Alden Avenue / Organized: 1915

In the early 1900s a large number of Polish immigrants came to Thompsonville to work in the carpet mills. They began to move into the north end of Thompsonville, into homes provided and built by the carpet company. Because they understood and spoke very little English attendance at St. Patrick's Church was not very satisfactory for them. Consequently, sometime before 1915 small groups began meeting in a building owned by the company in an area called "French Town" which was west of Pleasant Street. Polish priests traveled there and preached in their native tongue, which brought great satisfaction to all. As these gatherings grew they felt it was time to form and support their own church.

St. Adalbert's was actually organized in 1915 and a search for land was immediately begun. It was felt that the church should be located in the northern section of town and close to the mill houses where the majority of the Polish people lived. A large piece of suitable land was found on Alden Avenue and this has been the home of St. Adalbert's ever since.

Immediately after Mrs. Alden's land was acquired, a church foundation was put in; but the necessary funds were lacking to build a sanctuary. The sanctuary was not built until 1930 but previous to this services were held in the basement. The Depression of the 1930s took its toll in St. Adalbert's as in other churches, and a great deal of effort was needed to keep the church open and maintain on-going programs. The church was over-burdened with bills and mortgages and the priest (who was the original priest) was in failing health.

In 1938, however, new life was breathed into the parish when Father Paul Bartolewski was assigned here. His name is of particular significance to many people throughout the town. He was young, dynamic, and had strong convictions about the direction and importance of the church. "Father Paul" was well known to most of the town, Roman Catholic and Protestant alike. He was respected for his strong will and determination to furnish his church and acquire those things he felt important. In short, he was a very colorful man. Soon after his assignment here, he made the usual rounds of his parishioners to introduce himself; but he also asked for donations of money so that he could provide the necessary paintings for the interior of the church. This was done.

He planned a systematic expansion and the programs to support it. Much of the material was donated or sold to the contractors at reduced prices. Father Paul saw to it that the parish had the facilities necessary for a successful church life. In 1956 he completed a convent, and in 1958 a school. The school is available for social functions and for town use, and is one of the largest public assembly halls available.

As the church building was showing the effects of time, he undertook a massive redecorating program, including new pews, in 1972, and a new organ in the same year. Also, parking was becoming a severe problem as the church was attracting more than just the north end residents; and so the field directly across the street (that once served as a baseball field for the Bigelow employees) was acquired.

Father Paul retired in 1972 and is now dead—yet his memory lives on as probably the strongest Roman Catholic priest ever to serve in Enfield, and he will long be remembered for his accomplishments here in an era when progress was hard to come by.

ST. NICHOLAS GREEK ORTHODOX
23 Church St / Organized: 1916

The St. Nicholas Greek Orthodox Church occupies a unique place in Enfield. It not only is the sole Greek Church in the town, but its parish also includes East Windsor, Ellington, Rockville, Somers, Stafford Springs, Suffield, Vernon, Windsor Locks, and Windsor.

Although there were Greeks in Enfield prior to 1900, it was at this time that many of them were brought into town by the "Company Agents" of The Hartford Carpet Co. to work in the carpet mills. As any local or newly congregated people would naturally like to do, they were anxious to keep their old ways and traditions intact. No local church met their needs and the language barrier was forbidding. At first the Greek Orthodox faithful attended church in Springfield. In the case of a wedding or baptism the pastor of the Springfield church came to the town and the sacrament was performed in the home. One pioneer member remembers that a group went to Springfield by trolley to attend the Anastasis (Resurrection Service) and then it took them two and a half hours to walk back since there was no public transportation after midnight.

As more Greek people arrived in town, it became apparent that a church must be provided. A concerted effort was launched and sites were reviewed on Pleasant Street and Church Street, but to no avail. It was then learned that the old Orpheum Theater on the present church site was to be sold. A purchase price of $4,300 was agreed upon, including all furnishings, and the necessary renovations started. In December, 1917, only nine months after the Certificate of Organization was authorized, the "church" opened for worship. This ended about seventeen years of frustration and searching. For much of these seventeen years the services were held in Emmett Hall at the corner of Pearl and High Streets. The name St. Nicholas was chosen because many members came fron Koniska, Greece, and the patron Saint of Koniska was St. Nicholas.

The converted theater served as a church for eight years and was destroyed by a fire in early 1925. Such tragedies often happen at an inopportune time, yet much good can result.

Emmett Hall again served as a temporary sanctuary while hurried plans were assembled to rebuild. Plans were submitted at no cost by a Springfield architect who also agreed to supervise the building free of charge. Almost two years went by before the present building was completed and opened on October 25, 1926. It would no longer be necessary to conduct committee meetings in a bakery, coffee house, candy store, grocery store, or barber shop. The new building with the church proper on the main floor and hall in the basement met their needs for a place of worship and a place for meetings and socials.

The Depression hit this little group and from 1932 to 1942 there was no priest and little money to keep the organization going. It fell to the Parish of the Sts. Constantine & Helen in Chicopee Falls to keep the church together, but only one service a month was provided. During these years, and later when the church really did not function, an "ispraktor" would take a collection box to the members. As the Depression started to wane, the church began to show new interest and life, and in spite of not having a full-time priest the mortgage was paid off in 1940. Three years earlier a piece of land in Suffield had been given to the church and used often for recreational purposes until its sale, several years later, for $100. In 1940 the present pews were added to the church from the Springfield church. A church bell was added in 1944 as a gift from one of the members. In 1945 a usable pump organ was added to the church physical plant and replaced in 1950 with a new reed electric organ which itself was replaced two years ago by the current electronic organ, a gift from the St. Nicholas Philoptochos Society members.

As in the case of most churches, the conduct of the church schools and other religious training continues to be done by lay people. This system works well and keeps family and church interest high. Through these efforts many improvements have been added and the little church continues to add to its attractiveness. In 1968 the present priest's residence was purchased. In early 1970 the beautiful maroon wall to wall carpeting was added as a gift, also from the ladies' society. In 1974 the two-family house at 25-27 Church Street was purchased as an investment or for possible future expansion.

St. Nicholas Church is proud of its past and is ready to contribute in the future to the welfare of its members and the community.

POLISH NATIONAL CATHOLIC CHURCH
723 Enfield Street / Organized: 1934

The Polish National Catholic Church belongs to a group of independent Catholic churches whose aim is to carry on the traditions and customs and the language of their native land where the church was the center of the community. This sect originated in Pennsylvania in 1897 and since its beginning 162 parishes have been organized. It is a member of the National Council of Churches.

The Holy Cross Church of Enfield was started by a concerned group of Polish-speaking people who were interested in furthering the beliefs of this movement. They held their first meeting at the Polish National Home on Alden Avenue and it was the feeling that a church could be formed and become successful. The first mass was celebrated in the Greek Orthodox Church. It was clear from the start that the group must have their own meeting house if they were to survive. Their search ended when the present property on Enfield Street was purchased in 1935.

You must look closely today to realize that their church building is a converted barn. A huge effort was made immediately when as many as forty volunteers undertook to change its structure to one suitable for a church. Their efforts were well spent. Much of the funds was raised as a result of a lawn festival that lasted seven days and nights, something never done for such an extended period in Enfield. The bell in the belfry was originally in the old White Mill of the Thompsonville Carpet Company in 1828, and was rung for years as the curfew bell until 1906. This is probably the oldest bell in Enfield as it predates the re-cast bell in the Congregational Church by two years. It was donated to the Polish National Church in 1936.

There is now a congregation of 280 members and masses are given in both Polish and English. These people are now actively engaged in a complete remodeling of the church. If results compare with the original effort in 1935 the church will be an attraction to those who are oriented toward the Polish National faith and to those who enjoy different church interiors.

LUTHERAN CHURCH OF OUR REDEEMER
20 North Street / Organized: 1958

In 1956 the Missouri Synod sent a vicar to northern Connecticut to conduct a survey to determine if there were enough interested people in the area to support a Lutheran church. A minister was assigned here in 1958 and a membership drive resulted in seventy-seven charter members. Their first meeting place was the Hazardville Memorial School. A site committee was appointed and a drive for funds begun. This resulted in the purchase of a large plot of ground on North Street in Hazardville and here the church was built at a cost of $94,000. The cornerstone was laid in 1963. Although operating originally as a mission, they have been self-supporting since 1975.

FIRST BAPTIST CHURCH
253 Brainard Road / Organized: 1960

The First Baptist Church owes its origin to a Fellowship group from Grace Baptist Church in Springfield. They attempted first to found a church in Longmeadow but found little local interest in the project. Some Enfield residents expressed an interest in this and a survey was made which encouraged the group to transfer to Enfield as there was no Baptist organization here at the time.

A tract of land was offered and accepted on the corner of Brainard and George Washington Roads. A building was immediately erected and worship began in 1962. It was not long before this building was crowded and an educational wing was added. This served well for seven years when it became apparent that a more permanent religious center must be built to support their growing membership. A third building was added to the previous two so that the complex as it appears today comprises three buildings. The main church seats about 185 and is most attractive. The members of this church are strong and dedicated believers in the Calvinistic approach to God.

ST. MARTHA'S ROMAN CATHOLIC CHURCH
214 Brainard Road / Organized: 1961

As the town began to expand on a small scale in the late 1940s and to an explosive level in the 1950s it soon became apparent that the three Roman Catholic churches could not accommodate all those wanting to attend. St. Bernard's was the church most affected because it absorbed the new families from Green Manorville and Southwood Acres but St. Patrick's and St. Adalbert's were also involved.

The new parish of St. Martha's dates from September 21, 1961. It was decided that the best location for the new church was close to the two housing developments in the northern and eastern sections of the town, Whitacres and Green Manorville. It was felt that the southern section would eventually need its own church, which proved to be true in about four years.

Early masses were conducted in the Knights of Columbus Hall, baptisms, weddings, and funerals in either St. Bernard's or St. Patrick's. The first building completed was the rectory, and in a small chapel in the rectory daily masses were held by the newly assigned priest. Groundbreaking for the new building was on December 15, 1962. The official opening of the church was on September 22, 1963. It was designed with the finest appointments. From the two-ton marble altar table from Italy to the fine Wurlitzer organ and Schulmerich carillon bells, the church is a fine example of dedication and concern to have a building worthy of the name church.

Later a school was built. The total cost of church and school was about $650,000.

As is evident from reading any of the local newspapers the church is one of the most active in town. Many functions have very large followings and St. Martha's Players rank as a superb acting group well known throughout the area as a truly professional team.

FAITH BAPTIST CHURCH
182 Broad Brook Road / Organized: 1961

Anyone who has lived in Enfield for any length of time is probably familiar with the white school busses that weave their way throughout the town on Sunday mornings. These are the buses from Faith Baptist Church on Broad Brook Road. They cover the entire area of Enfield and parts of Manchester and Rockville. They will pick up any person, adult or child, member or not, who wishes to attend their service.

In 1961 a group of twelve people who had attended a Baptist Church in another town decided that they would like to establish a Baptist Church in Enfield. On September 16 of that year the Faith Baptist Church was incorporated. For the first four years the foundation of the present congregation was being established. The first pastor who served the congregation was the Reverend Melville Stewart who served about three years.

In July, 1966, the second pastor, Rev. B.W. Sanders, was called to the small congregation. At that particular time the congregation was meeting in the living room of a house on Green Manor Road. They immediately began plans for a building program and moved into their first building on Broad Brook Road in January, 1967. Due to an increased Sunday School attendance another building was erected in 1968. As the congregation continued to grow it became necessary to have a larger building for worship services. In November, 1970, the existing sanctuary was dedicated for that purpose. The congregation was also responsible for building the parsonage behind the church and they also erected a garage for the maintenance of the Sunday School buses.

The congregation believes in total involvement on the part of the members of the church, and consequently provides all of the labor for construction, maintenance of buses, and any other work the church needs performed.

Over a period of years a vast outreach from the church has been established. The church provides Sunday School for all ages, worship services Sunday morning and evening, Bible study and prayer on Wednesday evening, several choirs, a Ladies' Fellowship, a Men's Fellowship, an Adult Fellowship, Summer Camp, Winter Retreats, a twenty-four hour telephone service called Gospel-Line, free Sunday School bus service, Daily Vacation Bible School in summer, a radio ministry, convalescent home services, condolence letter ministry, weekly visitation program in homes, a shut-in ministry, a tape ministry, and an extensive missionary program which supports home and foreign missions.

The Faith Baptist Church has also founded the Enfield Christian Academy which is a private Christian school offering kindergarten through twelfth grade.

The Faith Baptist Church is independent of any ecclesiastical authority outside its own congregation and is self-governing. The church is fundamental in its doctrine. It holds firm to the belief that the Bible is the sole guide for faith and practice.

Faith Baptist Church is established to minister to Enfield and the surrounding areas as well as to the world. Faith Baptist Church is here, not to receive, but to give. Faith Baptist Church has a desire to be an asset and a blessing to the town of Enfield.

AMERICAN BAPTIST CHURCH
127 Post Office Road / Organized: 1964

The Baptist faith in Enfield is quite difficult to trace, and from what little is known it appears to date from 1750. Thus Baptists were probably the second religious group to settle in town (the Congregational being the first). Although very little is known about the early Baptists a minister and some parishioners were here in the mid 1700s and they probably lived in the eastern part of town near Somers. Records about their beginnings are very sketchy and we must refer to official Baptist publications to obtain any insight into their early life in Enfield. In these books we see that there was probably a succession of different Baptist organizations until 1851 when the last entry concerning the Enfield Baptists was made to the Hartford Baptist Association. That entry indicated that the Enfield organization had ceased to exist in 1851. Perhaps when a detailed history of the Baptists in Enfield is written long forgotten records will come to light and show that there was a tie between all the old associations.

Also, of the three active Baptist churches now in Enfield, the American Baptist probably might be the closest to those ancient organizations, but there is no direct tie. No record can now be located of any Baptist Church between 1851 and about 1960. It is possible that either the First Baptist Church of Enfield or the Faith Baptist Church may be even more closely related than the American Baptist to the early church. However, time and research are necessary to prove or disprove any connection. Suffice it to say that the current Baptist Churches in Enfield are not the only Baptists to have settled here, and Baptist roots go deep into our town's history.

As you can see from the history of the other Baptist Churches the current Baptist movement was initiated in 1960. There is every reason to hope that all these churches are operating from a stronger base than did the effort originated in 1750.

The third Baptist church to form here in recent times was the American Baptist which can trace its origin to 1964. The fellowship which formed met in homes and later that same year moved to the Harriet Beecher Stowe School on Post Office Road for Sunday morning services. Their early furnishings were, as expected, temporary, being set up in the auditorium on Saturday and stored again after the Sunday services.

In order to maintain an active church life, committee and Bible study meetings were held in private homes.

At this time the first minister was living at 43 Raffia Road. Late in 1964 he was moved to the newly acquired parsonage at 27 Post Office Road directly across the street from the proposed church site. It was another four years before he would look out on a completed meeting house. In 1972, during a general church reorganization, that parsonage was sold and a new one built on the church grounds.

The present meeting house is located near the Harriet Beecher Stowe School on land obtained from George W. Smith, Jr. Some of the land required fill and this was obtained from the I-91 construction project. Lee and Crabtree Associates, the architects who designed the building, styled it to be centered around a combination worship and general purpose room, seating about 170. In order to accomplish this, the furnishings are moveable. The exterior appearance of the structure gives the illusion of a building considerably larger, due to the high pitched roof. The first worship service was held in the new building on August 18, 1968, and thus we have the third Baptist church established and perhaps the sixth Baptist effort to settle permanently in Enfield.

The church bell in this church is unique in that it is the only bell in the Enfield churches with a direct tie to World War II. It was obtained from the aircraft carrier USS *Tarawa*. The bell was formally presented to the church in November, 1973, by the Hartford Council, U.S. Navy League when it was placed in its separate brick foundation along with the church sign. The bell was actually brought to the church in 1969 and an attempt was made to install it in the peak of the roof, but the 750 pound weight proved too great a load for the structure to bear. The bell was made available to the church because a member of the church building committee knew a member of the Navy League. It is interesting to note that the bell still sounds as a calling device, this time to God instead of to war.

The American Baptist Church, because of its strong belief in religious freedom and its willingness to cooperate with varied faiths, is the only denomination in Enfield to allow these groups to use its facilities. Three other congregations are currently holding religious services in the church: the Kingdom of God, the Associated Churches of God, and the Seventh Day Adventists. Although all organizations using this church benefit from such an arrangement, it takes a large Christian heart to allow it to happen. The American Baptists are such Christians.

HOLY FAMILY ROMAN CATHOLIC CHURCH
38 Simon Road / Organized: 1965

There was no Roman Catholic church in the southern section of the town until September 16, 1965, when the Holy Family Church was formed from the parishes of St. Patrick's and St. Bernard's. The name derives from the many young families that were within its boundaries. Property was selected on Simon Road because of its central location. Ground breaking was July 9, 1967. A type of church architecture was chosen that reflects the modern life and times of its people. It is contemporary in style and trapezoidal in shape. As most people will agree, the church is really an imposing building. Until the church was completed, regular services were held in the Enfield High School.

Many functions normally held within the confines of a church were, by necessity, held elsewhere. The Saturday school of instruction was held at the Harriet Beecher Stowe School, committee meetings were held at Raffia's Shopping Center. Bazaars, food sales, fashion shows, and general entertainments were held which provided the much needed money to make a new organization work.

Dedication ceremonies were held on November 9, 1968. The rectory is now on church property instead of across the road. The children attend Saturday School at the church. Instead of one priest, as at first, there are now two priests and two full-time nuns. Although dedicated to the principles of Roman Catholicism, many of the church's social functions are attended and enjoyed by non-Catholics of the neighborhood.

KINGDOM OF GOD
127 Post Office Road / Organized: 1970

Most of the churches in Enfield are members or associates of larger parent organizations. The Kingdom of God, however, is a new faith which grew out of the Church of God and can claim Enfield as its original home. Although newly formed and still in its embryonic stage, this new faith has five churches, four of which are located in Mexico City.

The Kingdom of God, like most other faiths, can trace its birth from other religions and was formed because the teachings or hierarchy did not suit their immediate needs. Some years back a man named Julius Shacknow was a very active speaker and had several religious groups scattered throughout New York, Connecticut, and New Jersey. A religious organization, strong in the south, known as the Church of God, invited Julius Shacknow to speak to the Church of God's Tennessee church. He indicated that there were several groups of people in Connecticut which should be formed into churches and particularly singled out Windsor Locks as containing an active group. An investigating team was sent to Windsor Locks and a Church of God was established in July, 1970, with about forty people comprising married couples and singles. For two years they met in private homes but realizing that in order to survive they must have a central religious center, they moved to Memorial Hall on Main Street. This building was not completely satisfying. It was also about this time that the group began to experience a change in theological direction.

In October, 1972, they moved to Enfield and changed their name to the Kingdom of God. Their first meeting house was the old United Presbyterian Church on High Street. When the town bought the building the members were forced to move again to private homes. In January, 1976, they moved to the American Baptist Church where they now have twenty active members. Part of their activity is centered around their five white motorcycles which travel throughout the area in search of young people's gatherings to pass out literature informing them of their beliefs.

In short, the Kingdom of God brings the town a new approach to God, in a sense Pentecostal. The members treat Easter, Christmas, and other religious holidays as any other day, equal before God.

APOSTOLIC CHURCH
1 Shaker Hill Road / Organized: 1971

One of the newer churches in Enfield is the Apostolic Church located on Shaker Hill Road. Though not large in numbers, through hard work they have achieved a most attractive building. It is a round church with a high-peaked roof. Entering the main body of the church one is struck by its unique beauty. The auditorium has a sloping theater-like floor, focusing on a lectern and an immersion baptismal font. The walls are paneled and there are handsome pews. The skylight in the high-peaked ceiling captures the late afternoon sun and adds meaning to their services. The building was designed with expansion possibilities and the 200 person capacity auditorium can be enlarged to 300 simply by removing a window and seating the overflow in a portion of the hallway which surrounds the main room.

The services are not formal, since they accept the will of those present so that a more meaningful message can be received. If it is their will to sing hymns, or talk, or exchange ideas and concerns among themselves, it is accepted.

The coming of this denomination to Enfield was the result of a gradual drifting away from the United Pentecostal Church in Springfield. A few of the present Apostolic Church members first rented a store on Pearl Street and for three years offered a complete program for young and old. Their children's religious education is varied and in depth. Their adult beliefs are, to some, stern and unyielding, to others, fair and in the true words of the Bible. They believe in the second coming of Christ and condemn drinking, smoking, dancing, and the movies.

A great deal of thought was put into the planning of their unique church building and it should serve the Pentecostal movement well.

CALVARY PRESBYTERIAN CHURCH
1518 King Street / Organized: 1972

In the history of Enfield churches many denominations have expanded but the only merger has occurred, with the Presbyterians. This merger brought together the First Presbyterian Church and the United Presbyterian Church and closed a rift that had lasted more than 120 years. This has resulted in a stronger, more unified church than either could probably have achieved on its own.

In the late 1960s and early 1970s there were some private discussions in the United Presbyterian Church that it would be in their best interests to join with the First Presbyterian Church. But how to do it? United Church services were a little more unorthodox, they had property to dissolve, invested funds, etc. The overture to merge, however, was made by the United Church. It was well received, but many members on both sides were hesitant and wary. The merger to be successful must be smooth at all levels. The minister at the First Presbyterian was an interim minister who would leave when a new minister, acceptable to both sides, was found. The minister of the United Presbyterian unhesitantly agreed to leave also. Joint services were held at both churches so that each could get to know the other again, and social functions were attended by both. Committees were equally split and decisions then would be unified. No bias could be charged. The selection of a minister was also a joint decision and the merger went smoothly. The union officially took place in 1972 and the name Calvary Presbyterian was chosen.

UNIVERSALIST-UNITARIAN FELLOWSHIP
Organized: 1974

The Universalist-Unitarian Fellowship had its beginning in September, 1974, when one of the future members gathered the names of other women who were interested in forming a fellowship. Because there was a gas shortage and prices were high they preferred to remain in the Enfield area and interest more local people. Thus this might be called an "energy crisis church."

The fellowship was begun with five women who met at a house on Abbe Road and wrote the by-laws during September, 1974. They were able to interest an additional seven and, together, they signed the charter the following November.

Because it was difficult to conduct meetings in a private home, during November, 1974, they moved to the Grange Hall in Scitico. A drive was commenced to interest others in the organization. As each new member joined he signed the by-laws and by February, 1975, another seven had joined, bringing the total to nineteen. These members do not represent family units but individuals.

In October, 1975, the fellowship moved to the Scantic YWCA at 96 Pearl Street. There is no minister as yet, consequently most of the meetings are discussions presented by the members and chosen from topics in pamphlets sent from the Boston Universalist-Unitarian headquarters. Occasionally guest speakers are available. Although the group is small it is completely self-sufficient and has a small treasury. There is no pledging but regular collections are taken.

JEHOVAH'S WITNESSES
322 North Maple Street / Organized: Date Unknown

The Jehovah's Witness congregation is relatively new in Enfield and it was not possible to obtain any information about this group.

The Ecumenical Movement

Prior to the formalization of any inter-church relationships individual parishes did enter into informal agreements such as the one that allowed the founders of St. Mary's Episcopal Church to hold their first worship services in the parish hall of St. Bernard's Roman Catholic Church.

The formal coming together of the various worshipping communities began with the organization of a local Ministerial Study Group. It was on May 27, 1937, that the Protestant ministers of the surrounding towns met to organize a study group and establish a common calendar, a project that has yet to be accomplished. The ministers from the following parishes were at that first meeting:

The Enfield Congregational Church
The United Presbyterian Church
Saint Andrew's & Saint Mary's (at that time one man covered both Parishes)
Hazardville Methodist Church
Warehouse Point Methodist Church
Suffield Congregational Church
Broad Brook Congregational Church
The Second Baptist Church of Suffield
The Thompsonville Methodist Church.

The following year (1938) the Enfield Christian Endeavor Union, in conjunction with the minister's study group, proposed and carried out a Lenten series entitled "The Living Church." This series culminated in a three-hour Good Friday Service at St. Andrew's Church. The Lenten series did not survive, but in the following years a musical service of worship was held at St. Andrew's on Good Friday.

Sometime after that original organizational meeting in 1937, the local churches formed a Men's Dart League which flourished in those pre-World War days for eleven years. This somewhat unorthodox activity aided in the creation of inter-church friendships in much the same way as the present day's Inter-Church Bowling League has done. It was this feeling of friendship that enabled the Christian community to plan and carry out town-wide projects.

The Ministerial group continued to meet, though somewhat smaller in size with the withdrawal of the out of town men. They exchanged papers, usually theological in nature, and planned the few inter-church services that were held. For instance, they once again held a

Lenten program that ended with a Service of Thanksgiving at St. Andrew's on Good Friday.

In 1945 this small group of Protestant churches combined with the Roman Catholic Parishes in town to establish a released time education program. The classes in this program began on October 1, 1945. This first experiment in Roman Catholic and Protestant cooperation lasted only one year and the program was cancelled by the school system in 1946. It was also in this year (1945) that a meeting of Protestant ministers and laity met to form a Council of Churches; it was a bad year, that failed too.

The first town-wide "World Day of Prayer" was held in 1948, again planned by the minister's group. This group, in 1949, was responsible for the printing and distribution of a folder that listed all the Protestant services. This was at a time when it would never have occurred to them to include those of the Roman Catholic Parishes.

In 1955 the Protestant and Roman Catholic Parishes again cooperated to establish Released Time Education. Each cooperating Parish was "taxed" $150.00 to cover the cost of the teachers' salaries.

Two years later, in 1957, the ministers again met with members of their laity and began the discussions that would result in the formation of the Enfield Council of Churches. This time they succeeded. On May 16, 1957, the Enfield Council of Churches was formally established and the sponsoring ministerial group turned over to them their small bank balance.

With the establishment of the Council the ministers could go back to their monthly meetings and present papers and exchange ideas. In the 1960s, under the sponsorship of Father Paul Bartolewski, the town's Roman Catholic clergy joined the group. The union of the two groups of clergy not only brought about new friendships, it also brought about a new name, The Enfield Clergy Colloquium. This new group met quarterly and because it represented both Protestant and Roman Catholic Churches it took over the responsibility for the planning and carrying out of the ecumenical services that were beginning to be held. It was this group that brought into being the successful Ecumenical Days of Prayer during the Octave of Unity in January of each year. It was during one of these series of services that Thomas Barbour, minister of the Enfield Congregational Church, died.

For some years there existed this inter-communion group of ministers and priests and the Enfield Council of Churches. The existence of both groups tended to weaken the Council but it continued to provide the town with a series of study groups such as Sex Education for Children, The Art of Parenting, a course on preparation for marriage, and during the sixties a six-week course on the plight of urban areas.

After nineteen years of life the Council of Churches came to an end. This was not caused by failure but by success. In the spring of 1975 an Ad Hoc Committee of clergy and laity from both the Roman Catholic and Protestant Communities met to reorganize the Council into a group that would include all the Churches of Enfield which would care to join. This new organization, now called the Greater Enfield Conference of Christian Churches, began its official life in September of 1975. Cooperation between the churches in this new conference is growing. Respect for each other's point of view and acceptance of differences is the strength that this new group will bring into the future.

CHAPTER 6

GOVERNMENT

laying the foundation

The nation's bicentennial year loosed a new and pervasive spirit in the land. Americans began looking backward! They were becoming curious about the past! They were busy digging out the facts of their beginnings, unearthing stories of the early settlers, collecting and preserving artifacts. It is in this spirit of curiosity and wonder that we ask: How did Enfield grow? How did the town that began with thirty families become a town of fifty thousand people? What spirit prevailed? What principles guided? What wisdom succeeded and what failed? Those "first families" had no blueprint to follow; no traditions to uphold or scorn. For in 1680 (Enfield's settlement year), merely sixty years after the landing at Plymouth, this was truly a new world to shape and to mold and to call home. What was their purpose? What manner of men were they? What did they seek and dream? What did they accomplish?

From the beginning Americans have always latched on to certain words as their personal property: words like free, independent, self-government, liberty, commonwealth. And it is true that in some degree these ideas of independence and freedom through self-government still persist after centuries.

Elias Sanford in his nineteenth century *History of Connecticut* describes the beginnings thus:

When a company of persons wished to settle– or plant as it was called– a new town, they made their purpose known to the Court [in the case of Enfield it was to the General Court in Massachusetts]. A tract of land was granted to the company: if it was found that they were able to support a minister, they were authorized to establish a plantation and a church. The Court appointed a committee who fixed the bounds of the land, that at first was held by the company as proprietors in common. From this time they could assemble in town meeting and transact matters connected with their local affairs. The location, size and cost of the meetinghouse was the first order of business. Then they decided as to the admission of new associates, distributed the land among individuals, voted as to the location of new roads and looked after the general interests of the community very much as towns do now.

When it became inconvenient for proprietors to meet often for all orders of business Select Men were chosen to administer town affairs between meetings.

In nearly three centuries of existence—1680-1975—a close look at Enfield's records of town meetings and Enfield's Annual Town Report reveals no diminution in those primary concerns: schools, protection of citizens, care of the poor and dependent, and the building and upkeep of highways. The programs to implement those concerns and the money to carry out the programs have come from the common consent of the people. Both Connecticut's Fundamental Orders and the Massachusetts General Court stated that the government of the colony was to be chosen by the inhabitants but this did not mean every person. Only adult males were considered "inhabitants and free men" according to Joseph B. Hoyt in *The Connecticut Story.* He further explains that these were a select group who were friends and members of the same church. Usually they were a church group who followed a minister and migrated together to Connecticut. A new man coming into the colony did not automatically become a voter; the older residents held the right to decide whether or not he would be accepted as an "inhabitant and freeman." The voters were rather a select club and in the first one hundred years the number in that club didn't increase

The Old Town Hall, built in 1775 as a church and meeting house, was moved across the street from its original location in 1849 and converted to the town hall. It is now being restored by the Enfield Historical Society.

very much even though the total population of the state increased. Newcomers were permitted to settle in towns but they were not all accepted as "inhabitants and freemen." If the newcomer belonged to the church established in the town it was easier to receive acceptance. It was also helpful if he owned a large amount of property. Also one might be accepted at age twenty-one if his father or grandfather was a voter, provided he had been a good citizen. "Even in the middle of the eighteenth century only one man in every nine was a voter." (*Connecticut Story*, Hoyt, p. 209). This situation did not provoke discontent because the prevailing belief at that time seemed to be that government should be left in the hands of the most capable men.

Even though early Enfield had its beginnings as part of Massachusetts and from 1680 to 1749 owed loyalty and allegiance to that entity the governing climate under which Enfield settlers struggled and lived was far removed from the democratic principles of our present day. True to those times the new settlement, at first referred to as the Freshwater Plantation, was a church group obtaining grants of land under the auspices of John Pynchon, a Springfield entrepreneur.

By 1683 as many as thirty families had settled in Enfield (an English place name meaning cleared land). The boundaries extended six miles down the Connecticut River from Longmeadow Brook and thence to the east to include what is now the Town of Somers. Even before a local governing body was established, a church building twenty feet square was built in 1683. This was subsequently replaced by a larger building and then in 1775 by the old Town Hall that is still standing.

These thirty families petitioned the General Court at Boston for the incorporation of the plantation with Town privileges by the name of Enfield. Their petition was granted and in 1688 the first Town Meeting was held. At that time the people chose John Pease, Jr., and Samuel Terry as their Select Men.

The early church was by far the town's most important building. It was not only used as the meetinghouse for services of worship, but also as the town hall and the civic center. In early America the church was the government and the government was the church. The church was the Congregational and one has only to look at these towns that are truly early New England and to identify their white spires rising so majestically above the tallest trees to understand a bit about the church's influence on the lives of New Englanders. The choicest spot of land in town was chosen as the site for the church, and the land nearest the church was chosen by those who could afford it for their homes. Even those living away from the village chose land that afforded a view of the church. For many years, in fact until 1818, the Congregational Church was the established denomination in Connecticut, fostered and provided for by the government.

From the very beginning, not only Enfield but all of New England carried on lengthy boundary disputes. So that it was not unusual that Enfield together with Suffield, Woodstock, and Somers (which had become a separate town in 1734) felt more comfortable and compatible with Connecticut than Massachusetts. Enfield petitioned in 1715 that "we be joined to Connecticut where we properly belong." This request was not realized until 1749. There was much argument about the way the original surveying had been rather arbitrarily done and in the end Enfield "joined with" Connecticut.

The early settlers were all farmers. Even the minister, the school teacher, and the surveyor farmed. Here at Enfield settlers found the rich agricultural land of the Connecticut River Valley. Each community had to be self-sustaining, each town must and did take care of its own affairs. A survey of the officers of the town chosen in town meeting in

Enfield for the period March 13, 1748/49, as found in Allen's *History of the Town of Enfield*, shows just how self-sustaining a town had to be:

Moderator
Constables (2)
Town Clerk
Selectmen (5)
Assessors (3)
Town Treasurer
Two men "chosen to take care for ye Prevention of Killing Deer"
Tything men (2)
Sealer of Leather (1)
Surveyors of highways (4)
Fence Viewers (2)
Hogreves—also called a Hayward (2) (men charged with im-
    pounding stray hogs)
    Added to above by 1751:
Grand Jurors (2)
Gager, Searcher and Packer (one who inspects dutiable goods)
Sealer of weights and measures
Key Keeper
Packer of Tobacco
Collector of Rates (taxes)
By 1752 men were being chosen: "to take Care about the schools
    and to Call meetings when there shall be need"
By 1754 Town Meeting voted: "to chuse a Committee to divide the
    town into districts for Schools and to Establish the places
    where the Several School houses shall be built"

It is easy to believe that all matters were decided by a vote of all the townspeople since that is the modern idea of the government by town meeting, but in early New England this was far from the truth. Those allowed to vote were only those who were "admitted inhabitants" and "freemen." First of all that eliminated all women. But it also eliminated all who did not belong to the Congregational church, all who did not own property and all who were not models of behavior, for an "admitted inhabitant" was a resident of honest conversation, a godly man and substantial landowner who had taken an oath of allegiance to the Commonwealth testifying that he was neither Jew, Quaker, or atheist. When voted in at town meeting the new voter could take part in town affairs, cast a ballot for town officials or for deputies to the

General Court; he was eligible for election to an inconspicuous local office but could not participate in state government.

Free men were the more distinguished "admitted inhabitants" who through exemplary citizenship and church going had been approved by the General Court itself. Only the "freemen" could vote for higher officials, i.e., governor.

It became more and more clear that while all men were taxed, all men did not vote. For example, in 1750 all males between sixteen and seventy with property valued at eighteen pounds or over were liable to payment of rates with certain exceptions which included officers of state, ministers, college tutors, schoolmasters, and students. In the valuation of land, house lots of three acres were rated at 20 shillings (1 shilling = 1 quarter approximately), upland pasture at 8 shillings, meadowland at 15 shillings an acre, boggy meadows at 5 shillings an acre. An ox was valued at 4 pounds (1 pound = $5 approximately), a cow and a horse at 3 pounds, and swine at 1 pound each. A voting freeman had to have an estate yielding at least 7 pounds per year or taxable personal property worth 13 shillings.

Since, in the distinctions given in "admitted inhabitants" and "freemen," there is stress on the "godly man" and "exemplary citizenship" it is not difficult to understand that those who ruled while in no way royal with a "divine right" were nevertheless not representative of the common man.

Connecticut justly or unjustly has been dubbed the Land of Steady Habits and perhaps this honeycombing of church and town had more than a little to do with the name. Early records show fines received for not attending town meetings or for breaking the Sabbath. While much about Connecticut blue laws has been exaggerated there were directions on how the Sabbath should be observed that precluded cooking, travel, signs of affection and frivolity. It did include two long church services with a noon break. And here again it was in church, from the minister who in most cases was the most learned man in town, that questions political as well as theological were examined and dealt with.

the religious influence

The Congregational ministers were a dominating force in the political thought and action of early Connecticut. They were freely acknowledged as expert politicians and one of the year's great events, Election Day, began with a lengthy and judicious sermon on the event about to take place.

The Tercentenary Commission of the State of Connecticut notes:

Since early Colonial days Connecticut had supported Congregationalism as an official church. Its ministers played an important part in politics and its parishes were subsidized by funds secured from public taxation. Because of this situation nearly all the members of the Congregational church were also members of the dominant political party, the Federalist, and conversely, most Episcopalians, Methodists, and Baptists flooded into the Republican fold.

Toward the end of the eighteenth century more and more people who were not Congregationalists were settling in Connecticut. They objected to an established church that they must pay taxes to support pay its minister, replenish its psalm books. It was a new voice in the land. The old ways must give way to the new. The result was really the blossoming of a new political party. The Republicans, or the Democrat-Republicans as they were officially called with Thomas Jefferson as their leader, were the Dissenters. They argued for religious equality, open suffrage, separation of church and state, and a liberal constitution. The Federalists supported an official church (Congregational) and an aristocratic form of government (the select club of "admitted inhabitant" and "freeman"). This dichotomy of thought resulted in a new Constitution in Connecticut in 1818 that swept away the old government, struck down the established church, and established three levels of government at the state level—legislative, judicial and executive. The Federalists, the "friends of religion and order," were defeated by a majority of 1,554 votes (even then the voters were only about one tenth of the population). The Republicans, the "friends of liberty and Constitutions," were in.

the suffrage problem

Noah Webster was only one Federalist who brought eloquence to his argument:

Equally absurd is the doctrine that the universal enjoyment of the right of suffrage is the best security for free elections and a pure administration . . . a liberal extension of the right of suffrage accelerates the growth of corruption, by multiplying the number of corruptible electors and reducing the price of venal suffrages.

He agreed that all men should have equal protection before the law whether they possessed a single cow or a thousand acres but not equal power to make that law. It would be an injustice and a danger to allow the class who held but a twentieth of the wealth to rule. He also said:

The very principle of admitting everybody to the right of suffrage, prostrates the wealth of individuals to the rapaciousness of a merciless gang, who have nothing to lose and will delight in plundering their neighbors.

Indeed, Webster further believed that if the vote was extended the "landed man" should be given a plural vote.

But Noah Webster and those who believed as he did were not in the majority. There were enough men with property who believed that all men should have a voice in their government, and in this way another growth in self-government was achieved. These concepts of liberty, equality, sovereignty, so identified with Americans, were the source of keen examination in this early nineteenth century America. Political wisdom had been crystallized and condensed in the Constitution. Liberty meant equality of opportunity for the individual. Sovereignty gave liberty and in the minds of the Americans it also gave equality. President Andrew Jackson in his message to Congress in 1829 said, "The duties of all public offices are or at least admit of being made so plain and simple that men of intelligence may readily qualify themselves for their performance." At the same time Ralph Waldo Emerson was exclaiming from his study at Concord, Massachusetts, that all men were "divine." Both feelings one historian asserts are a "sure key to the treasures of heaven and earth." Even if nineteenth century Americans were expanding their opportunities to grow and to develop they were aware as they had always been of those who were dependent either because of poverty, sickness, or because they were mentally handicapped. As early as 1788 Enfield's Town Meeting voted that the "Selectmen Shall hire a house Somewhere in the Town of Enfield and put the poor of the Town into the same." Just when and how this was done is not known. This practice of providing a home for those who could not help themselves continued until about 1953, when the federal programs of old age assistance, social security, and aid to dependent aliens removed the necessity for it.

provision for education

Just as the poor were taken care of, so, from the beginning, was there a provision for education. In 1703 at Town Meeting it was voted to hire a schoolmaster and in 1708 construction of a school was authorized. The size was eighteen-by-sixteen.

Just twenty-eight years later it was necessary to create three school districts in the town:

1. South: east and west of the Scantic River
2. North of the Scantic
3. North side of Freshwater

At the same Town Meeting, 1736, two men were chosen to administer each district and "to hire a woman to keep school there." This system of dividing the town into school districts was continued and by 1881 there were fourteen school districts and each district had specific responsibilities. They were: (1) to provide a proper building for "scholars" of that district; (2) to elect to the district committee a person who will efficiently manage the school; (3) to give to the district officer the responsibility of hiring the teacher for that school. Each of the three largest school districts also taxed its citizens and the district representative was the tax collector.

This policy of districting the town to share the burden of education was not new. In 1836 the town was divided into districts, fourteen to be exact, for maintaining and providing highways. Persons were chosen at town meeting to be the surveyor of highways and to collect the taxes in their respective districts. It seems logical that the fourteen highway districts and the fourteen school districts would be identical.

health protection

As the nineteenth century established itself, Enfield as well as other Connecticut communities was moving from a farming town to a manufacturing center. Even though there had been a turpentine industry, a grist mill, and a saw mill of some size—as well as other smaller manufacturing works—it was not until the carpet mills were established in Thompsonville in 1828 and the gun powder works of Powder Hollow in 1833 that the tide was turned in favor of industry. For one thing this innovation developed two major concentrations of population and the villages of Thompsonville named after Orrin Thompson, the carpet man, followed some years later by Hazardville, named after Augustus Hazard, the gun powder man, were formed. True to the original boundaries Enfield remained the seat of government and consisted of four villages: Thompsonville, Hazardville, Scitico, and Enfield. The industries attracted many new people, so much so that Enfield—which boasted of 2,661 persons in 1820—had increased to 6,755 with a grand list of $2,647,193 according to the Connecticut Register of 1887.

With the growth in population, the concentration of people in two distinct areas, and with the change in occupations from farmers to factory workers, the demands upon the town government increased yearly. Concerns for the health and safety of its citizens were of prime importance. A look at a report of the local health officer, Dr. George Finch who served for more than twenty-five years and who wrote cogent yearly reports on the Town of Enfield, will give the reader an eye-witness report of town problems and town progress:

Report of the Town Health Officer

The following is the report of the Town Health Officer for the year ending August 31st, 1920:

With the writing of this annual report the Town Health Officer is rounding out the 25th year of continuous service as Health Officer for the town of Enfield. A quarter of a century is rather a long period of time and naturally it has brought marked changes in the civic life of our community. Enfield can never be accused of vegetating and it is a decided pleasure to take a backward glance.

We will leave to another pen to chronicle the phenomenal increase in our grand list during this period; the coming of a carpet manufacturing corporation, a giant among the carpet plants of the world; the increase of our industries, the installation of a lighting system in our town, the introduction of trolley transportation, the building of miles of sidewalks, the widening of our roads, the wonderful growth of our school system with its beautiful new school buildings, the splendid increase in our fire protection and many other modern conveniences and adjuncts to comfortable living. These things come to all progressive towns in the natural course of events. The people demand them and they get them.

For the purposes of this report the two most important achievements of this twenty-five year period, the two that stand out most prominently, that bring comfort and satisfaction to the greatest number of people, that minister more particularly to public health and happiness, that are reflected more openly on the general well being of this community, are our Water system and our Sewer system. One must needs be an inhabitant to appreciate to the full what these twin aids to public health have accomplished for us. Today we turn a faucet and we have for our use, in abundance for all our needs, water that is above reproach. Its source is under official inspection and control, the water is analyzed at intervals to determine its chemical content and fitness for use. This has practically eliminated all water borne diseases. In former years we expected a crop of Typhoid Fever just as we expected a crop of potatoes or apples. We called it Autumnal Fever and thought it came in the ordinary course of nature like other maturing crops. We know now that it came from nasty, polluted well water. That during the summer the wells were lowered and contained less water and that in the fall we got a stronger dose of the filth that had filtered into them. Typhoid Fever of the type of thirty years ago is practically unknown.

A sewer system is an absolute necessity for a community that desires and seeks protection, and even immunity from filth born diseases. In former years our town was dotted over thickly with hundreds of privies. Many of them had no vaults and the contents were washed over the ground. If there were vaults, the walls were fallen in and soil saturation was promoted. Every house had either an open sink drain or a make-shift cesspool. The soil receiving the outflow of sewage year after year was soaked to saturation and could absorb no more. In such soil and under such conditions wells were located and we in our ignorance and innocence were actually drinking the water from these wells. Naturally we

Main Street, Thompsonville, after the blizzard of 1888.

contracted Typhoid Fever, and we regarded it as a dispensation of Providence. Our Sewer System has changed these conditions entirely, and in the change has eliminated innumerable sources of danger to which we were exposed.

There is one very important factor, perhaps a vital factor that must not be overlooked while we are reviewing the improvement in health conditions in our town, and that is the splendid public spirit that has grown up among us with the passing years. Slow of development, meeting many setbacks, encountering considerable friction and opposition, there is today in the town of Enfield a civic pride, a community of interest, a spirit of co-operation and helpfulness in all matters pertaining to health protection and betterment of living conditions that cheers the heart of the Health Officer and makes his duties much easier to perform. It is simply a matter of education; people have learned that they cannot maintain an offensive nor a foul smelling sink-drain where they have access to a sewer. People have learned that they cannot maintain a nuisance of any sort. The placarding of contagious diseases causes no trouble. The orders of the Health Officer, given in a kindly way, are complied with readily and willingly. All complaints are investigated; some are trivial, some are even ridiculous; some are from spite and quarrels between neighbors. It is the aim and intention of this office to accord fair treatment to all.

The government and the state are putting forth every effort to take the public into their confidence, to show the people the imperative necessity for measures to safeguard the public health, to enlist their hearty and whole souled co-operation. This modest report of a Town Health Officer aims to impress its public with the inspiring idea that we, a small country town, are an integral part of one of the grandest, the most humanitarian, the most unselfish systems that was ever inaugurated to help the human race. It asks for appreciation of work done, for sympathy in measures adopted, for a thorough system of team work, that Enfield may share to the full in the benefits that are justly hers. The thought that is expended on matters pertaining to public health, the investigations and analyses making such study definite and effective, the legislative regulations passed to suppress or to control factors inimical to public welfare, will never reach the highest point of possible efficiency until the public has been awakened to a full realization of their importance and is prepared to enter into partnership with health officials in ferreting out, suppressing or controlling, regulating by statute, all of these evils, these deviations from standard sanitation, these sins against accepted hygiene, that are constantly threatening the health and well-being of our citizenry. Such efforts must find soil in which to flourish, such appeal must be made to open ears.

As part of a publicity campaign to awaken interest in the public health question, Dr. Blue, former Surgeon General of the United States, sent to the mayors of all towns in the United States having a population of over 5,000, to all Boards of Trade and Chambers of Commerce, to all chapters of the American Red Cross, a letter entitled: "Is Your Community Fit?" It is hoped that this will stimulate active interest in public health matters throughout the country and that the state and local health officers will translate this program into effective action. This letter asks a number of pertinent questions and it is gratifying to note that Enfield will score a very good mark in answering them.

1. — Who is responsible for the health of your community? Have you a Health Officer? Does he give all his time to his office, or are you depending on a busy doctor who accepts this position at a nominal salary for the honor he feels attached to it?

It is well to bear in mind the truth of the motto: Public Health is purchasable. In a large measure a community can limit the degree of prevalence of disease within its borders. It is practically impossible for the ordinary country town to employ a full time Local Health Officer and in this respect Enfield is fortunate. The advantages of a full time man are appreciated in epidemics such as Infantile Paralysis and Influenza when the Health Officer's time is fully taken up. A doctor who is not engaged in practice does his work with far less friction with other doctors in the community. When we realize fully that public health is purchasable we will feel satisfied that the money spent by the town in garbage collection, street cleaning, pay for health policing, is well invested and will bring satisfactory returns.

2. — Have you any definite information as to the prevalence of preventable diseases in your community?

Without such information health officials cannot direct their activities in a way that will yield the largest returns in disease prevention. All doctors must report such diseases as part of their responsibility to the community. The law is very plain on this point. If no doctor is in attendance on a case of contagious disease the family in which it occurs must report the case. A doctor having such a case in his care must report as soon as he has made a diagnosis, and, if he is alive to his responsibility, he will report suspicious cases. The reporting of cases is all important as it is the sole basis for action on the part of the Health Officer.

3. — Have you a safe water supply? How do you know it is safe? Among the many valuable assets possessed by the town of Enfield our water supply stands out like a bright and shining light. In safety it is practically absolute, in purity it is unsurpassed. This we know from frequent and regular bacteriological examinations. To our pure drinking water we attribute the comparative freedom of our town from Typhoid Fever, Diarrhea, Dysentery and other water born diseases. The water used for domestic purposes in our town is practically never ponded, never at rest. It flows pure and sparkling from natural springs, it is conducted in natural pipes to a small reservoir at the pumping station, from here it is pumped almost immediately into the distributing system. It has no time to become stagnant and little chance to become contaminated.

4. — Is your town adequately sewered or are there still many homes with cesspools and unsanitary privies?

District No. 2 Thompsonville, has a sewer system that is serving its people in a very satisfactory way and is capable of expansion to take care of future needs. District No. 1 Hazardville, a well populated, rather thickly settled community, cries aloud for sewers. (Note: Yearly reports of the Health Officer have emphasized the need for sewers in Hazardville.) The village is dotted with unsanitary privies and disease breeding cesspools. The soil has become supersaturated with sewage and conditions in general are an open invitation to epidemics. Many communities similarly neglectful of safeguards to public health and safety have been awakened to duty by a deadly epidemic of some filth born disease that has taken a death toll of scores of children. Such lessons are learned at a fearful cost.

5. — What effort has been made to ascertain whether or not your milk supply is safe? Enfield has a system of milk inspection measuring up to the requirements of a country town whose milk supply is at her own door. Samples of milk from various producers and dealers are sent frequently to the state laboratory for analysis. Measures are constantly being taken to insure the safety of the supply.

6. — Are your schools provided with medical supervision to control the spread of communicable diseases among the children and to limit the number of sources of contagious diseases which often spread rapidly when carried to susceptible persons? We operate under a system of medical inspection that has been complimented by health authorities for its simplicity, its practical features and ease of application, its efficiency. It is yielding us satisfactory results. . . . . .
. . . .
Our town water is most satisfactory in quantity and quality. Every school room in town has been thoroughly cleaned and fumigated and necessary repairs have been made in preparation for the opening of schools in the Fall.

When we stop to consider what has been accomplished during a period of twenty-five years in measures for health protection, and remember the splendid public sentiment that has been built up in our town toward public health safeguards during that time, the future is bright with promise.

Enfield is on the threshhold of marked growth and development; all the signs of the times point in no uncertain manner toward advancement, progress, forward movement. With our public water supply, our sewer system, our garbage collecting systems, our school inspection, and the varied machinery that has been brought into service, we feel that in health protection we shall be able to keep step with our civic growth and be able to fortify our commonwealth with a citizenry that is physically strong and healthy. After all, health, with its vigor of mind and body, is the one important consideration, the worthwhile aim in life.

DR. GEORGE T. FINCH,
Town Health Officer.

new town services

As early as 1890 there were sewers of some sort in Thompsonville proper and as the twentieth century began "every property owner having access to a public sewer will be expected to use it." There was no doubt about the seriousness of this project. On the same subject a public official comments: "The average cost for entering a private house into the sewer is about $25 . . . . the cost will be considered the best investment of a lifetime." Fire and Sewer Districts were established by legislative act and remain to the present day. Town water followed in 1899 or 1900, and shortly afterward in 1902 the town installed electric street lights for Thompsonville and Hazardville.

During these early years of the twentieth century Enfield was fast losing its rural village atmosphere and initiating areas and departments that were to experience phenomenal growth as the century wore on. In 1903 a police department was established with an expenditure of $350. Edward Bromage, the first chief of police, had under him one full time patrolman. Others served part time as needed.

In 1896 the town appropriated $400 to open a free public library. Here was a whole new area of government service to citizens. In its first year of operation the new library had acquired 1,800 books for public borrowing.

Garbage disposal was added to the town's services. In 1913 Enfield initiated a rubbish collection (dry garbage) and a garbage collection. The latter was usually a job that a farmer offered to do for a certain price because he could use the garbage to feed his hogs.

Even though the town had greatly increased services to inhabitants and while there were more than the Selectmen of early years to administer these services, the authority for what was done in the town remained the same. The authority was the Town Meeting. In other words, proposals were made as to what the town should do, an amount of money was suggested, and *if* the residents of the town agreed by voting for it at a town meeting, the proposal became a certainty. There were some exceptions when state and federal government might intervene but the day-to-day operation of the town was accomplished by the will of those voting at Town Meeting. It would not be until 1962 that Enfield would find it necessary to give up this time-honored method of town government.

town administration

Two acts of the Legislature can be cited as influencing the way the town operated. In 1919 the State Legislature enacted a law which "placed the actual laying the tax in the hands of a Board of Finance." Previous to this the Selectmen determined what the tax rate should be. Then in 1931 an act of the Legislature removed the control of the police from the Board of Selectmen to a commission of six members to be appointed by the Chairman of the Board of Selectmen.

Growth brings increased government and this is demonstrated by the list of Town Officers for the year ending August 31, 1931:

ELECTIVE

Town Clerk and Treasurer	Assessors (3)
Board of Selectmen (3)	Board of Relief (3)

In 1902 the "Bigelow" Fire Department augmented the town's fire fighting services.

Constables (7)	Board of Finance (6)
Auditors (2)	Library Board (9)
Collector of Taxes	Board of Education (9)
Registrar of Voters (2)	Zoning Commission (5)
Park and Playground Commission (5)	

APPOINTIVE

Civil Service Commission (3)
Personal Tax Collector (1)
Board of Appeals (5)
Dog Warden (1)
Sealer of Weights and Measures (County Sealer)
Tree Warden
Health Officer
Police Commission (6)
Town Plan Commission (5)

The "second" Town Hall, at the intersection of Church and North Main Streets, from an old postcard.

In 1924 one of the first Zoning Commissions in the state was established and in the same year a Park and Playground Commission came into existence.

Positive evidence of the town's growth rests in figures—population and budget. The population was over twelve thousand in the thirties and the town needed something under a half million dollars for expenses. The tax rate? Twenty-four mills.

This steady growth in population that showed no signs of reversing in the foreseeable future led thoughtful townspeople to try to provide for the future. One such group was the Town Plan Commission. In 1940 they submitted a number of recommendations to the town that showed foresight. It would be at least twenty years before their acumen was appreciated.

Recommendations of the Town Plan Commission of 1940 in the interest of better town government included:

a. A change to the Council-Manager form as being more economical, more efficient, more up to date
b. A new Town Building for Enfield or its equivalent
c. A Town Fire Department instead of District Companies (Note: Fire Districts continue to operate)

d. A town-owned Sewer System, expense to be paid by the users
e. A long term school building program

It seems fairly certain that town growth and overburdened town facilities were a concern. At separate times at least two groups were appointed to study the town government and to make recommendations for change. The recommendations were made but were defeated by the townspeople. The Town continued to operate as it had from its very beginning with a Town Meeting, a Board of Selectmen, and the state-initiated Board of Finance and Police Commission. In addition Enfield was governed by State Law, forty-eight Special Acts, and twenty-four Ordinances.

problems of growth

The years after World War II brought an abrupt change to the living patterns of Americans. The city was no longer the "in" place to live as it had been in decades earlier. There was a mass exodus of people from the cities and the suburbs became the "ideal place" to live and bring up children. Since Enfield lies between the cities of Hartford and Springfield and astute builders saw the market for homes if the price was right, the town entered into a period of unprecedented growth. Between 1940 and 1970 the town more than tripled in population. In every area the facilities of the town were overburdened. Those people coming to a small town from a large city were impatient with the school system, the public works, the methods of financing. That old New England custom, "the revered town meeting," was not working for Enfield as a town of 32,000 people. Disgruntled townspeople met with frustration and disappointment when they spoke for increased services.

Once again there were two main groups—those who felt that "the old ways are the best ways" much as the Federalists had argued at the beginning of the nineteenth century and those who saw that new conditions needed another way of governing. This ferment culminated in the election in 1961 of Joseph Tozzoli who had campaigned for First Selectman on the pledge that he would appoint a committee to study the best form of government for the town. Those people who wanted the town to keep step with the population saw this as a means to change. True to his pledge, Mr. Tozzoli initiated the Charter Study Committee shortly after taking office in 1961.

As a result of their study a proposal for a change in the form of

Enfield's third and present Town Hall, built in 1964, reflects the growth of the community.

government was again placed before the voters of Enfield. The Charter Study Committee recommended a Council-Manager form of government.

Those who favored the recommended form argued that it gave Enfield a "technically sound charter which can provide a responsive and responsible structure of government for the town. It provides for a continuing legislative body (the council) representative of the people and for a unified administration for the management of the day-to-day affairs of the town." Those who were opposed argued that the voters of Enfield were giving up their voting rights because they would not be choosing the most important town officials. Many responded that in Enfield's budget approximately one half (2.5 out of 4.4 million dollars) was spent on schools and that the Board of Education had a trained professional, the Superintendent of Schools, administer the spending of that money. The other part of the budget also needed a trained administrator, they argued. Opponents of trained personnel feared that the cost of this government would be prohibitive.

On December 5, 1962, with Enfield's population at almost forty

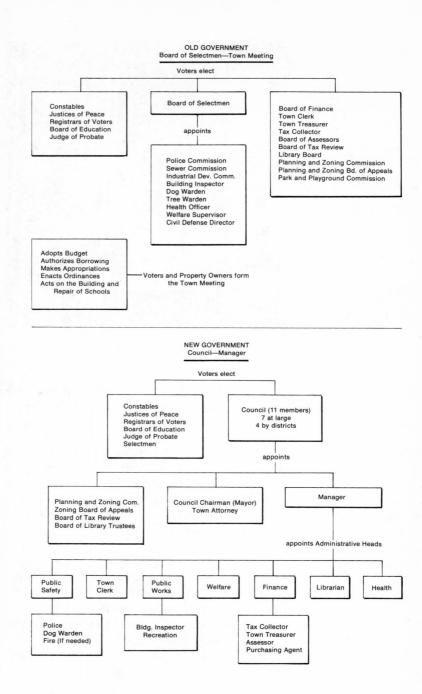

OLD GOVERNMENT
Board of Selectmen—Town Meeting

Voters elect

Constables
Justices of Peace
Registrars of Voters
Board of Education
Judge of Probate

Board of Selectmen

appoints

Board of Finance
Town Clerk
Town Treasurer
Tax Collector
Board of Assessors
Board of Tax Review
Library Board
Planning and Zoning Commission
Planning and Zoning Bd. of Appeals
Park and Playground Commission

Police Commission
Sewer Commission
Industrial Dev. Comm.
Building Inspector
Dog Warden
Tree Warden
Health Officer
Welfare Supervisor
Civil Defense Director

Adopts Budget
Authorizes Borrowing
Makes Appropriations
Enacts Ordinances
Acts on the Building and
    Repair of Schools

Voters and Property Owners form
the Town Meeting

NEW GOVERNMENT
Council—Manager

Voters elect

Constables
Justices of Peace
Registrars of Voters
Board of Education
Judge of Probate
Selectmen

Council (11 members)
7 at large
4 by districts

appoints

Planning and Zoning Com.
Zoning Board of Appeals
Board of Tax Review
Board of Library Trustees

Council Chairman (Mayor)
Town Attorney

Manager

appoints Administrative Heads

Public
Safety

Town
Clerk

Public
Works

Welfare

Finance

Librarian

Health

Police
Dog Warden
Fire (If needed)

Bldg. Inspector
Recreation

Tax Collector
Town Treasurer
Assessor
Purchasing Agent

140 / *the challenge of change*

thousand, the town voted to relinquish the highly revered Town Meeting for the Council-Manager form of government.

A vivid description of Enfield with all of its problems appeared in an area newspaper early in 1965. The reporter wrote thus:

Town Planning Saving Enfield from Chaos

This once-fading community is responding to a beauty treatment.

Uncontrolled growth and an outmoded government system almost turned Enfield into a modern day dinosaur. But an aroused community came to the rescue.

The growth boom is still on but a new manager-council form of government that went into effect in July, 1963, has taken up the dusty reins of leadership and organization. It replaced the traditional selectmen-town meeting system.

The result: The tidal wave of new families, the force that created the sprawling monster, has been stemmed.

The new government brought vigorous leadership and the creation of new departments to deal with the problems of the past and the future.

The first major revision in an almost worthless set of zoning regulations dating back to 1925 was passed last August with new subdivision regulations. This is beginning to create an atmosphere of planned growth. It almost came too late.

Population Boom

From 1950 to 1964 Enfield's population jumped from 15,464 to 38,100. Just during the 1950-60 census period the population more than doubled. In fact it led the state in growth for those ten years.

New housing starts peaked out a few years ago at more than 900 for one year. Last year there were only 266 new homes started.

How did it happen? Enfield was one of the last Connecticut communities to adopt modern zoning and building regulations. Before 1963, when the major revisions were adopted, there were few restrictions for builders. The old 1925 zoning regulations didn't even specify lot sizes.

For some developers, Enfield was the pot at the end of the rainbow. With almost a free hand they were able to offer homes well below the cost of builders in other parts of the state.

And the 34 square miles of gently rolling tobacco valley countryside eased the technical problems of home construction.

Low Cost Housing

The low cost homes attracted young couples, who provided a steady market for the builders.

Some homes were built with front footages as narrow as 60 feet.

Today the picture has changed dramatically. Enfield has two residential zones R-A and R-B which provide for 25,000 and 17,000 square foot lot sizes. Front foot requirements range now from 110 to 125 feet.

The building code is stronger and subdivision requirements call for better roads, curbing and similar improvements.

The great migration of young couples meant school children.

.....More than 46 percent of Enfield's families have children under six, compared to the state average of 30 percent.

School Needs

The young couples and the steady flow of new babies put the pressure on the schools, where double sessions have been a way of life for years.

But this September with the opening of a $2,820,000 junior high school and an elementary school, the system should be free of the double sessions. All of Enfield's 40 class-rooms of second graders will go off the double shift.

At least one new elementary school was built every year for the last few years plus a new high school. Looking ahead, plans are on the drawing boards for another junior high school in 1968 and two more elementary schools in 1966.

Enfield's economic stability has remained relatively strong despite the fact that industrial development was almost non-existent for the big growth period.

For years the Bigelow-Sanford Carpet Co. was the mainstay of the community but in the last five years employment at the firm has dropped from 4,000 to 900.

Today, more than 84 percent of the combined male and female labor force works in Hartford. This has threatened to turn Enfield into a bedroom town.

Continued residential growth was bound to start pushing up the tax rate beyond reasonable bounds.

One of the answers was industrial development. Last December town officials sent questionnaires to 10,000 families seeking opinions on the future character of Enfield. Ten percent replied and two-thirds of them stressed the need for industrial development.

From this survey and earlier studies came a plan for rezoning 1,000 acres of land for industrial use along the new Interstate 91. On March 11 a public hearing will be held on the rezoning.

If Enfield gets this tract under its belt officials plan to work on rezoning another 2,500 acres.

Streamlined Government

City Manager Francis Tedesco who took over the new post in August, 1963, is obviously proud of the progress although he has his critics who claim the town went too far too fast.

He replied simply that when he took over he saw the need for quick responses to obvious problems and he worked hard at meeting the challenge.

His proudest achievement is the zoning revisions and the prime mover behind this was William Kweder, the town's new Director of Planning.

Mr. Tedesco also likes to point to expanded town services such as the street resurfacing program, modern garbage collection system, expanded recreation programs and construction of housing for the elderly.

Both he and Mr. Kweder like to emphasize the team idea in organization and leadership, something they try to practice as much as they preach.

The climax to all the planning will come with the completion of Enfield's master plan started last April. It is scheduled to be completed by September and according to Mr. Kweder is unique. Most master plans are developed along a general line. Enfield's will be specific to the point that it will pinpoint the exact location of a school or other community projects. It will also refine earlier zoning revisions.

Mr. Tedesco feels that Enfield is finally meeting its problems, although he admits there is still a lot to be done in changing the image of this town.

The organizational charts show the difference in the old government (Board of Selectmen-Town Meeting) and the new government (Council-Manager).

The new government planned to meet needs which had been touched upon in the past but had not been answered. The year 1966 witnessed great strides forward. In that year a sewer ordinance created a Sewer Authority under the jurisdiction of the Town Council. To do this the Thompsonville Fire and Sewer District dropped its rights to control the sewers and plans were then made to sewer the whole town. In May, 1966, Enfield adopted a Master Plan that would provide for orderly and effective expansion. A Mental Health Clinic opened in August, 1966, and the next month a Redevelopment Agency was formed.

The new look that Enfield was sporting and the enthusiasm for planning and problem solving helped to make the town a finalist in the All-America City contest that year. The pride in that designation reached its zenith in 1970 when Enfield was chosen as an All-America City.

CHAPTER 7

ENFIELD SCHOOLS

elementary schools

Today's free, compulsory, tax-supported system of public education developed from the persistent concern of the colonists that their children should not grow up in ignorance in the wilderness. The importance of reading the Bible so that they could understand the laws and religious principles of the colony dominated their thinking in New England. The Puritans of the Massachusetts Bay Colony had a strong centralized government controlled by the clergy, and a high proportion of university graduates as their leaders. In 1647 they passed a law requiring every town of fifty families to support an elementary school where reading, writing, and arithmetic were taught. Every town of one hundred families was to have a Latin grammar school in which boys could be prepared for college. Samuel Eliot Morison observed that "in a community so well provided with ministers, school-masters, and birch trees" they felt that their children would be brought up to be virtuous and educated men and women.

In 1650 Connecticut passed a similar law. It was their fundamental belief that a knowledge of the Scripture and an understanding of the principles of the Christian (Puritan) religion were necessary for salvation and that every man was able to judge for himself in its interpretation. An education was identical with self-preservation. The leaders, being men of social experience, religious character, and wealth, saw a need for carrying out their beliefs in pioneer days.

How much education the girls of pioneer days received from early schools is a question. Many New England women were literate, so they learned somewhere. Dame schools privately supported by tuition and sometimes by towns were common. Sewing and embroidery were often taught so that an orphan girl could be self-supporting. There was concern to train children to earn their own living. Mothers taught their own and often their neighbors' children so that they could become self-sufficient. As there are many references to money being allocated to certain individuals in different areas of the town "to keepe school," Enfield must have hired teachers to teach in homes before 1754. The construction of only one school is reported before that time.

THE FIRST SCHOOLS

In Enfield, which was settled in 1680, pressures were made upon the town fathers to make provision for the religious needs of the people by 1689. This was closely followed by demands for the establishment and support of a school. The committee voted "an allotment of forty acres of land in some convenient place for and toward the support of a school to be improved for that use forever."

In 1702/3 it was voted to hire a school master to teach the children. In 1708 it was voted to build a schoolhouse eighteen feet long and sixteen feet wide, in the most convenient place in town.

It is not known just where this spot is located but probably it was on Enfield Street somewhere between the cemetery and the stone commemorating the sermon of Jonathan Edwards. From that time provision has been made annually for the support of a school. The decision was made on December 8, 1707, that all children from five years to nine pay a third part of the charge of maintaining a school and the other two thirds be paid by the inhabitants. Support of the school caused much dissension and problems were often left to the Selectmen for settlement. Town meetings were full of tension and the elected officials had serious decisions to make.

Edward Whittington's name is mentioned as the first school master but it is doubtful if he did teach school. He came to Enfield with some of

The Wallop District School, shown here in 1909, was built in 1800 and used until 1947.

the settlers in 1689 and was accepted as an inhabitant and given a home lot and field lot. He left town so that the grant was forfeited to John Richards who was accepted on March 13, 1703, to "keep school" at a salary of fourteen pounds. Twenty acres of land were promised to Mr. Richards if he continued to teach for five years. Apparently he did not remain for the required time as no land was granted to him permanently.

In 1714 it was voted "to hire a woman to keep school for four or five months, if the Selectmen see cause and think convenient." For one reason or another this probably was not done because on October 12, 1715, "The Selectmen Hath Agreed With Jonathan pear's to Keepe Scoole and for ye Time Ye Keeps Thay are to Give him after ye Rate of four and twenty pounds a year and Cleare his Rats" (His rates, meaning taxes). He was still receiving money in 1721.

Joseph Sexton, Jr., was also teaching in 1718 and continued until at least 1722. John Collins taught from 1741 through 1743 and Ezekiel Pease in 1745. In April of 1753 Wallop and Scitico were allowed "their part of the money raised for schooling for which they had kept in the year 1751/2." As there was no record of any other schoolhouse than the one near or on Enfield Street, private homes must have been used as schools.

SCHOOL DISTRICTS ESTABLISHED

On April 8, 1754, an important town meeting was held. It was voted to draw 300 pounds "old tender" out of the treasury for the use of schools. As the town had expanded and population had increased it had become necessary to build more schools. Five districts called North End, South End, Center, Scitico, and Wallop were established. On October 21 of the same year 500 pounds "old tender" were voted to build the necessary new schools. The separate schools in the various sections which were constituted districts were controlled by one central school committee throughout the Colonial period.

Each of these districts was allowed the liberty of carrying on the business of its school in the manner that seemed best for its area. Certain men were selected in each district to have charge of the money allocated to the district, and together they served as a School Committee. Later in the 1800s they were called Acting Visitors. They were civic-minded men working without pay, appointed to visit and manage the affairs of the school. It was their duty to hire a good teacher and find a place for him to live where food and shelter would be supplied. This helped the parent where he lived to meet a portion of the taxes required of him. It was the duty of the Acting Visitor to use the school fund to pay all bills. The state required this Board of School Visitors to make annual reports starting in 1890. These reports not only contain a great deal of information concerning the problems faced by this important group of men but they also made the townspeople aware of the intense interest and unceasing effort of these men to provide a good education for the children of the town.

During a teacher's absence a Visitor might think it necessary and advisable to take over the classroom and thus learn what was going on day by day. [Such a day I can well remember. Our teacher that year was a very weak disciplinarian. We had reached the stage of no control, but what an awakening we had! Woe unto the pupil who dared to test our substitute's patience with any of our tricks of misbehavior! The punishment justly deserved was promptly and forcibly administered upon the offender who considered it much wiser to refrain from telling his parents about it as that would only mean additional pain inflicted at home.]

There was constant pressure for funds to carry on the educational program. Acting Visitors sympathized with the teachers. A salary of six dollars a week for thirty weeks of the year made the committee feel that long before she had made up the cost of her education a good teacher might become disgusted with teaching and be willing to risk the hazards of matrimony rather than try to satisfy her appetite for fifty-two weeks at $180 a year. They reported, "Our teachers are the pick of

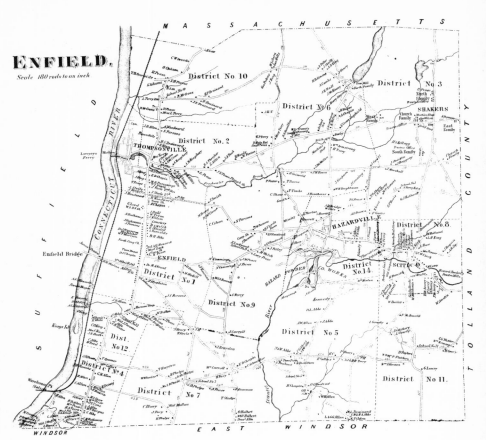

Enfield School District map published in 1869

the state. We are raided by hungry superintendents who are looking for choice teachers. Let us encourage good teachers by kind words and occasional visits, see that our children attend school and are punctual, impress children that teachers are to be obeyed implicitly, promptly, and cheerfully."

PRIMITIVE FACILITIES

Today it is difficult for us to realize the inconveniences of the schools during the 1800s. In the one-room schools water was obtained from a near-by well or spring and carried to the school in pails by the pupils. Franklin Sheldon, who started school in 1850 at the Bement's Brook

School at the age of four, tells that one of the pleasures of his school-days was to be allowed to go for a pail of water at the top of the hill to the west of the school. A kindly neighbor allowed the school the use of her well on the condition that during the time of year when it was necessary for her to use the well for refrigeration the children would take every precaution to avoid spoiling her food. They should not get it wet or forget to return it to the cool area of the well after taking the water they needed. A long-handled dipper was kept in the pail for the use of all the pupils. In June of 1910 the Board of Education approved the first bubbling fountains. Two were to be put in the High School and one each in North, South, Thompsonville, Hazardville, and Enfield Street Schools. In 1911 a well was dug at the Wallop School with the help of the Gleaners. In 1914 Weymouth School had one. As late as 1930 it was voted for the first time to purchase paper drinking cups for the schools without running water.

This lack of running water meant outhouses. It was not until 1911 that toilets were placed in the basement of the Enfield Street School and even then the children on the second floor had to go outdoors in order to get to the basement. Stairs to overcome this difficulty were installed by August 31, 1913. Hazardville Grammar School, one of the larger schools at the time, did not have toilets in the building until 1918, at which time a heating system was installed to improve working conditions there. Chemical toilets were placed in some of the rural schools and were considereed very satisfactory.

Most of the rooms were heated with stoves located, if possible, in the draftiest part of the room. Whether a child froze or roasted depended upon the seat the teacher chose for him. The hungry monster devoured huge amounts of fuel. The all-too-often arrival of the janitor to feed it the wood or coal that was necessary was really a nerve-shattering experience.

The child who sat near a window was a fortunate one. As there was no way of lighting the room except by the sun, on a cloudy day it was the best place for one to see to read or "cipher." The pupil might be most uncomfortable with the draft from the window or the glare of the sun on a bright day, but he, at least, had as much light as possible on the bad days. Electric lights were put in the halls and upper rooms of a few schools in 1916. The eighth and ninth grades in the High School had them in 1911.

Rooms were sparsely furnished in the first schools. Benches and tables for the children, a desk and chair for the teacher, and shelves for books were about all they had. Double seats were used in the 1860s. By

Early photo of the Hazardville Grammar School, used as a public primary school for 100 years.

1911 Enfield had replaced most of these with single seats although some had been used since 1862. The seat was attached to the desk of the pupil in back. It is easy to imagine the annoyance that one who was in the mood for teasing or disturbing could cause the other. Dipping the braids of the girls' hair into the inkwell conveniently located in the upper right corner of each desk was one common way of relieving boredom. What a blessing the invention of the ballpoint pen was to the classroom teacher!

A TEACHER REMINISCES

Records show that in 1839 a direct method of taxation was inaugurated. It was voted to lay a tax of two mills on a dollar for education. The salary of a principal was to be seventeen dollars a month and board. The salary of a woman teacher was to be fourteen dollars a month without board. Teachers were chosen by a show of hands at the school meeting. In 1866 applicants for teaching positions took an examination in the conference room of the old Enfield Street School.

The reminiscences of Mrs. A.S. Brainard, written many years later, tell this story:

I shall never forget the conference room on Enfield Street where I took my first examination as teacher . . . It fell to my lot to bound the city of Hartford. I asked to be excused as I came from Worcester. Reverend Mr. Brigham asked me to bound that city, and thinking that probably I knew as much about it as anyone present, I boldly accomplished the task. I'm quite sure I put in towns enough and felt quite elated until I later learned that Mr. Brigham was a native of Boylston, just over the Worcester line! I value greatly my certificate signed that day by Mr. Brigham, Reverend Mr. Adams, Albert Abbe, John Houston, and Dr. Adams. I taught in a little brick schoolhouse, now demolished, in Brainard District and had about eighteen children. The dark pine woods around the school, the crow conventions every day, the box stove whose back often fell out if the sticks were too long, scattering coals in every direction, and the large number of ungraded classes were very bewildering to a novice like me who had never been away from home before— or even seen the inside of a district school. Still, it was a happy and pleasant winter and when, after teaching from December first to March fifth, I returned home with thirty dollars in my purse, I felt pretty rich. I don't know how much salary I did have but I did not spend a cent of it and I know my board was extremely modest so I guess the stipend wasn't very large.

In 1851 a plan was proposed to put a charge upon all children of the town over five years of age. Children from five to ten should pay a tax of twelve and one-half cents and those over ten years of age twenty-five cents to supply books, pens, paper, etc. This money was to be collected by the teachers. How successful this plan was or how long it existed is not recorded.

EDUCATION IN THE LATE 1800s

In 1882 a statute of the state government required that all children between the ages of eight and fourteen of physical and mental ability should attend school for sixty full days of the year.

By 1880 the Districts in Enfield had increased. They were as follows:

SCHOOL DISTRICTS AS OF 1880

No.	Name	Cost to Operate	No. of Teachers	Date of Establishment
1	Enfield Street	$ 937.00	2	1708

2	Thompsonville			
	Bell School	310.00	1	1750
3	Shakers	265.00	1	1794
4	King Street	285.00	1	1750
5	Wallop	285.00	1	1735
6	Jabbok	260.30	1	1775
7	Weymouth	265.00	1	1775
8	Scitico	590.00	1	1730
9	London	265.00	1	1775
10	Brainard	217.00	1	1792
11	East Wallop	213.70	1	1764
12	Bement's Brook	262.33	1	1750
13	Thompsonville			
	North	2,977.00	10	1750
14	Hazardville	1,854.00	5	1854

The numbers of these districts were frequently changed but this table states them as they were in 1880, except for the date of establishment (which is as near as I can place it from my research). Many of the one-room schools were opened or closed as the population of the area dictated. Even though the number of pupils attending might be extremely low these schools were kept open until the townspeople voted for consolidation.

In the school year 1891-1892 there were sixteen schoolhouses, thirty-two teachers, and 1,507 pupils in the Town of Enfield. The cost for the education program was $17,389.55. The attendance in many of the outlying districts was very low, making the proportionate expense high. Closing some of these schools and consolidating others was considered most advisable by the School Visitors. This idea met with a great deal of opposition. One Board member wrote:

The fewer schools operated, the more money available for those in operation. The halo, the radiance which shines around the traditional little red schoolhouse, is a sacred flame. It must be a bold hand indeed that will cause it to shine less brightly, a daring one that will extinguish it.

How true this is today!

The act to consolidate the schools was passed on October 3, 1892, to be tried for five years. It was adopted on June 3, 1893. All districts legally lost their identity. By 1895 Bement's Brook, London, Jabbok, Hubbard, and East Wallop Schools were temporarily closed. Problems of transportation, apathy, and parental dissension caused a great deal of turmoil for all concerned but financially the plan was beneficial.

Teacher, pupils and Enfield Street/Brainard Road School, circa 1880.

Transporting children, especially small ones, to consolidated schools was very unpopular.

The School Visitor report in 1898 made this appeal: "Times are hard, money is scarce, and it is difficult to pay our taxes, but don't let us begin to economize by cutting down on the educational advantages of our children. **** We can wear our clothes for a longer period, we can run our wagons until they are more shabby, we can endure rough roads and mud, but let us leave the schools all they require, not to be spent extravagantly, recklessly, carelessly, but prudently, thoughtfully, getting value received for every dollar spent. ***** As citizens we must decide just what kind of schools we want and can afford, and having settled that point, we must appropriate the money accordingly."

HIGHER STANDARDS

By 1901 the wisdom of having a Superintendent of Schools was suggested but it wasn't until 1913 that this vision came true. The men who have filled this position so far are as follows:

1913-1917 Edward B. Sellew—starting salary $1,800
1917-1922 Grover C. Bowman—   "   " $2,200

Second grade at South School in 1897.

1922-1926	Anson B. Handy—	”	”	$3,400
1926-1941	Edgar H. Parkman			
1941-1959	Karl D. Lee			
1959-1965	Maurice Smith			
1965-1968	Charles Syberla			
1968-1971	Maurice Smith			
1971-	Louis Mager			

By 1907 it was decided to consider no applicant for a teaching position unless the qualifications of a State Normal diploma or an Elementary State Certificate were met. The demand for competent teachers was far in excess of the supply so that the current wage compelled the committee to take those teachers that other school officials had refused or to depend entirely upon the supply of "home girls." The committee knew that it must face increased salaries for teachers. With the cost of living average of $5.50 a week, a salary of $380 a year was not reasonable. It was thought that teachers could live in hope if they received $400 a year with an increase of fifty cents a week each year for five years and $500 on the fifth year.

Enfield ranked ninety-first among Connecticut towns in the yearly expense per pupil and yet it stood among the first in average attendance, standard of scholarship, quality of teachers, and condition of schools.

In the Town Report of August 31, 1907, on page 45, the following praise was given to the school system:

Owing to our excellent and popular High School, we are sending a group of bright smart girls to our Normal Training Schools every year. Many of our schools today are taught by home girls, fashioned in our grade schools, finished in our High School, polished in our State Normal Schools, and they are noble girls doing a grand work. They are a credit to our town, an advertisement for the Enfield school system. They are a part of the glorious harvest our town is reaping from the judicious sowing of the years.

The reports of the School Committee showed that they were completely satisfied that school money was not misused. The judgment of its members was at a high level compared to the notoriously explosive excitement of the Town Meetings. It is interesting to note that it wasn't until 1931 that a state law requiring the furnishing of textbooks and supplies without cost to the pupils was passed, but the School Committee of Enfield had voted for free textbooks, free supplies, free transportation for Enfield students, and evening school at seven cents a night per pupil in 1906.

THE EVENING SCHOOL PROGRAM

This quote from the Town Report of September 1, 1907, on page 49, shows the effort of the School Committee to try to meet the needs of education at that time:

The subject of free evening schools has long been agitated in Thompsonville. The Town School Committee has considered the matter in an informal way for a number of years . . . The State, recognizing fully the severe tax entailed upon the smaller towns in maintaining their public schools, has fixed upon 10,000 population as the limit when evening schools are mandatory. We have assumed the obligation voluntarily and an appropriation of five hundred dollars was made for the maintenance of such schools . . . Enfield has the honor of being one of the towns able to carry on such schools for the prescribed period of seventy-five nights . . . The evening school cost the town seven cents a night for each pupil in attendance . . . The vast majority of people attending had no knowledge whatever of the English language, none had much . . . They now have a working basis. If this work can be done at the same reasonable figure, it is a good investment.

Enfield's evening school program for adults has been a credit to the town. Two hundred forty-eight registered for the seventy-five night course of study. No town in the state had a larger Americanization problem than Enfield, as it had an enormous foreign element who desired to speak and read the English language. Later on, besides English, classes discussed health, food, dress, and sanitation. Men were interested in having their wives taught American ways. The aim was to help them become real Americans, fit for citizenship and ready to be loyal to American ideals. Adult evening classes today are widely attended but of a very different nature. The subject matter is very much expanded—crafts of all types, various academic courses, homemaking projects, physical health programs, etc., are available. There are exciting possibilities for all.

EXPANDED SCHOOL SERVICES

Superintendent Bowman (1918-1922) had proposed that provision should be made for a school nurse. In December of 1928 the Woman's Club of Enfield requested permission to provide a school nurse for the rest of the school year at thirty-five dollars a week. The Board accepted this offer in February of 1929. From that time on a very beneficial school nurse program has been in effect. There are now thirteen nurses serving sixteen schools. A system of periodic health examinations of all school children was required by the state in 1945. A Dental Clinic was established about that time.

The first hot lunch program started in the High School in 1924. Now both high schools, both junior high schools, the Intermediate School, Hazardville Memorial School, and Enfield Street School employ a staff to provide prepared meals at each. All other schools have satellite lunches brought to the schools.

Enfield's phenomenal growth with a 158.7 percent increase in population from 1950 to 1967 has caused serious problems for the Education Department. In 1973 there were 12,692 dwelling places compared to 2,880 in 1949. The town grew into a city in less than thirty years. The population doubled from 1950 to 1960. Through the 1960s Enfield was averaging one new school a year, making a total of sixteen elementary schools, two junior high schools and two senior high schools.

The following table gives some idea of what has happened in 200 years:

Year	No. of Schools	No. of Teachers	Cost to Maintain	Evaluation
1776	5 One-room	5	$500	Approx.$500
1876	11 One-room 5 Two- (or more) room	Approx. 28	$12,197	?
1976	16 of sixteen or more rooms	645 33 Admin- istrators	$12,254,396	$46,241,580

What of the future? No one can tell. One hundred, even fifty years from now, an Enfield resident will probably have as much difficulty visualizing the Enfield of today as we have understanding school conditions in the eighteenth century.

high schools

The desire to give every young person an education that would prepare him for adulthood has always been one of the prime concerns of the people of Connecticut. In the *Story of Connecticut* Lewis Sprague Mills states that free high schools were established in Thompson in 1829, in Hartford in 1838, in Middletown in 1841, and in New Britain in 1850.

THE ENFIELD HIGH SCHOOL ASSOCIATION

In the small town of Enfield on May 29, 1848, the following business took place at a town meeting. It was voted

That the town buy the Meeting House belonging to the first Congregational Society at the price of five hundred dollars for a town house and that an association of any number of inhabitants of the Town of Enfield has the privilege of converting the upper part of their Town House into a school room fitted for a High School and by them so occupied free of any expense to the Town.

At a town meeting on October 2, 1848, A.L. Spaulding reported that such an association had been formed in September by the name of the Enfield High School Association and they then asked the town to recognize them and confirm the privilege offered. It was voted to grant the request on condition that a committee of three persons examine the lease on which the town house stood to see if the lease was sufficient for

Enfield High School.

NAMES OF PUPILS,

WITH THEIR

Relative Rank in Scholarship and Deportment,

For the Month Ending October 1st, 1875.

PUPILS.	Scholarship.	Deportment.	Half Days Absent.	Times Tardy.	PUPILS.	Scholarship.	Deportment.	Half Days Absent.	Times Tardy.
EXCELLENT.									
Homer Patten,*	48.0	50.0			Nellie Tryon,	38.0	46.0	1	1
Olive Abbe,	48.0	48.7	1		Howard Parsons,	41.5	44.5		1
Lilla Alexander,*	46.6	50.0			Katie Pease,*	34.2	48.2		
Mary Parsons,*	46.7	49.1			Maggie Miller,	35.7	46.5		1
Frank Booth,*	46.3	48.6			Asher Allen,*	38.0	44.0		
Carrie Olmsted,*	45.3	49.5			Anna Parsons,	34.5	44.0	4	
Mary Pease,	45.0	49.5		1	Henrietta Parsons,	35.5	42.2	4	1
Fred. Chapin,*	44.5	49.6			Anna Pierce,	35.5	41.0	5	1
					Herbert Mathewson,	35.2	40.6	4	3
MEDIUM.									
Jennie Loomis,*	40.8	49.0			**INFERIOR.**				
Jennie Alden,*	40.5	48.5							
Julia Hannigan,	39.2	46.5	1		Normie Allen,	32.2	41.5		3
Emma Hohl,*	38.2	48.5			Ada Bancroft,	27.2	44.6	3	1
Nellie Strickland,*	38.7	47.5			George Alden,	31.9	41.0		1
Thomas Abbe,	37.2	46.0	1		Victor Hohl,	29.4	32.7	10	
Allie Allen,	43.1	43.5	3		Florence Tryon,	25.5	46.5		1
Edith Pease,	41.5	44.5	4		James Miskill,	18.3	19.7	16	4

* Perfect in Attendance for one month.

Highest mark, 50. Pupils whose average in scholarship and deportment is above 45 are considered excellent; 37 to 45, medium; below 37, inferior. Pupils, when absent, are marked zero in both scholarship and deportment.

E. Y. Parsons

Parents are respectfully requested to examine and sign this report, and return to

F. H. BREWER, Principal.

Parsons' Printing Office, Thompsonville.

the purposes of the Town and the association, and if it was not adequate to procure a satisfactory lease. Then the town would grant the request. Aholiab Johnson, A.G. Hazard, and Asa L. Spaulding were to comprise the committee to examine the lease.

On April 2, 1849, it was voted to rescind all votes on the subject of granting the privilege of using the upper part of the Town House for a high school. For some reason this first attempt to have a high school did not materialize. Perhaps the time was not ripe for such a venture.

However, academies for young people, especially boys, were very popular then for those who could afford to send their sons and daughters to private schools for higher learning. Most of the young people who desired further education attended Suffield Academy, then called Connecticut Literary Institute, if they lived in the western part of the town. Those who lived in the eastern part usually went to Wilbraham Academy.

In the ten or fifteen years after the first attempt failed, the need for a public high school must have become evident because several districts tried to meet it though the records are not very clear and are far from complete.

THE FIRST HIGH SCHOOL CLASSES

In 1856 high school classes were held in Session Hall. This building, located on Church Street where the Greek Orthodox Church now stands, belonged to the First Presbyterian Church and was used as a parish hall.

At the Connecticut State Library in Hartford, a book entitled *Enfield High School* (Call number 974.62 En 2hs) states on page 162, "It took until 1857 to get high school classes started in what was then called #7 School." Its location is not mentioned. District 7 is shown on maps at the southern end of the town.

By the 1860s the town had grown so that in some districts a one-room school was not adequate and new schoolhouses were built, this time of brick. Enfield Street's new building was two stories high with a "conference" room on the second floor, intended for public use. Thompsonville then had three schoolhouses, each with two classrooms—the North School, the South School, and the Bell School. Hazardville had a six-room building, which is still there but with a 1927 addition in front of it. With these larger buildings high school courses could be offered to the older scholars. By the middle 1870s the Thompsonville, Enfield, and Hazardville Districts had a two-year program of high school sub-

Report cards in 1875 left nothing to the imagination.

jects. But there was still no building exclusively for high school students.

THE THOMPSONVILLE HIGH SCHOOL

This problem was tackled by the Thompsonville district, the largest and most flourishing part of the town. The first real high school building, called the Thompsonville High School, was approved by town vote in 1867. Land was purchased and construction began about 1870. The building cost $16,934 and was located on North Main Street in Thompsonville where the Neighborhood Youth Center now stands. F.E. Moody was hired as the first principal at a salary of $600 a year. No students living outside of the district were allowed to attend at that time. (The first diplomas were issued in 1879.) The curriculum was broadened, a Literary Society was soon organized, and a school newspaper was published. The members of the Board of Acting Visitors, later called the Board of Education, were very proud of the accomplishments of their program in the High School.

By 1890 this building was inadequate. The town report of that year states:

Too much praise cannot be bestowed upon the people of District 2 for what they have done during the past year for their school . . . A special tax was levied and even more than the usual amount of money was furnished for the schools . . . Three thousand dollars was voted to enlarge the high school building and the result is a credit to the district and the town . . . The whole building will be heated by steam, and it has been provided with marble basins, mirrors, water closets, and all the conveniences found in the modern school building . . . One pupil has been prepared for college and will enter Yale in September.

In 1892 the town voted for consolidation, bringing all schools under town management. The School Board voted to take over the Thompsonville High School (which had been started by the citizens of District 2 and very successfully developed) and maintain it as the Enfield Public High School.

However, high school classes continued in the Hazardville Grammar School until September of 1904. That year the total number of pupils in grades nine through eleven was one hundred eighty-six. There had been twenty-six such pupils during the school year of 1888-1889. As the eastern part of the town was considered the rural section, Hazardville Grammar School was educating its fair proportion of high school students. When the high school classes were discontinued in 1904, the Board hoped that it would "cause no regrets."

Elmer Randall, Principal of the Hazardville Grammar School from 1891 to 1903, must have been a man of great ability as a teacher. The school is reported as one of very high standing in the town reports during that period. He was an exceptionally strong disciplinarian according to the stories told by the oldsters who attended the school, but respect for him was high, and with good reason.

INSURING QUALITY IN EDUCATION

The following quotations from the Town Report of August 31, 1896 (page 58), support the paragraph above. Professor W.H. Newhall, Principal of Wilbraham Academy, wrote:

The students from Hazardville all show that they have received careful training, and not only in textbooks but in general discipline, they were better equipped than the majority who came to us from towns of Massachusetts, Connecticut, or New York.

Professor Gill, also of Wilbraham, wrote:

The best mathematicians that enter our school come from Hazardville.

Regular attendance and punctuality were known to be of great importance as shown by this statement in the Town Report of August 31, 1896—pages 50 and 51:

The great state of Connecticut, which gives large sums of money each year to the various towns to aid them in maintaining their schools, claims the right to make laws compelling school attendance. Through the machinery of her courts she possesses the power to bring this about . . .
We intend to trace very child of school age in the Town of Enfield . . . It is not pleasant to resort to severe measures but indications point to the inevitable

Enfield High School,
Thompsonville, Conn.

Enfield's first high school building from an early miniature postcard.

conclusion that a few examples of the operation of the law will be necessary to impress the sense of duty upon the careless, indifferent, and defiant . . . Tardiness, irregular attendance, and absenteeism constitute the greatest menace to efficiency and good work with which we have to deal.

Pride was confirmed by the following statement found on page 57:

Our High School is gaining in reputation . . . In the entering class at the State Normal School in New Britain last fall, six of the fifteen chosen as the first division were graduates of the Enfield Public High School.

In 1897 on pages 60 and 61 it is stated:

We feel proud that the Enfield Public High School has been selected as one of the eight in the state whose course of study, teaching ability, and general organization is deemed worthy of publication in the annual report of the State Board of Education.

At the present time it [the school] requires two large session rooms and four recitation rooms to accommodate it besides a smaller room for the use of typewriters. There were one hundred twenty-one scholars registered last year and in June we graduated a class of eighteen. Six teachers are employed and five courses of study are offered to pupils. We have scholars from surrounding towns and over $800 is turned into the town treasury from tuition.

Very early we established a high standard and determined to maintain it, if the school only numbered twenty-five. Occasionally we sent a boy or girl to college, but it was hard work, and they were obliged to study in school and out, and to recite at all hours of the day and evening. Gradually our High School began to make a name for itself. Our boys and girls who went to college were found to be well-prepared. Scholars who came to try our entrance examinations found it was difficult to pass them and so were anxious to get in, until our school was in demand and began to grow.

(Tuition pupils from the Towns of Suffield, East Windsor, and Somers attended our high school classes through the school year of 1935.)

Two rooms were added to the south of the High School in 1890 at a cost of $3,000 and in 1902 a two-room addition was put on the north costing $5,500. Six upper grades at the elementary level were housed in the building at that time. The high school occupied the second floor. It was not until the school year of 1914-15 that the building was used for high school classes exclusively. At that time there were over 200 students in the high school. This included many tuition pupils from nearby towns.

The zealous efforts of Edgar H. Parkman, Principal, developed what proved to be a very satisfactory course. The New England Entrance Certificate Board, an extremely rigid examining group, investigated the Enfield Public High School in 1909 and placed it on the accredited school list. Students could be admitted to a large number of colleges on certificate. The Massachusetts Institute of Technology was one of which the Board was particularly proud.

Mr. Parkman was considered a "veritable Moses" because out of uncertainty and inefficiency he had brought the standard of the school to a position where definite, accurate work was accomplished. It was considered a school for the people. The curriculum was so varied and the scope so broad that it could meet the needs of every pupil at that time. One of his favorite quotations was, "Our todays and yesterdays are the stones with which we build." It was proving true.

NEED FOR A NEW HIGH SCHOOL

In 1906 there was some sentiment for a new high school but the town fathers did not feel that it was a necessity. A building costing $70,000 to $75,000 when fully equipped would place a tremendous burden upon the taxpayers. It was deemed wiser to "pay our debts, and when we have a clean slate, if we want to indulge ourselves in the luxury of a new high school building, we can do so." However, land was scarce and valuable and a committee was appointed to make a general survey of the town to find what was available and suitable for a site. Dr. Thomas Alcorn worked very diligently on this project. The school had only just opened in September of 1925 when he died on November 28. He was a man who was greatly respected by the townspeople and they were happy that he lived to see his dream materialize. He had been instrumental in obtaining the land, which is located on Enfield Street near New King Street, site of the building which is now known as the Intermediate School. The original building cost $277,500.

In 1913 the elementary school was changed to eight grades instead of nine for graduation. This made it possible for a child of fourteen to finish elementary school and perhaps enter high school in the years that he was legally required to attend school.

When Mr. Parkman retired in 1951, G. Stephen Potwin, a former tuition pupil of the Enfield Public High School from East Windsor, recalled conditions in his high school days as follows:

It was not the usual thing to continue from grades into high schools forty years ago. Those who did decide to pursue their studies further had a harder row to hoe than pupils have nowadays.

Transportation in my day, demanded as a right today, was unheard of a generation ago. At 7:40 I set forth for the trolley station which was two miles away. In the spring and fall a bicycle was often used but there was always a horse and a two-seated buggy, which families shared. Despite cold, rain, snow, and mud we went. There was no cancellation of sessions. We bought our own books. The town reimbursed our trolley fare but we were on our own getting to and from the trolley.

[I can well remember walking the trolley tracks from Thompsonville to Hazardville when a severe snow storm made it impossible for the trolley to get us home. Some of my friends had to continue on to Somersville and Somers. One family lived on Hall Hill Road very near the Massachusetts border. One day we trudged both ways, but I am sure that was for a daring adventure.]

The past fifty years have brought increasing changes in all conditions of life. Time does that! Enfield's astounding population explosion has caused unbelievable problems. The town has become urban rather than rural. Fundamentally unprepared for this rapid growth and change, the education system has had the enormous task of adjusting its program to fill the needs of its students, both children and adults.

MEETING THE DEMANDS OF THE POPULATION EXPLOSION

The educational system has done its utmost to meet the challenges of the present. Constant vigilance and zealous effort have caused repeated adjustments for the improvement of the curriculum, not without many difficult problems. Infractions similar to those of the past can be observed such as: poor attendance, defiance, indifference, lack of cooperation of people involved, etc., plus the new and very disturbing conditions of life. Education today is really a "big business" and a most difficult one.

Two new junior high schools housing grades seven through nine have been constructed. The Thaddeus Kosciuszko School on Elm Street was ready for use in 1965 at a cost of $2,257,700. The largest of its type in the state, it was constructed to run on a house plan of organization which was based on the idea of maintaining the best features of a small school but also taking advantage of the facilities available for a large school. A student is assigned to one "house" and one group of teachers for the three years of the Junior High program in all basic academic subjects. Students are integrated for the specialized subjects. A team-teaching program is now being tried and evaluated. Each team has about 120 students with four teachers—one in English, one for Science, one for Math, and one for Social Studies. Home Economics, the Industrial Arts, Music, and Physical Education are integrated. After experimentation and adaptation this program may be established in all three years of the Junior High School. John F. Kennedy Junior High School, located on Raffia Road, cost $3,900,000 and was ready for occupancy in 1969. Both schools conduct a similar pattern of instruction. Kennedy has a swimming pool that serves the town residents during school hours, vacation, and evenings.

Two beautiful high schools are now being used to instruct teenagers and adults night and day. The Enfield High School on Enfield Street, completed in 1963, is held in high esteem by the residents of the town, especially those who are older and well remember the inadequacies of the buildings in which they struggled for an education. The increased spread of the curriculum, the beauty and conveniences—even luxuries—of the improved facilities, and the many specialized departments are too phenomenal to have been even imagined fifty years ago. Today the curriculum is so broad that any scholar has the golden opportunity to start, at least, preparation for any field of work.

The Enrico Fermi High School on North Maple Street in the eastern part of the town was ready for occupancy in 1971. The total cost of building and land was $6,255,000. It is one of the finest schools in the state. The planetarium is used by all the students in the town. The swimming pool and its facilities are enjoyed by residents of all ages. The three-level Library Resource Center is so centralized that it is easily accessible to all departments. Another special feature of its program is the Food Service Department. Some of the student cooks may become the famous chefs or restaurant owners of the future. The curriculum is extremely expansive. The programs established are designed with an awareness of the importance of the individual which requires flexibility and adaptability to teaching techniques.

The tremendous building program and the continual need to expand and change the curriculum comprise only some of the problems faced by the Board of Education, the administrators, teachers, and residents of the Town of Enfield, especially during the past twenty years. If you can also visualize the additional areas of concern with which all have had to contend, you will better understand how serious and difficult the adjustment has been. The demands placed by state law upon towns to supply adequate instruction for the individual child, no matter how severe the handicaps may be, has forced unbelievable financial burdens upon towns in all departments. It requires people with courage, patience, intelligence, determination, understanding, and love of mankind to carry such a load. To succeed they must also have the cooperation of all concerned—students, teachers, and parents. If Enfield is to continue to be a town of which we can be proud, we must try to educate our children to the complexities of life. What a responsibility for all!

parochial schools

Parochial schools have had a distinct influence on the educational growth of Enfield. In the last hundred years they have expanded from one to four elementary schools, one Montessori, an academy, and for a short time a Junior College. These developed because Catholic and other Christian families felt the need of religious as well as secular education for their children.

EARLY SCHOOLING

In 1871 Father John Cooney was appointed Pastor of St. Patrick's Parish. His first major decision was to invite the Sisters of Mercy to teach in a parish school to be known as St. Joseph's School. His dream became a reality in August, 1872, when four Sisters of Mercy arrived.

The first setting for St. Joseph's School was in the basement of the old frame church which was divided into two large classrooms. The older boys were taught in the larger room and the girls in the other room. The younger children were taught in the back of the larger room. Two hundred children attended.

An Academy was also opened in the first week of September, 1872, using the Convent parlor and refectory.

A Night School for Boys, conducted by Father Michael Kelly and the Sisters, opened in October, 1872, but closed in April, 1873. In place of this, religious instructions were taught two nights a week.

In 1873-74 a four-room school was built, but within eight years this building proved inadequate. An abandoned six-room public school was purchased and relocated near the church. This was opened in 1882.

When the new church basement was completed, the old church was divided into two classrooms and a large hall, providing the Parish with eight individual elementary classrooms which served until 1958.

A modern sixteen-room school, constructed under the direction of the pastor, Father William P. Kilcoyne, was dedicated on Sunday, September 28, 1958, and was filled to capacity during the prosperous years.

At present nine rooms are used as classrooms, one for a library, one for a science laboratory, and one for the Confraternity of Christian Doctrine office.

FELICIAN SISTERS' CONTRIBUTIONS

On December 13, 1933, the Felician Sisters bought the thirty-two-and-a-half acre Mifflin property on Enfield Street, known as Longview Estate. It then became known as Our Lady of Angels Convent, which eventually initiated three special education programs:

1. A private kindergarten, known as Our Lady of Angels School, opened September, 1949, with an enrollment of 34 children, and reached 312 in 1969. With establishment of kindergartens in the public schools, the enrollment dwindled and the school was closed in June, 1970.

2. On September 13, 1965, the Enfield Montessori School opened its first Primary Montessori Class with an enrollment of nineteen. This child-centered approach to education met with the parents' approval so a second class was opened in 1967, and a third in 1972. Application of Montessori principles leads to the development of order, intellectual concentration, mutual help, and self-discipline. Simple in design yet functional special educational apparatus is used for the development of control of the hand, exploration of environment, and preparation for the spoken and written word in many areas of learning (language, mathematics, biology, geography, history, and the arts). The enrollment grew to eighty-six.

3. The third educational development was the opening of Our Lady of Angels Reading Clinic in 1963. This project was a small but crucial response to a mounting need. The clinic sponsors a remedial plan of instruction for children from grades three through twelve who for various reasons have not been able to grasp one or more basics of reading. As many as thirty pupils have benefited from this program one summer alone.

On the secondary level Our Lady of Angels Academy became a reality in 1944 with purchase of the Graham Estate and twelve acres of land diagonally across from the provincial house. This day school for girls, comprised of grades nine through twelve, was affiliated with Catholic University of America in 1945 and accredited by the New England Association of Colleges and Secondary Schools. A single curriculum provided excellent preparatory training for the college-bound student. The larger goal was to promote the kind of guidance and instruction that would encourage an intense Christian response to life.

Prior to 1949, the student body consisted primarily of aspirants to the Sisterhood, but in 1950 seventeen day students were registered and at its peak there were one hundred thirty-two students enrolled. Today the curriculum is completely individualized to suit each pupil's needs.

OTHER EDUCATIONAL OPPORTUNITIES

Our Lady of Angels Teacher Training Institute opened its first summer school in July, 1945, with seventy-two sister students. The name was changed in 1950 to Our Lady of Angels Junior College. In 1957 a new convent, a fine library, offices, gymnasium, and auditorium were constructed and in 1966 the college received official recognition by the State Commission of Higher Education. Once again it changed its name—to Longview College in 1970. It then offered an expanded two-year co-educational program which the Sisters placed at the disposal of Enfield citizens. However, rising operational costs, decline in student body, high tuition, and lack of civic need for the college necessitated its closing in June, 1972.

On October 4, 1954, St. Adalbert's Parish opened a kindergarten under the direction of the Felician Sisters.

Under the direction of the Pastor, Father Paul Bartlewski, St. Adalbert's School was constructed and opened on September 9, 1959, with an enrollment of 286 pupils. It was staffed by the Felician Sisters and contained grades one to seven. Later an eighth grade was added and the enrollment reached 312.

St. Bernard's School in the Hazardville District was officially opened under the supervision of Father Edward J. Reardon, pastor, on September 4, 1958. Four Felician Sisters taught Grades six, seven, and eight. Other grades were opened until there was a full complement of grades one through eight by 1970 with an enrollment of 317 pupils.

Soon after establishment of St. Martha's Parish in 1961 under Father John B. O'Connell, Pastor, plans were made to build a church and school. On September 5, 1963, St. Martha's School was opened with seven grades being taught by four Felician Sisters and three lay teachers. The original enrollment was 296 pupils.

All of these parochial schools have contributed greatly to the civic and religious leadership in Enfield. Their programs have inspired love of God and Neighborhood, as well as a well-rounded intellectual education to assist their graduates to assume their responsibilities as Christian members in their civic community.

CHAPTER 8

MANUFACTURING IN ENFIELD*

W HEN THE FORESTS had been cleared and the settlements were secured from hostile Indians and wild beasts, the first problem facing the early Enfielders was to win a bare living. Families must be fed, clothed, and sheltered. Thus while the prime occupation was farming, with the dawn-to-dusk assistance of numerous progeny, most of the farmers developed an auxiliary skill which constituted the manufacturing industry of that day. Hides were tanned for shoes and harness; wool was sheared, spun, and woven; abundant wood was worked into houses, furniture, and tools; soap was made from fats and wood ashes: usually at the home of the farmer, himself.

The horse was the main source of power and transportation. However, swift-running streams soon became dotted with saw mills, grist mills, and fulling mills. Blacksmiths set up their forges and had plenty of activity keeping the horses shod. Yankee genius for invention and tinkering brought forth tin pots and pans, shoes, hats, and buttons; but

* Numbers in text refer to bibliographic references.

kitchen utensils were still rare enough to be individually mentioned in wills.

the first mills

The year 1674 marked the appearance of a sawmill on Freshwater, erected by Major John Pynchon of Springfield.[17] It seems to have been burned by the Indians the next year.[18] In 1679 a Springfield committee made allocations of land for settlement and these plans persuaded two white men, John and Robert Pease, to spend the winter of 1679-80 in a hillside dugout, not far from the Congregational Church. By 1683 there were thirty families in town; a petition was made, with the agreement of Springfield, to the General Court in Boston, and on May 16, 1683, the Town of Enfield was established by that Court.

Isaac Meacham and Jonathan Bush erected a sawmill on Freshwater, and the former also built a fulling mill. The first corn mill on Freshwater was in 1688. Totaps, the Podunk Indian chief (alias Nottatuck) on March 16, 1688, sold to the English the land between Asnuntuck (Freshwater) and Poggetoffee (Boleyn Brook?), eastward to the hills, reserving the right to share hunting and fishing with the English.[17]

In 1689, Benjamin Jones settled just east of Somers center, returning to town during winters. Two years later, Benjamin Parsons, Samuel Terry, and Isaac Morgan received a grant for a sawmill at Sawmill Brook (Terry Brook) at a site which was later used by Gowdy distillery. Israel Meacham erected an iron works about 1714 at Powder Hollow to smelt bog iron, and Nathaniel Gary built a grain mill in Scitico.

The next half century saw the continuation of the agricultural-personal artisan activity on a laborious and humble scale. The settlers were struggling just to maintain their existence. Heavy pine forests in the east were wastefully burned off to clear land for cultivation—the ashes were good potash fertilizer—while turpentine and pine tar were produced for local use and to support the flourishing shipbuilding industry along the coast. To this day, turpentine, pine tar, and rosin—in fact, all the terpene derivatives—are referred to as "naval stores." Lumber was cut. There were no luxuries, and only river boats, horses, and a few farm wagons for transportation. In 1749, when Massachusetts relinquished claims to Woodstock, Enfield, Somers, and Suffield, colonial Connecticut assumed jurisdiction over these towns. By 1756 the population was 1,050.

Important and sometimes grim events were in the offing, however. In 1745, French-English wars began, draining off some of the finest young men; and military action continued, to culminate in the Revolution.

The power situation was about to change. In England, in 1698, Savery had invented a water pump which used the alternate generation and condensation of steam to create a vacuum and raise mine water by suction. In 1705 Newcomen made the steam engine a practical success by using a separate steam boiler and actuating a piston; while James Watt, in the 1760s, kept the cylinder constantly hot, boiled and condensed steam in separate vessels, and applied steam pressure alternately to both sides of the piston.[23] This new source of power, depending only on supply of water and fuel, would completely revise industry in the next century.

A sort of culmination of the farmer-artisan idea occurred at the turn of the century. Five Shaker families were set up in the area from East Longmeadow to the Scantic. The Shakers were a devoutly religious sect, based on hard work ("hands to work and hearts to God"), celibacy, and communal property.

While they had been started near Albany in 1776 by Ann Lee, who maintained she was the female counterpart of Jesus Christ (an early example of Women's Lib), it was her successors, Joseph Meacham of Enfield and Lucy Wright, who built the productive organization which lasted over one hundred years.

The first local meeting, in June, 1782, resulted in widespread deeding of property by converts around 1800, and by 1828 they owned about 3,000 acres, with twenty-three dwelling houses, a grist mill (still existent at Shaker Pines), three saw mills, three cider mills, a carding machine, a pail factory, plus a trip hammer and lead pipe plant. Their garden seeds were widely purchased, and their everyday living products—furniture, fabrics, clothes, hats, leather, harness—were noted for their plain, sturdy, and dependable construction. They were credited with the invention of flat brooms, screw propeller, Babbitt metal, rotary harrow, circular saw, cut nails, and the common clothespin.[2] In 1840 they built the Scantic dam at Scitico. In 1917 the Enfield families dissolved.

early industry in Enfield

The industrial revolution had started in England. Hargreaves invented the spinning jenny (multiple spindles); Arkwright in 1769 invented the spinning frame; Crompton came up with the "mule"; and Cartwright applied power to looms in 1785. In 1782 Jefferson was wholly content to develop agriculture as the only true source of wealth and leave manufacture to Europeans; but Alexander Hamilton's *Report on the Subject of Manufacture,* 1791,[14] forecast a balance of industry and farming, pleaded for protective tariffs, and convinced Jefferson that manufacture was coming, even recognizing that the new-fangled steam engine might be applied to machines and ships.

Thus the factory town was born. On the Blackstone River, Samuel Slater, supported by William Almy and Moses Brown, built carding and spinning machines for cotton and started schools for the children. These had to be on Sunday, for entire families, including children seven to eleven, worked from ten to twelve hours a day, six days a week, as on the farm.[23] A child's pay was forty-two cents a week. Fortunately, the Puritan ancestry discouraged child labor, and it was gradually abandoned. In 1807 Jeremiah Wadsworth, whose stockholders included the Colt family, started the Hartford Woolen Manufactory. The stage was set for Enfield's major industry.

In Enfield, however, another steam operation was to forestall the engine. The main Connecticut industry in 1810 was woolen goods, still made mainly in the home; but the second greatest industry was still-made gin and cider brandy (value, $811,194), centered in Enfield and the Windsors. Two hundred distillers produced over 700,000 gallons annually, and some of the best was made in the Gowdy plants— especially the one on Sawmill (Terry) Brook. In 1875, when operated by Loren Gowdy, the plant reported a capacity of eight forty-gallon barrels per day, worth sixty dollars a barrel. Connecticut consumption was five gallons per capita per year. This ameliorated the hard life, and there was firm belief in the medicinal properties: but western competition and high import taxes throttled the business.

The Enfield Society for the Detection of Thieves and Robbers adopted its constitution January 30, 1823,[4] with provision for a suitable number of "Pursuers to hold themselves in readiness with each a good Horse on the shortest notice to pursue after any person" to recover stolen horses, money, or goods. For this pursuit of thieves or felons, fourteen cents a mile expense money (one-half the actual miles traveled) was authorized. Initial subscribers included:

Henry Terry	Horace Medcalf	Ebenesor Chapin
William Dixon	Simon Olmsted	David Gates
L.T. Pease	Timothy Abbe	Geer Terry
Lot Killam	Mathew Thompson	Christopher H. Terry
Peter Raynolds	John Olmsted	Jabez Collins
Joseph Olmsted	Solomon Terry	Horace Pease
Heber Pease	Ephm P. Prudden	Reuben Pease
Timothy Killam	Orrin Thompson	George Allen
Daniel Abbe	Henry Kingsburry	William Adams
Levi Abbe	George Meacham	John Bartlett, Jr.
John King	Harris Meacham	Henry Thompson
Fletcher Prudden	Selah Terry	Samuel Booth
Sylvester Lusk	Daniel Gowdy	Elisha Parsons
Thomas Knight	Hill Gowdy	Samuel A. Stillman
Walter Collins	Robert Gowdy	Isaac Wright
		John Burbank

The Society has continued to this day, but mainly as a social and slightly political group.

carpets

The creator and driver of the Enfield carpet effort was Orrin Thompson.

Born in Suffield on March 28, 1788, this imperious, energetic, and daring entrepreneur had his own store in Enfield by 1814. He joined the carpet importing firm of Austin and Andrews in New York in 1821, and two years later purchased a partnership, the firm becoming Andrews Thompson & Company. At that time, carpet imports—mostly from England—were running at a half-million yards a year. The carpet duty in 1824 persuaded the Scottish manufacturers, Gregory Thomson & Company, to set up weaving in the United States, and they were willing to support Thompson's ideas with capital, skilled workers, and knowhow. In 1828, duties on carpet imports were increased again.

Thompson purchased the power site on Freshwater, where there was a 50-foot fall, built a 118-foot dam, 14 feet high, and obtained a charter. Andrews, Thompson, and James Elnathan Smith subscribed for 71 shares of stock at $500, an investment of $35,500.[12] The Thompsonville Carpet Manufacturing Company started when there were about fifty inhabitants in the district.[21]

The first Scottish weavers arrived in the fall of 1828, long before

Orrin Thompson

anything was ready, so they were housed in boatmen's taverns and worked on the dam, the factory, and houses. In their haste, the Scottish firm had even included weavers of linen, who knew nothing about wool, and had most precarious living. The White Mill, astride the stream, complete with cupola and bell, was finished in 1829, and by early summer the first pieces of carpet were woven.

The bulk of production at first, and during the early years, was low-cost, flat-woven ingrain as opposed to the more expensive pile fabrics. Three-ply ingrain, rugs, and loop brussels (a wire-formed carpet pile) were gradually added, and by 1846 there were 230 looms. The business was always at the mercy of style preference, strong competition, the vagaries of wool supply, and price: from the very beginning the path of the enterprise was rugged. Constantly, abandonment was threatened; Robert Thomson, of the Scottish interest, retired; and Orrin Thompson bought out Lusk, his brother-in-law, several Enfield stockholders, Andrews (at his death), and the shares of Gregory Thomson & Company. The selling agent in New York was now Thompson & Company.

The flour mill which had been converted to a dye house went up in flames in 1834, leading to the formation of a strong, regular fire department.

The expanding market and the constant style changes encouraged

Early view of the White Mill looking south from the monument.

Thompson to continued addition of looms and spinning equipment, and in 1841 another company was added bodily. The Tariff Manufacturing Company had been started in 1824 by three Hartford men: William H. Knight, Henry Leavitt Ellsworth, and Nathan Allen. They set up on the Farmington River to weave broadcloth but soon expanded to carpeting. Boston money came into the company, and the McLane report of 1832 on manufacturers of the United States listed the output at 114,000 yards in the year, worth $120,000. There were 136 employees: 81 men were paid about $1 per day; 38 women 35 cents; 17 children 25 cents. Notes to Hugh Kendall in Boston could not be paid; in 1838, after litigation, Kendall took possession; in 1841 Orrin Thompson and the Beach family bought the property and ran the business as the Tariff Manufacturing Company, along with Thompsonville. The product was still mostly ingrain.

A major technological advance had occurred meanwhile. Erastus Brigham Bigelow, born April 2, 1814, in West Boylston, Massachusetts, had tried bookselling, manufacture of twine, and teaching. He then commenced textile invention, producing a power counterpane loom and a loom for coach lace, used in the trimming of stage coaches. The Lowell Manufacturing Company, a well financed competitor of Thompson's, started in 1828, taking over an effort launched in 1826 by Alexander Wright. Wright and George W. Lyman of the

176 / *the challenge of change*

company saw the possibilities of the power loom, and in 1837 persuaded Bigelow to turn attention to it. Mechanical problems were complicated: two and three plies must be interwoven, accurate takeup was necessary, the selvage had to be even and firm, patterns needed to match geometrically, and all the shuttle boxes must be handled. Promptly Bigelow planned the loom, submitted drawings, and produced an experimental loom for Lyman. In May, 1842, patents were received, more looms were built, and it was soon demonstrated that they could save 6 to 12 cents a yard on ingrain, or 10 percent on the selling price.

Faced with this competition, Thompson first cut wages 25 percent; then, with characteristic vigor, he signed a contract with Lowell on August 31, 1847, to own and use 125 to 150 power looms with 2 cents royalty on two-ply and 4 cents on three-ply. Tariff executed a similar agreement. A new brick mill, 330-by-60, was built; and from July 1, 1848, to July 1, 1851, $350,000 were spent for machinery. In 1850, $322,000 were spent for materials, mostly wool. The power loom also eased out the hard-core Scottish unity of the weavers, who were proud, stubborn, independent, and expert: who resorted occasionally to strikes, but by and large worked cooperatively and efficiently. By 1850, 250,000 yards of carpet per year were being made in Thompsonville, and output was increasing rapidly.

Erastus B. Bigelow

Epstein & Son truckload of carpets destined for Marshall Field in 1918.

The profit picture had changed. The good years from 1830 to 1847 were succeeded by losses and bad debts just when heavy financing was required. Thompson and Company, in New York (Orrin's son, Henry G. Thompson, and Joseph Dean), who had provided funds for the factory and held its bonds, went bankrupt. The plant was mortgaged; creditors took over. Orrin Thompson lost his equity, bondholders were paid fifty cents on the dollar, and other creditors received nothing. A group of Hartford men, headed by Timothy Allyn, Edmund G. Howe, and William R. Cone, organized a new company, raised $500,000 in new money, and hired Orrin Thompson as superintendent, with an interest in the company. The mill was returned to operation just in time for a business recession in late 1854! The Hartford Carpet Company was under way.

From 1855 to 1878 the company was headed by George Roberts, Sr., a sound, experienced businessman, with Orrin Thompson as mill superintendent until 1861. The years before the Civil War were prosperous. In 1859 the mills, including Tariffville, had looms for 1,700,000 yards of ingrain; 500,000 yards of venetian; and 200,000 yards of brussels—per year. Sales in 1859 were 1,200,000 yards, worth $775,000 (1). The year 1866 was most profitable, at $677,000. There had been two bothersome fires: in 1864 the brick spinning and carding mill burned, and in June, 1867, the Tariffville plant was destroyed. Workers transferred to Thompsonville. The mill was expanded, and by 1871 was turning out 1,200 yards of brussels a day. There were 247 ingrain looms good for 6,000 yards a day. Surplus reached a record high of $987,000 in 1875.

Three years later, Roberts died suddenly and was succeeded by John L. Houston, president from 1878 to 1894. In addition to sound judgment and great consideration for his employees, he continually sought out new ideas and techniques, including the Alexander Smith (competitor) moquette line. This was a modified axminster. Wilton, another expensive wire-formed cut pile, was a natural extension of brussels. In 1896 the company had the most extensive line in the country. Other improvements included substitution of electricity for open-flame lights. The work week was down to 56 hours. Only a few (30-40) children were used, in a work force of 1,800. However, reserves had been depleted by generous dividends, and when Houston suffered a stroke in November, 1894, there was no seasoned manager to take over.

Opportunity for merger soon developed. In New York, Alvin and Elias Higgins had started a carpet company in 1837, which was continued by Elias and his brother, Nathaniel, as E.S. Higgins & Company in 1856. They prospered, especially in tapestry, but had labor troubles. The depression of 1895, coupled with the disinterest of Elias' son Eugene, led to the need to get out of New York and abandon the Higgins name. But Higgins had acquired a most able young manager in Robert Perkins, a Harvard graduate, born in 1861. The banking houses of Kidder Peabody and F.S. Moseley bought out Higgins, then proceeded to merge with Hartford Carpet Company to form, in 1901, the Hartford Carpet Corporation, with the New York equipment moved to Thompsonville as soon as new buildings could be completed. Robert Perkins became president; and Alvin D. Higgins, agent. The company was set for the business growth of the early twentieth century.

Higgins was very civic minded. He assembled the land where the Town Hall and the Alvin D. Higgins School now stand. In 1975 his daughter, Grace (Mrs. William E. Lyford), bequeathed the town $250,000 to maintain the school.

Great expansion and modernization took place. The 400,000 square feet built in 1901 included a 900-foot tapestry mill along Pleasant

The Carpet City Band.

Street; a worsted mill; finishing, fulling, and scouring mills; a color house; and a rug finishing department in the old Lozier Bicycle Works. The next year a $175,000 axminster mill was added, along with some of the new broad looms, which were already being exploited by a competitor, Stephen Sanford. A 4,000 H.P. electric plant furnished power for new large and small motor drives. By 1910 there were 2,900 workers, and Italians and Poles were supplementing the original Scottish, English, Irish, and Canadians. The company owned more than one hundred houses, and social and athletic clubs grew up. The panic of 1907 dropped prices; but these recovered and in 1909 the huge mill was turning out seven-and-a-half million yards, at production costs of $0.32 to $1.47 per yard. Subdued tones, huge flowers, and picture rugs were in the patterns. Advertising boomed and movies were made to help sales. Working capital plus fixed assets had increased by $4,000,000—all from profits.

Another consolidation was imminent. Back in 1828 the Boston Lowell Manufacturing Company, based on an earlier (1826) Medway effort, had been set up in the great Lowell Textile complex. Erastus Bigelow, the power loom inventor, and his brother Horatio had started the Bigelow Carpet Company in Clinton, Massachusetts, in 1849. These two concerns merged in 1899 to form the Bigelow Carpet Company, and under the management of the Fairbanks family an enviable surplus was built up. In 1914, the same bankers engineered the combination of Hartford and Bigelow. This strong new company, Bigelow-Hartford Carpet Company, was the third largest concern incorporated in New England, with capacity for 8,000,000 yards at Thompsonville; 2,850,000 yards at Lowell; and 2,300,000 yards at Clinton. In Enfield, a new steam turbine was installed, looms were moved from Lowell, shipping facilities were expanded, and a huge coal storage area was constructed. Lowell closed in 1917. Clinton turned largely to duck for the war effort, and cut carpet.

By 1920 the trade was tending toward axminsters, wilton, and velvet; but most of the company's looms were narrow. Robert Perkins, who had acted as Red Cross Commissioner to Italy, contracted a severe illness there, never fully recovered, and passed away in 1924. The short, sharp depression of 1921 lowered prices, wages, brought on a brief strike, and practically destroyed the union. For a short time—to 1927—John F. Norman, the vigorous salesman, took over. He showed unusual consideration for the employees, but his cavalier propensities

Stephen Sanford

led to his replacement as president by another Bostonian and ex-naval officer, John A. Sweetser, in 1927.

Meanwhile, woolen carpeting was in the doldrums, and linoleum and asphalt-base, hard-surface coverings had achieved twice the woven woolen volume. Sweetser strengthened marketing and exploited raw stock dyeing (of stock before spinning); and his engineers brought out rayon-cotton combinations, originated the "Domestic Oriental" sheen, and produced an eighteen-foot velvet loom adapted to jacquard weaving. Attention focused on manufacturing, and Richard G. Knowland, an M.I.T. chemical engineer, became at first assistant to the president, then vice president in 1930. The year 1929 was a good one.

Back in 1836, William K. Greene, Jr., and John Sanford imported six hand looms and set them up in Amsterdam, New York. Sanford bought out the Greenes, and in 1844 his son, Stephen Sanford, entered the business which was to merge with Bigelow-Hartford in 1929. Stephen Sanford learned every phase of carpet manufacture and directed his company to a commanding position over the next seventy years, in spite of spectacular fires in 1849 and 1853. A straightforward, soldierly gentleman, cautious but bold to act, he followed his own maxim, "wise men dip into the future," and was the first general operator of broad looms. Throughout his long career he sensed product trends with uncanny foresight, and by 1929 was operating 346 looms over 72 inches, against 227 such looms for the larger Bigelow-Hartford Company. His son John had entered the business in the 1870s. Stephen died in 1913, and by 1929 John Sanford was willing to retire, with no family successor manager in sight. John sold his company for $5 million in notes and 85,000 shares of new company stock, based on a Bigelow-Hartford valuation of $100 per share, after "Black Tuesday"—October 29, 1929—on Wall Street. Sanford interests owned 26 percent of the new Bigelow-Sanford Carpet Company, Inc.

Depression hit the new company hard. Prices were cut, wages were lowered, dividends were suspended, auctions were demoralizing, and there was much pruning of personnel. Marketing was overhauled; advertising stressed high quality, "live wool," and the Bigelow weavers' knot; direct selling gradually reduced wholesales. The patented "Lok-Weave" construction prevented raveling of cut edges. A foray into linoleum failed. The Clinton plant closed in 1933, to the distress of that town. The business recovered, however, and by 1935 dividends were resumed.

The next few years saw enough improvement in rayon so that it was

182 / *the challenge of change*

used, with some struggling, to replace up to fifty percent of wool in some lines. There were labor arguments, and one carpet company, James Lees & Son, found that a move to Glasgow, Virginia, gave geographical advantage, low heating and modest construction costs, and cheap homogeneous American labor. At Thompsonville manager Petersen set up a defense training program, handled by the able mechanical engineer, E. Wadsworth Stone.

During the Second World War Amsterdam and Thompsonville made $56 million worth of blankets—more than any other manufacturer. Enormous quantities of duck were produced on 260 looms; nylon and rayon were treated with rubber for gas tanks and tires; and the machine shops furnished parts for submarines, planes, radar, and Oak Ridge. Stone's planning paid off, and quality control steadied the huge blanket supply. Still, profits were low, and by October, 1945, war surplus materials were offered to the market. Union shop was included in the 1943 contract, and personnel experts took over hiring and firing. Both Thompsonville and Amsterdam won Army and Navy "E" awards for excellence. In 1943 Sweetser dismissed Knowland and suddenly died in August, 1944. James D. Wise, a lawyer who had served as Under-Secretary of the Navy, rather reluctantly assumed leadership on December 1, 1944. Elliott Petersen became production vice president and James Jackson succeeded him as Thompsonville superintendent.

The next year Wise reorganized the company along divisional lines. The post-war boom brought total employment to 9,000 in 1948, but by 1949 reaction set in. The Korean war in 1950 brought renewed buying; wool was scarce. The company's higher prices encouraged buyer resistance, which with labor trouble resulted in substantial losses in 1951. Wise bought Hartford Rayon Corporation. W.N. Freyer was executive vice president. By 1952 over half the soft floor covering contained surface fiber other than wool. Bristol Mills, Inc., of Virginia was bought as a carpet yarn producer, and this was consolidated with the company in 1951 to a new Delaware corporation, Bigelow-Sanford Carpet Co., Inc., which had a broader charter to permit greater diversification.

Enormous technical and sales changes were in the wind. Purchase of a small tufting plant in Georgia started a major swing to this process, which permitted lower costs and prompt delivery; and rose from zero in 1950 to fifteen percent of the industry in 1952, forty-three percent in 1956, and sixty-six percent in 1960. Mr. Wise's own 1952 patent for the silo blending process permitted great uniformity. Increased use of

Bigelow Sanford's Thompsonville mill about 1950.

man-made fibers held down the wild price gyrations of wool: nylon gave tremendous wear and strength, acrylics had wool-like properties, and rayon offered bright, precise colors. The Locktuft process in 1965 brought in polypropylene. In manufacture, tape condenser cards appeared just after the war, and the Bigelow parallel system of yarn making appeared in 1965. Warehouses and truck deliveries sped products to the market. All during the period, the skillful organization and alert planning of Wise and his successor, Lowell P. Weicker, president 1956 to 1967, kept the company in the forefront of the industry, met the competition of many new domestic and foreign plants, and maintained the reputation for highest quality product and service.

As the old carpet types waned, the Amsterdam operation transferred to Thompsonville in 1955, in spite of a tight Connecticut labor market resulting from competition of the aircraft and machine tool industries. Amsterdam closed shortly thereafter. Depression conditions in 1957-58 made it clear that the aged Thompsonville plant could not compete with new southern plants, so in June, 1958, the Thompsonville plant was sold for $1,300,000 to Kratter Associates with leaseback of space to continue the declining axminster and wilton lines, while a new velvet plant was built in the Carolinas. Two interim manufacturing efforts at Thompsonville proved unremunerative: an attempt to introduce the successful tufting operation had difficulty from low ceilings and the reluctance of labor to accept automation whereby one man handled more machines, although the Thompsonville team, directed by John Roddy, maintained confidence in their ability to make it work; and a short-term manufacture of glass-polyester Crestliner pleasure boats missed the market.

In 1961, Hartford Fibers (Hartford Rayon), having served its purpose, was sold, along with Crestliner (1964). New tuft dyeing patents helped hold the company lead. It licensed its processes in most foreign countries. From 1962 on the company had good growth in the booming soft floor coverings. In 1967, Sperry and Hutchinson (S&H Green Stamps) made an attractive offer to stockholders, and ownership passed to them. For a couple of years (1972-74) Jennings and Mills were presidents, and in 1974 leadership came to Walter H. Wieler, who had spent many years in the company, had trained under both Wise and Weicker, and who promptly and ably continued the traditions of the founders (about the only feature which had not changed) of superlative quality, skillful flexibility in the shifting textile industry, high craftsmanship and style, and general service in the community.

In 1971 the Thompsonville saga ended. The plant was vacated the next year, and Enfield bade a sorrowful farewell to the fine Bigelow-Sanford teams which had played so essential a part in its history. This is an excellent example of the fundamental truth that for every product, medicine, communication, transportation, comfort, and security which we enjoy, there is somewhere in the background (a) an inventor who hammered out the idea, and (b) a producer who made it available to humanity at accessible price.

Inspection of tufted carpet manufacture at Bigelow Sanford.

gunpowder

Just after the carpet mill started (1835), a Suffield man, Allen Loomis, was trading with trappers in Vermont and New York State, exchanging whips from Westfield, cigars, and gunpowder for furs, which were shipped by boat to the Astors and others,[16] in New York. Loomis saw the advantages of manufacturing his goods: he set up a cigar factory in Suffield, and in 1836 purchased five hundred acres of pasture in Powder Hollow from Dr David Allen, a Revolutionary War surgeon.

To manufacture gunpowder, approximately equal parts of sulfur and charcoal were ball-milled to a fine powder. One part of this mix was compounded, wet, with a little glue and with three times its weight of saltpeter (potassium nitrate), which had to be imported from the English colony at Calcutta. The mix was ground by heavy vertical roller wheels working in a circular bed trough. The wet powder was pressed hydraulically to slatelike plates; these plates were cracked ("corned") with zinc rollers to a coarse powder, from which the commercial product was screened. The powder was further dried in warm rooms, tumbled—sometimes with additional graphite—to complete the drying and to glaze, and after a final sifting was packed in canisters, kegs and barrels.

Loomis took as partners his two brothers, Parkes and Neeland, and Allen A. Denslow of New Haven.[22] By the fall of 1835 a small cylinder mill—rawhide drums with brass balls—was operating, and in the next year wheel mills were installed. In 1836 the business incorporated as Loomis, Denslow and Company. Important personages were added at this time. From England came William and Henry Prickett, with gunpowder experience from John Hall and Sons' works in Faversham, Kent, England. They later induced other skilled workmen to emigrate, so good expertise developed. In 1837 a quarter interest in the firm was acquired by Colonel Augustus George Hazard, the New York general agent, who guided the successful enterprise for the next thirty-two years.

Colonel Hazard, born in South Kensington, Rhode Island, April 28, 1802, was a direct descendent of one of the twenty-seven Rhode Island families associated with Roger Williams, the original founder. The Hazards came to a farm in Columbia, Connecticut; Augustus Hazard spent five years in house painting and when twenty years old moved to Savannah, Georgia, to deal in paints and oils. His business prospered. He came to New York as a merchandising agent and part owner of packet ships between New York and Savannah. His commission business included zinc, cotton, and gunpowder. His title of colonel stemmed from his association with the Georgia state military organizations. The panic of 1837 caused him huge losses, but he repaid all of his debts and emerged with still stronger credit.

The Hazard holdings were gradually increased, and in 1843 the Hazard Powder Company (what name could be more appropriate!) was incorporated, with the Colonel as principal owner. He moved to Enfield, built the spacious French Colonial home on Enfield Street, which only recently was destroyed by fire, and entertained lavishly. Among the visitors were Daniel Webster and Jefferson Davis.[16]

In 1845 John Mathewson became superintendent. Meanwhile, in 1842 the second (upper) dam was built on the Scantic and a canal was dug along the north side of the river to power a new mill—later known as the "mankiller"—and a new corning mill. The plant thus consisted of six wheel mills, two corning houses, two presses, a glaze house, and a drying house.

The war with Mexico—May, 1846—to establish the southern Texas boundary, brought urgent demands for powder, further augmented by an unfortunate explosion at the du Pont Brandywine plant, killing eighteen men (9). In one year, to July 1, 1847, the government bought 730,000 pounds. The year 1849 saw the discovery of gold in California, which meant new demands for blasting powder. Steam-driven mills

Col. Augustus George
Hazard

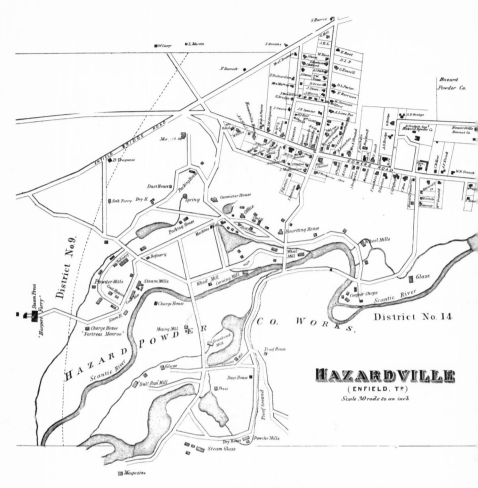

Map of Powder Hollow published in 1869

were installed; the horseshoe dam was completed; new mills, magazines, and a saltpeter refinery were built; all in time for the Crimean war in 1854. Hazard Powder furnished 10,000 one hundred-pound barrels which the British ordnance officers certified to be of very superior quality.[22] The company was reincorporated by the Connecicut legislature under new corporation laws.

Meanwhile, in 1849, Paul Greeley (a Hazard employee), Tudor and

Frank Gowdy, and Wells Loomis formed the Enfield Powder Company, erected a plant east of forge bridge, and operated it until it was absorbed by Hazard Powder in 1854. It produced until 1902. In those days the railroad would not accept powder for shipment so it was carried by wagons to the east bank of the Connecticut River, flatboated to Hartford, and taken by schooners to Constable Point, New Jersey.

Both England and Russia purchased Hazard powder through Grinnell, Minturn and Company in New York, at prices from 16½-18 cents per pound. England complained that sale to Russia was a violation of neutrality and briefly prohibited the export of saltpeter to any but British possessions, while Russia secretly sent a representative to deal directly with the powder companies, Captain Lilieafeld. Hazard and Henry du Pont freely communicated to each other the actions taken by their respective companies.

In the spring of 1854 Sylvester Charter opened a hotel in Scitico, and at a banquet there,[13] following the suggestion of William Colvin, a Hazard Powder Company foreman, it was voted to name the village at the west end Hazardville—although a similar vote was reported at Scitico schoolhouse in 1849.[6]

The powder companies survived the depression of 1857 largely because of powder demands for railroad building and metal mining plus the cooperation of du Pont and Hazard.

Colonel Hazard had the misfortune to lose both of his sons. Horace was killed by a premature powder explosion in a testing device on April 4, 1855; and George, who was so much at odds with his father that he publicly condemned the Hazardville installation,[15] died of consumption shortly afterward. One daughter was reported to be engaged to John Alexander Garesche, who was killed—along with William Colvin,[16] Stephen Pace, and Thomas Ball—when engaged in experimenting with dry-mixed powder—1,800 pounds. The risk of powder making is underscored by the melancholy roster, which follows, of sixty-seven persons who lost their lives at the plant by such explosions. Dr. Bridge remarked:[6]

The fear of these explosions hung over the people of this village during the entire period when the manufacture of gunpowder was carried on here . . . Of the five members of the Prickett family who came to work in the mills, three were killed by explosions, and another was injured in the same way.

Just before the Civil War, Hazardville was doing a million dollar business. Immediately after the South seized Fort Sumter, Colonel

Powder wagons at packing house.

Hazard instructed Southern agents to sell all their stocks for cash, an
large Southern stocks were merely appropriated. Initially, the go
ernment was quoted an eighteen-cent price and the powder compani
settled down to massive wartime production. The Hazardville an
Scitico plants were described by Bishop:[5]

This Company has eighteen sets of rolling mills with thirty-six iron wheels, eac
wheel weighing eight tons; seven granulating mills; five screw press building
and three hydraulic presses of 500 tons each, in different and separate buil
ings; and about fifty buildings used for dusting, assorting, drying, mixing
pulverizing, glazing, and packing houses—with extensive saltpeter refineries an
magazines, cooperage, iron, woodworking, and machine shops—in all, abou
125 buildings at their main works at Hazardville and Scitico, extending over
mile and a half in length and half a mile in width. To propel this vast amount
machinery, twenty-five water wheels and three steam engines are required.
The company manufactures annually over a million dollars worth of powder

various kinds, known as Government, Sporting, Shipping, and Mining Powder.

The capacity was 12,500 pounds per day. The stepped-up wartime production was briefly hampered by British strictures on saltpeter export; California markets were practically cut off by privateers; and the Government caused a severe financial bind by paying one third cash and two thirds notes (3). South Street was often referred to as Smoke Street, there being no environmental protection from the burners which made charcoal from willow and alder.[6]

In 1864 a unit was built for refining nitrate of soda from Chile. By August of that year powder at retail commanded 55 cents to $1.15 per pound.

Colonel Hazard gave a new church to St. Mary's parish, which served the many Anglican workers employed in the powder mills.

Readjustment after the Civil War saw huge stocks of government powder—some good, some bad—auctioned off, and ruinous competition ensued. To add to the unsettlement, Colonal Hazard died in May, 1868, without suitable executive replacement. A formidable explosion in 1871 destroyed much of the plant and installation, and the fluctuating economy culminated in the panic of 1873. In 1874 the company needed "both money and orders." By 1876 the main stockholders, tired and discouraged, were glad to sell out to du Pont. In the same year the railroad through Scitico was completed. It accepted powder, brought to the siding by wagon, up Long Hollow Road. Francis P. Leary of Hazardville, the station master after 1883, remembered (*Springfield Union*—August 8, 1928) that nineteen tons of powder a day were shipped in carload and less-than-carload lots to every state in the union.

Just before the sale to du Pont in 1872, the three powder companies (including Laflin and Rand) set up the "Gunpowder Trade Association of the United States" to restore health to the industry by "equitable adjustment of prices and terms for sales of powder throughout the United States."[20] The sale of Hazard Powder to du Pont was not publicly known for a decade, during which time the trade association stabilized the industry, absorbing new companies and actively discouraging new enterprises. By various agreements, du Pont, Hazard, and Laflin and Rand dominated the industry until 1890, when the agreement of 1886 expired. On July 2, 1890, President Harrison signed an anti-monopoly bill which became known as the Sherman Act, but for some years it had no practical effect on the gunpowder trust or the du Pont partnership.

"View of Thompsonville, Conn. / 1878"
(O.H. Bailey & Co., Boston)

Powder wagons at Scitico station siding.

Colonel Henry du Pont died in the summer of 1889. He was succeeded by his nephew, Eugene, who continued the policy of buying out new companies. In 1895 high explosives (based on cellulose nitrate and nitroglycerine) were transferred to a new firm, Eastern Dynamite Company. The du Pont partnership was dissolved in 1899, and du Pont Company was incorporated in Delaware. Two years later Eugene died, whereupon three able, driving du Pont cousins—Alfred I., Pierre S., and T. Coleman—took over in 1902,[11] purchased control of Laflin and Rand, and set up E.I. du Pont de Nemours Company, which by 1906 was selling 70 percent of the explosives consumed in the United States. T. Coleman du Pont, a superb organizer, integrated and rearranged dozens of the controlled companies, aiming to liquidate the Gunpowder Association and Hazard, among others. The Hazardville operation clumped along routinely.

The year 1907 saw a government suit against du Pont, instigated by a former employee, Robert Waddell, and after four years of exhaustive litigation, the court found du Pont guilty of violating the Sherman Act; but the horde of companies was so tangled up that the government invoked the help of the Company to effect a dissolution.

The explosives business was divided into three firms: Hercules Powder, Atlas Powder, and E.I. du Pont de Nemours and Company. Hazard mills were transferred to Hercules December 15, 1912. On January 14, 1913, a heavy explosion damaged the plant so much that Hercules moved the remaining equipment to Valley Falls, New York, and Powder Hollow gradually reverted to open field and became a favorite locale for athletic contests.

194 / *the challenge of change*

Plant Superintendents over the years were:

Allen A. Denslow	1835-1845
John Mathewson	1845-1858
J.A. Garesche	1858
Edward Prickett and Joseph Sexton	1859-1867
Edward Prickett	1867-1905
Edward L. Prickett	1905-1908
	1909-1915
A.E. Colvin, custodian	1908-1909

Personnel killed by explosions at Hazardville and Scitico were:

March 11, 1839	Hiram Pierce	
	Robert McChesney	Press building
Fall of 1839	N. Dunn	
	William Leanard	Graining Mill
August 25, 1842	George Prickett	Rolling Mill No. 10
June 27, 1844	William Luce	Graining Mill
October 16, 1844	William Prickett	
	N. McClester	Rolling Mill No. 10
	H. Durfee	
March 31, 1845	Name lost; man came from the Schaghticoke Mills, New York	Graining Mill
July 9, 1845	William Hall	Graining Mill
March 26, 1846	Dan Bert	Rolling Mill No. 9
August, 1849	James Bisker	Clothing caught fire during noon hour
April 10, 1851	James McKenzie	
	James Pierce	Rolling Mill No. 10
May 20, 1853	William Murry	Rolling Mill Scitico
June 9, 1853	Walter Luce	Graining Mill Scitico
April 6, 1855	Horace Hazard	Killed at Mortar, proving powder.
November 28, 1855	James Murphy	With powder wagon on plant.
July 12, 1856	Charles Elcock	
	William Lowrie	Lower Engine,
	A. Whitehead	Rolling Mills
October 27, 1857	John Burns	Rolling Mill, Scitico
September 13, 1858	John Garesche, Superintendent	
	William Colvin, Foreman	Mixing Mill, experimenting
	Stephen Pace	
	Thomas Ball	

October 19, 1859	Michail Burns	Rolling Mill No. 9
July 23, 1862	Arthur Beach	
	James Beach	
	H. Clark	Explosion started at Press.
	Pat Carney	Two presses, one graining
	L. Monseau	mill, and two rolling mills;
	Edward Gramond	one following the other in
	James Neelands	quick succession.
	Pat Fallows	
	Miss Smith	
July 5, 1864	John Howarth	Graining Mill
	John Haggerty	
December 22, 1865	William Fahey	Mixing Mill
May 7, 1866	John Keshan	
	William Agnew	Press building
	Edward Burke	
	Pat Bailey	
December, 1867	Peter Havey	Mixer
June 30, 1868	Frank Richardson	Rolling Mill, Scitico
February 11, 1869	Joseph Yates	
	Thomas Turner	Rolling Mill No. 9
February 11, 1870	Pat Turneran	Rolling Mill No. 9
May 30, 1870	Peter Ryan	Rolling Mill No. 10
May 25, 1871	O. Taylor	Graining Mill. Taylor
	A. Racine	was with horse and cart.
	Loseau	
May 19, 1875	Moses Bolac	
	John Lamere	Press
	George Richards	
August 14, 1883	James Leanard	Graining Mill
March 16, 1886	Charles Luce	Graining Mill
June 29, 1892	Dennis Bailey	Graining Mill
August 7, 1894	George Raiche	Graining Mill
June 18, 1897	Mat Pierce, Foreman	
	B. Stratton, Machinist	Graining Mill
	Richard May	
May 27, 1898	Alfred Blunden	Graining Mill
February 26, 1901	Eugene Bowen	Rolling Mill No. 9
January 14, 1913	Jacob Stocker	
	Charles Blunden	Upper Sporting Press

the Scantic Gap

At Scitico, the Scantic River foams through a breach in the north-south ledge of rock and drops thirty feet in its tumultuous rush to the lower meadows. By the turn of the eighteenth century, a dam just east of the present railroad bridge at forge pond furnished power for a water wheel driving a carding mill. This was operated by John Mason, a descendant of Captain John Mason of the Pequot War and the father of Jeduthun T. Mason, who lived near the site of the first Post Office (August 27, 1835) at Leary Road.[10] Another wheel drove a forge on the south side of the stream.

In 1840 the Shakers built the dam just west of Broad Brook Road. A gristmill at the site was run successively by Wheeden, Preston Abbe, and finally by Leroy Spencer, who purchased and operated it until 1886. An old-fashioned up-and-down sawmill was run by Treat Steele, and by Wells Spencer as S. Spencer and Company. Just east of these two mills, on Water Street, L.A. Johnson had a store and the Post Office.

A few rods downstream, beyond the Gowdy distillery, the Enfield Manufacturing Company, which had its main plant just south of the carpet mill in Thompsonville, built a stockinette factory, with an office on the main road. William C. Medlicott was a large owner; placed in charge of the Scitico mill was William Tansley. Fashioning of the underwear was carried out by neighboring women in their homes. The business languished after the Civil War, and the plant was purchased in 1873 by J.D. Stowe of Suffield for manila paper production. He equipped it with two 200-pound beaters and a 48-inch cylinder machine.[19] The 800-pounds-per-day output of wrapping paper, tobacco paper, and counter paper was sold mainly to Gordon Brothers. An interesting water supply construction diverted the Scantic water at night to a large area south of the river for accumulation, and this could then be run back to the dam and down through the machines for greater throughput in the daytime. In 1905 the plant burned. A small leather-board unit, working from leather scraps, lasted a few years, and in 1925 it was sold to Gordon Brothers.

Gordon Brothers had its genesis just after the Civil War. David G. Gordon, an Army lieutenant, was encouraged by Colonel Hazard to start a business. Together, David Gordon, George B. Gordon, Andrew Gordon, Amos D. Bridge, and Edward Prickett set up the Hazardville Bonnet Company on Oak Street, just north of the Hazardville fire station, to make Shaker type bonnets. After a few years, styles changed

The Gordon brothers.

and the business faltered. Meanwhile, a few years earlier, Albert Olmstead had developed a tin and rag enterprise in Hazardville, and was succeeded by his brother-in-law, Franklin Smith. Needing partners, Smith took in David Gordon and John Spencer. Later, the Gordons acquired the business and in 1875 operated on the north side of the Main Street with fifteen hands in their tin shop and rag rooms and thirteen peddlers. They shipped several hundred tons of paper stock each year to the Holyoke mills, and handled three tons of wrapping paper a week from J.D. Stowe, to whom they supplied stock.[19]

After a disastrous fire, the brothers bought the Shaker grist mill and moved their business there. They built the riverside brick buildings, incorporating in 1901 as Gordon Brothers. They installed twenty-five woolen cards and imported a dry carbonizing unit from Scotland. The acid treatment of rags destroyed the cotton "dust," so they were able to buy waste from the mills, separate the shoddy, card it, and recycle a very good grade of wool back to the same mills. For power they used the 20-foot waterfall to develop 260 horsepower, transmitted by a forest of belts and pulleys to the cards and pickers. David Gordon, the driving manager, became known as "Push" Gordon, and George B. was treasurer. They were considerate of their employees: they owned most of the houses nearby, which were rented to the workers at $1.40 to $2.50 per week, and no rent was charged if one was sick or out of work. The loyalty they engendered was well personified by Fred Gemme, who with Herman Billings built an office building from bricks from the distillery chimneys and who faithfully stayed with the plant long after the Gordons relinquished it. When the chimney was raised for the

The Gordon Mill

power plant, William Gordon personally soldered lead sheet around the cap, high in the air.

The interest of Howard and William Gordon, sons of David, was purchased by the other members of the family. Howard and William developed an alternate dry carbonizing process which they operated for a few years. This would handle scoured wool, removing burrs. At the main plant, a large new north-and-south building was put up with the idea of making cloth, but it was not carried out. For some time the first floor was used for storage, with sorting on the second floor. The business languished, and this building was picked up by DeBell & Richardson. The riverfront property was run by A.W. Dolge & Company for a few years, then sold to DeBell & Richardson as Dolge moved to Stafford.

Henry M. Richardson and John M. DeBell, born, respectively, in Beardstown, Illinois, and Great Barrington, Massachusetts, were engineers who had spent many years building up the plastics business of General Electric. In 1945 they set up a development laboratory in the upper floors of a building in Springfield, Massachusetts; but when the lower floors were seared by fire, these two men purchased one large Gordon Brothers building in 1948, then the office building, and in 1955 the riverfront property. On August 18-19, 1955, a tremendous storm dumped 14 inches of rainfall on the Scantic watershed, and all of this poured through the Scantic Gap, smashed the dam, and knocked

J.M. DeBell and R.H.M.
Richardson.

out four stories of the south wall of the old Gordon mill. With the help
of Hartford National Bank and Standard Builders, Inc., the company
rebuilt and reinforced the structures, and converted the Stowe
pond—a tangle of swamp, fallen timber, and debris—into a sylvan
meadow and trout pond.

While the company tackled any phase of plastic invention, manufacture, fabrication, patents negotiation, and litigation, it specialized in
the creation of new plastics businesses, doing work for most chemical
and oil companies, and carrying projects which showed promise into
pilot plant verification. In 1946 it had published *German Plastics
Practice,* a 360-page compendium collected for the Army the preced-
ing year, which proved to be a handbook for the next twenty years.[10]

Successful patent-protected projects included new polyester molding compounds, new methods for fluorocarbon polymerization,
shaped glass fibers, Orangeburg pipe fittings, foam radar lenses for
fighter plane navigation, and deep-drawn oriented thermoplastics
sheet (cigarette packages). Of course, as in all development, there were
also unsuccessful efforts! About fifty patents were issued in the period
1948-1968, and the company was instrumental in refurbishing the
Mitsui plastics effort, inducting Foster-Grant into styrene polymer and
monomer manufacture, making special moldings and fabrications for
undersea cable, and experting litigation. In 1968, the plastics library
was probably the finest in the world.

DeBell and Richardson plant after the 1965 hurricane.

The professional team which built the company in the early days to a two million dollar annual business included: Dr. M.H. Nickerson, chemist; Kenneth Barker, chemical engineer; Fred E. Wiley, mechanical engineer; Wesley S. Larson, molding and fabricating specialist; Herbert S. Schnitzer, chemical engineer; William J. Eakins, glass technologist; and Sven Richter, chemical engineer and technical information specialist. For many years the directorate included Margaret E. Ganley, attorney; and A. McK. Gifford, retired engineer of materials, General Electric, Pittsfield, Massachusetts. Two affiliates—D&R Pilot Plants, and D&R Plastic Welders run by Rolland C. Trudeau—were essentially pilot operations which were absorbed into the main company later. There were 150 employees by that time. Three new buildings were put up between 1964 and 1972, and a tobacco storage structure on Park Street was purchased.

On retirement of the principals, Arthur J. Warner served as president from 1967 to 1972; Richardson returned briefly to active management. Since February, 1972, the effort has been headed by Dr. Robert Springborn (of Geneva, Illinois, and a graduate of the Universities of Illinois and Cornell) who built the Borg-Warner polymer business and introduced new products for W.R. Grace & Company. From the early days financial affairs were handled by Machado Mead, now vice president and treasurer. Supplementing pursuit of the original objectives, a strong marketing group has been built up by E.S.

Childs and polymer analysis and elaborate mechanical testing have been greatly expanded. Wiley, Larson, Schnitzer, and Childs are still active as vice presidents. Arthur Karszes, also a vice president, has nursed the testing and analytical laboratory to an internationally recognized Testing Institute. Dr. Bernard Baum, vice president, is now in charge of the chemical department (Materials Research and Development).

Rainbows, Inc. now located on the south side of the Scantic, was established in 1950 by three men, all of Enfield: Herbert Gerecht, Edwin Darling, and William Mangini—President, Vice President, and Treasurer, respectively. All of these founders of the company had been employees of National Printing Company prior to starting the new business. Since all three were involved in the lithographic color trade, each brought with him his own special craftsmanship. Herbert Gerecht was a cameraman, Edwin Darling was a platemaker and photocomposer, and William Mangini was a dot etcher. Gerecht and Darling are now deceased.

The first place of business was a small store on Main Street in Scitico, in a tiny area roughly thirty-by-forty feet where were placed a camera, a small proofing press, developing sinks, and platemaking equipment. Two years of hard work produced modest progress.

In 1952 four acres of land were purchased on Broad Brook Road; on this site was built the present Rainbows, Inc. The business was incorporated in April, 1953.

The principal products are pilot color plates and proofs for the lithographic printers in the New England area. Some of the work produced goes into the making of Limited Editions publications; some in the fine arts field of prints; some is used in the producing of games and puzzles for all ages, color brochures, and complete catalogs for a variety of products.

Basically, Rainbows, Inc., services printing concerns—web offset printers as well as those with conventional presses—and the employees number thirty-three. The latest acquisition by the company has been an electronic scanner that produces color separations at a high speed through the use of computers and, prospectively, laser dot generation.

Hazardville enterprises:
wood, boxes, and reels

Many enterprises followed the success of the powder business in Hazardville. In the northeast quadrant at the center, around the Hazardville Institute, Alexander, John, and James B. Law (later John Law & Company) had a box, metal forming, and canister plant, which in 1875 employed 25 hands and could turn out 300 wooden and 500 metal kegs per day.[19] They also made about 100,000 canisters a year for the powder company, and conducted a general tin business. The powder company contract lasted until 1886.

Captain John King manufactured wooden plow beams in Scitico on Leary Road and after his death in 1852 the business was continued by his son-in-law, Charles Clark. Large shipments were made by water from Enfield and Hartford to the South, but the Civil War greatly curtailed sales and the last shipment was made in 1883.[13] Potter and Parsons, plow makers, had similar experience in Enfield. George Tansley manufactured gloves on Water Street; J.M. Harris had a wagon shop just east of the present railroad line; John Olmstead had a tin shop on South Road (as mentioned above).

On April 28, 1842, Amos D. Bridge, then an infant, arrived in Scitico from Milton, Kent, England, along with his parents, three brothers, and a sister, behind a three-horse team and wagon which carried all of their worldly goods: after a six-week voyage and hard tack meals. They came to join the powder-making Pricketts, to whom they were related by marriage. Amos' father, John Bridge, worked in the powder plant, and the boys joined him at an early age: George Bridge was there in 1844, at age fourteen, and recalls how the youngsters dashed for the charcoal storage in thunder storms which might ignite powder.

Amos Bridge, as noted earlier, bought into the bonnet business on Oak Street and made an arrangement with Colonel Hazard to spend part of his time there. The bonnets were shipped in wooden boxes. In 1875 Amos devoted full time to the work, set up a sawmill (by Hazardville Water Company) and bought land south of Freshwater for the timber. He discontinued the bonnet business but rapidly expanded the box business. He also built a dairy farm west of School Street, pastured the cows there, farmed for fodder, and added a store retailing hardware, coal, and wood. Undiscouraged by bad fires in 1885 and 1892, he chartered the Hazardville Water Company in 1899 and entered road construction in 1893. As a local contractor he built houses

and churches, and manufactured tobacco laths and tobacco boxes. After his death in 1906 the company was incorporated as Amos D. Bridge's Sons, Inc., 1907, and operation was continued by his sons Stephen, Allyn, William, Homer, and Charles plus his nephew, David Bridge. In 1928, General Electric appliances were added, and the box division started producing cable reels.

The depression of 1932 brought trouble. Although solvent, the company had extended so much delayed credit that it was necessary in 1934 to go into receivership. Nothing daunted, the brothers fought through to a termination of their receivership in 1943, with all obligations paid—an unheard-of performance. They spun off three lusty units: Bridge Manufacturing, for reels and wood products; Bridge Construction for roadbuilding (mostly in Maine); and Bridge Insurance, which had been purchased in 1932 (40). All four businesses are operated by the fourth generation people: John and David, sons of Chester G. and grandsons of Allyn; Donald, son of Douglas and grandson of Charles; and R. Dudley, son of Robert and grandson of Allyn. J. Douglas Brown is manager of Amos D. Bridge's Sons, Inc.

Bridge had also started the Hazardville Water Company, specially chartered in 1899. This company services the area approximately from Somers to the Mall and from East Windsor to Moody Road. Water is from a string of wells in the southern area, stored in a 750,000-gallon

Amos D. Bridge

In 1892, Amos D. Bridge (foreground) designed and constructed a handsome windmill and water tower for Hazardville's public water supply.

The Bridge Manufacturing Company plant on Randolph Street.

standpipe on Buckin Road (no thoroughfare) and a 150,000-gallon tank on North Maple Street.

In 1927 Homer E. Bridge was president and manager. In 1935, when Bridge was working out of financial straits, the company was sold to Dewing, and then to Granite State Gas & Electric Company, which now controls it. Stewart B. Avery is president, and the local manager is Robert Goodby.

Service has expanded from 20 hydrants and 310 services in 1935 to 380 hydrants and 5,000 meters in 1975. Meters were first installed in 1936.

Alongside the Bridge installation, the Hazard Lead Works manufactured white lead paints for a time before transferring the actual production to Brooklyn, New York. William H. Whitney, Jr., was born in Enfield, October 4, 1869,[21] attended school in Brooklyn, New York, and Suffield Institute, and in 1889 became general superintendent of King Paint Company. He went into business for himself in 1897 and in 1907 with H. Stephen Bridge, Charles C. Mann, and F.A. Pickering incorporated the Hazard Lead Works. He rented a factory on the Bridge premises and installed power and equipment to grind white lead paint. He also conducted the Colonial Works of Brooklyn in the same field and a few years later consolidated all the manufacturing in that city, but retaining the company office in Hazardville for a considerable time thereafter. His father, William H. Whitney, was in the publishing business, and his maternal great-grandfather, Thomas Bostock, had fought in the battle of Waterloo.

industry in the twentieth century

In the latter part of the bicentennium, a great variety of enterprises—some large, some small—dotted the Enfield scene. R.E. Hamilton had a sash and blind factory in Jabbok (the north-central section of town) in the 1850s, and Cooper Brothers made needles for the Wilcox and Gibbs single-thread sewing machine.[13]

The Enfield Manufacturing Company was incorporated September 15, 1845, with initial subscriptions of $100,000. Incorporators were W.G. Thompson, H. Schoonmaker, H. Allen Grant, John Worthington, F.S. & D. Lathrop, Samuel Parsons, James E. Smith, Condit & Scott, Joseph Steele, and Steiger Enz, with H.G. Thompson (Orrin's son) as president. Their plant, south of Bigelow and Asnuntuck Street, produced hosiery and stockinette, with a broad textile charter. Although the unit appears in the maps of 1869, it was "legislated out 1880"[5] (sic) and the property passed to Bigelow. The same maps show G.W. Moseley harness shop; J. Watson grist mill; Joseph Bent, wagons and carriages—succeeded by Carl E. Miller; Isaac T. Pease, inventor of fire alarms; A.T. Lord, harness manufacturer; and the New Haven, Hartford, and Springfield Railroad.

Lyman A. Upson, later co-founder of the Upson-Martin Company, was born in Westfield July 23, 1841, and served in the Civil War. He was assistant to John L. Houston of the Hartford Carpet Company, and in 1878 became superintendent.[21] In 1902, with Henry G.T. Martin of New York, he built the plant at the east end of Central Street and by 1911 had fifty looms making axminster rugs. He was elected a representative in the General Assembly in 1875 and as a long-time member of the school board overhauled the Enfield educational system. The buildings, purchased by Hinsdale-Smith for a tobacco warehouse, were taken by the town for taxes in 1937 and sold to National Printing Company. A few years later the business was discontinued and the structures have just been demolished in the urban renewal program.

In 1893 the Westfield Plate Company erected a four-story building on the west side of the railroad, opposite the depot, for the manufacture of casket hardware. Albert H. Mathewson was treasurer and manager for fourteen years, followed by H.L. Vietts, who later became president.[21] The company sold direct to undertakers rather than through jobbers, and also produced shrouds and casket linings. In 1919, when they merged with International Casket Hardware, they had 125 employees. Lead nameplates were later replaced by cheaper plated steel, the building was taken over in 1954 by the Dow Mechanical Corporation, and in 1958 the plate company certificate was terminated by limitation.

The western part of town—i.e., Enfield proper and Thompsonville—has had water service since 1885 when Judge Charles H. Briscoe and colleagues founded the Thompsonville Water Company. The judge was first president, with William Birnie as treasurer and L.H. Pease as secretary. George F. Cooper and his brother, Henry R. Cooper, were early superintendents. On April 1, 1926, the company was absorbed by Northern Connecticut Light & Power, under the aegis of Walter Schwabe (below), and in 1956 was sold to the present owner, Connecticut Water Company. Supply is from wells in the north part of town through the Enfield Street pump station and from East Windsor via a booster station near St. Patrick's Cemetery. The local manager is Alexander Tarnowicz and Frank A. Shaw is operating vice president.

During 1875-1885 a nest of enterprises took form. At the south end of Prospect Street, which had been extended until it met the railroad, Horace K. Brainard operated a farm supply business complete with a steam-powered grist mill where he stocked harnesses, wagons, cultivators, feed, and fertilizer. This business passed to his son, Leslie, who sold it to George S. Phelps Company, and it ended up as Nutmeg Building Supply. Horace B., another son, so impressed the Hartford Carpet Company that he became one of their chief purchasing agents.

Just north of Brainard, the G.H. Bushnell Press Company relocated from Worcester and struggled along until James A. Colvin, a foundry expert born in Cranston, Rhode Island, and previously with plants in Worcester and Danielson, bought control on February 4, 1894.[21] With H.W. Bushnell as manager, Colvin produced heavy presses for the extraction of vegetable oils, knuckle joint and baling presses for cloth bales, and general machined products including looms for Upson-Martin. In the same area he set up the Standard Metal Works (1905), a pipe bending operation which produced pipe fittings and tail pipes for the expanding automobile business. The press business moved to Greenville, South Carolina, and on November 16, 1922, Mark Bushnell, then president of Standard Metal, announced its sale to Premier Manufacturing Company of Sandy Hook, Connecticut. Amos D. Bridge's Sons also had a unit in the same vicinity.

By the early 1900s gracious, comfortable living was available to anyone who was willing to work for it. While big city government was notoriously corrupt, the bulk of the population led happy lives, were close to the farm, and were definitely not predatory. In the average town, a bicycle left unattended at the curb in the early morning would still be there in the late afternoon.

The Dow Mechanical Corporation was incorporated in 1946. Its founder, Walter K. Dow, first located in the old court house on Central Street, leaving the inscriptions "Judge" and "Prosecuting Attorney" on the doors for a while "to add a little prestige," Mr. Dow humorously explained. This company makes a wide line of comparator gauges and stubs which permit checking the dimensions of machine work to extraordinary accuracy. It regularly adds patented devices, such as hones and specialized gauges, to its line. In 1954 it moved to the former Westfield Plate Building on 33 North River Street.

The Enfield plant of Hallmark Cards opened November 17, 1952, in the Central Street Building of National Printing, and was managed by Robert D. Payne. His successor, Arthur D. Coate, became active in 1957, and in 1961 opened the 200,000 square foot installation on Manning Road.

Hallmark, the leading manufacturers of greeting messages, started in Kansas City, Missouri, on January 10, 1910, when Joyce Hall of Norfolk, Nebraska, took a room in the YMCA, began distribution of picture postcards, and kept his stock in shoe boxes. Hall Brothers started regular manufacture in 1915, and in 1923 adopted the "Hallmark" term—both from the family name and silversmith tradition. It became the company name in 1954. The taste and imagination shown by their product, and the skillful advertising, vaulted the concern to its present commanding position. Its "Hall of Fame" television program won more Emmy awards than any other. Donald J. Hall is now president, the company prints its products in twelve languages in more than one hundred nations, and has about 5,000 employees in the Kansas City area. It produces eight million cards a day. Stationery, gift wraps, books, and candles were added, and Springbok Editions was acquired (1968).[9]

Expansion in Enfield continued and 12,000 stores along the Eastern seaboard were serviced from here. Martin L. Gleason became manager in 1963, computer ordering came in, and more space was needed. Omer S. Muchmore, Jr., took over in April, 1969, and constructed the large new warehouse facility in 1972, connected to the main building by conveyor.

Five hundred persons are employed. A liberal personnel policy heightens their effectiveness and encourages maximum quality of the product.

Wallace Manufacturing Corporation started business in West Springfield, Massachusetts, in 1949, specializing in the design and manufacture of pruners, shears, and loppers. Intensive engineering design studies resulted in sturdy, patent-protected equipment whose merit brought increased business and substantial exports. In 1958 the proprietor, Edward M. Wallace, built the Manning Road facility, and continues to expand from customer recognition of the skillful design and marketing constantly applied to the products, evidenced also by favorable reviews in Consumers' Reports.[9]

Arthur P. Wagenknecht started the company bearing his name in 1945 in Pittsfield, Massachusetts, to make a varied line of paper mill auxiliaries—suction boxes, covers, and blades—originally mostly from phenolic laminates. Many other starting materials, including stainless steel, were used in a continuously increasing line of products. In February, 1951, he moved the firm to Enfield, to the old "pretzel factory" (also fire station and grinding wheel plant) on Enfield Street, where the installation has grown ever since. He sold to Albany Felt Company in February, 1961, and retired in 1964. The Appleton Wire Company was also acquired. In 1970 the corporate name was changed to International Wagenknecht and formed polyethylene was added to the product line. In 1971 the name was changed again to Albany Engineered Systems. The present plant superintendent is Mitchell C. Turek.

The Peerless Tool and Machine Company, Inc., started in 1942 in a garage on Hazard Avenue with three employees. Henry Turbak built it to its present stature, moving to Spring Street in 1945 and incorporating October 30, 1959. Precision machines, fixtures, and elaborate plastic molds are produced, including aircraft tooling—along with a wide variety of close-tolerance metal shaping jobs.[9]

The Stanley Turbak and Jezek families founded Sterling Machine Co., Inc., in July, 1956. The company, now operated by Stanley Turbak and Alexander Caravella, specializes in aircraft parts and other construction, particularly involving specialty alloys.[9]

Alconn Plastics was incorporated in 1957 by Arthur W. House, formerly of Berkshire Plastics. It conducted custom and proprietary molding of thermoplastics, designed packages, and furnished special services to the milk container and packaging trade. Programs were seriously interrupted by the sudden death of Mr. House in 1975.

Walter's Machine Products Co., Inc., and The Topskill Manufacturing Co., Inc., constitute a father-and-son machine shop combination.[9] The former was started as Hilliard Machine Company in 1952 and was incorporated by Walter J. Topolski and his son in 1964. Topskill was incorporated in 1967.

Barnes Engineering Company, a Delaware corporation, was authorized in Connecticut in 1954 and has been active here since 1956. Operated by Jack Barnes, president, and his son Carl, it designs and builds special automatic machinery, especially for the screwdriver and printing trade.

In 1961 Ewart Weaver of East Longmeadow and Albert P. Vecchiarelli of Longmeadow decided there was still room for a small jobbing firm to produce bronze and aluminum sand castings. They founded Yankee Casting Company, Inc., obtaining modest orders from Standard Knapp, Gilbert & Barker, and Chandler Evans. With advice and bank loans from Enfielders, they commenced the Shaker Road plant and completed their building program in 1968. They tackled all of the problems of a small growing business and emerged as a nationally recognized source of parts for aircraft fuel control housings, machine tools, packaging machines, submarine valves, glassmaking equipment, pump housings, and ventilation systems for oil tankers. Their hard work brought enjoyment and prosperity.

Neighbors in Powder Hollow started their two independent businesses at about the same time, and with the same ambition—to run their own shows. In 1961, Adrian L. Raiche and Richard W. Leno were already expert in the fabrication of steel stairs, railings, and fire escapes; with large families, they had given plenty of hostages to fortune. They embarked on Colonial Iron Shop, Inc., and located in one of four venerable powder works buildings, which they purchased.[9] The shop was in a cinderblock structure, with offices in an upper story wooden adjunct. The old blacksmith shop and wagon barn were not used at first.

The business became well established by December, 1963, when a fire damaged the shop and completely consumed the office. Hurt but not daunted, the partners rebuilt by the next spring, working meanwhile from a cramped borrowed trailer. The years since have seen many changes. The small partnership—begun on a shoestring—is now a corporation, employs nine full-time workers, has four trucks, and works in Massachusetts as well as Connecticut. The old bumpy dirt roads have been paved and lighted. The carriage barn has been rented, but in the old blacksmith shop, now used for storage, remnants of early days are seen in the wall iron rings used to tie horses while they were being shod. The outfit still forges ahead.

About the same time (1962), S.N. "Pete" Johnson was operating the pump division for Associated Engineers in West Springfield. One spring Thursday in 1962 a creditor and the company treasurer proposed to Pete that he might purchase the business. With characteristic vigor, he assumed notes, purchased the inventory and equipment, moved to Connecticut for more favorable tax treatment, occupied the old Thompsonville Bank on Friday and started production on Saturday as the Manufacturing Service Company. For six months he built pumps and did necessary accounting in the tellers' cages and vaults. Much to Pete's surprise, before the six months were up the State insisted that he have a business number, collect sales tax, and perform the multitudinous duties required by bureaucracy. He negotiated peace with the authorities, moved to a Civil War carriage shed with 75 percent dirt floor, used an old wallpaper bench for a desk, and heated with an oil pot stove. Improvement continued and in 1965 a brand new plant was built, with Pete as architect and prime contractor—using sage advice from the town construction expert, Bert King.

Service is supplied mainly to the machine tool industry, effecting savings through design of efficient liquid filtration and positive displacement pumping. The firm's equipment is well recommended, and by 1974 annual sales were approaching the half-million mark.

Two major new industries are shaping up for the future: the generation of power from non fossil fuel rather than oil, coal, and uranium, and the useful conversion of solid waste. Sooner or later Enfield must evolve a rational plan for the latter, since it has one hundred tons a day to dispose of. S. Camerota and Sons, Inc., has a running start in the latter field. Founded in 1960 by Salvatore Camerota to collect and merchandise used truck and auto parts,[9] the company's name was changed in 1974 as Frank Camerota became active and specialized increasingly in the recycling of metals. It has a favorable location on a precarious rail line.

While house building is not strictly a manufacturing business, mention must be made of the wholesome influence exerted over a quarter of a century by the ardent home developer, S. Leger Starr. Hundreds of Enfield dwellings built by him have transformed the older farms into much needed shelter and staved off deterioration of residential areas.

For half a century the U.S. Envelope Company operated in

Springfield, Massachusetts, until management decided in 1965 to build a plant in Enfield. It went on stream in February, 1966, and now occupies 100,000 square feet, produces fifteen million envelopes a day, and is the largest envelope manufacturing unit in the world, employing close to two hundred.[9] The preeminent position has been maintained by continuing design work and patenting of new machines and processes.

At about the time of the Enfield move, Westvaco Corporation (successor to the old West Virginia Pulp and Paper Company) purchased controlling interest in U.S. Envelope and most of the remaining minority was bought out a couple of years ago. A strange anti-trust quirk is the requirement that the Company is not allowed to purchase its paper stock from its parent! Richard Laffargue is the manager, and he has found time to perform public service as Secretary of the Planning and Zoning Commission.

As the bicentennium closes, productivity of man has achieved enormous advance over colonial days. A worker is now backed up, on the average, by $25,000 worth of production equipment; tremendous inventions have been exploited in rapid succession; and the standard of living has improved correspondingly. Recognizing the need to bolster Enfield industry, especially with the departure of Bigelow-Sanford, the Town Council and Town Manager Kissinger instigated the industrial park idea, which a public referendum approved on March 23, 1971. This activity has led to a promising group of new enterprises to make history for the future, including Lego Manufacturing Company, the Danish toy maker; Eli Lilly, the drug concern; United Silk Screen; Dawson Manufacturing Company, fabricators of stoves and household service devices; Roncari Industries, the Windsor construction firm which is taking over the Tadeus Olko bituminous plant, and others in negotiation.

The problems of business have increased seriously in recent years. Savage multiple taxes are exacted by several taxing authorities. Prices have been driven steadily skyward by the Congress, which for thirty years has been appropriating money it doesn't have. Also, producers are beset by three parasite groups: the consumer advocates, government regulators, and government prosecutors acting under cover of anti-trust laws. The individuals in these groups have two characteristics in common: none has ever made significant innovative contribution to society; and none has knowledge, experience, nor skill in the production he attacks. The penalty for success is oppression. Nevertheless, intrepid spirits continue to drive toward new accomplishments, and it appears that this tendency to progress will endure so long as the great majority of the population continue honest and ambitious.

CHAPTER 9

TRANSPORTATION, COMMUNICATION,
AND ENERGY

IN 1635 MAJOR PYNCHON floated supplies up the river to Warehouse Point where he maintained the depot which originated the name. The Enfield rapids intervened there so the remainder was freighted by pack animals, on land, to the Agawam-Springfield settlement.[3] By the Revolution, heavy scows made their appearance, laboriously poled upstream by brawny rivermen, using spiked 12-20-foot ash poles. In turn, at the bow, they braced poles against the bottom, then walked along the scow to the stern, pushing mightily. Occasionally an assisting south wind would pick up the sail they carried. The boisterous characters renewed their spirits liberally at the Enfield end of the trip and sang lustily on the downstream run.

The ferryboat *Cora*, built in the late 1800s, preceded the Suffield Bridge.

the era of canals

Canals became important when the Erie opened in 1825. In May, 1824, a charter was granted to the Connecticut River Company to improve navigation, first to Barnet, Vermont. Further incorporation of the Connecticut River Banking Company, with $1,500,000 capital, took place in 1825. A steam-powered craft, the *Barnet*, was built simultaneously, towed to Hartford November 17, 1826, and proceeded to Warehouse Point that night. Sturdy polemen failed in their first attempt to breast the rapids but on November 22, with thirty straining fallsmen manning ship and scow lashed to the sides, the *Barnet* passed the rapids. Celebrations were held in towns all the way, but after a few trips the *Barnet* disappeared. The Connecticut River Company paid funeral expenses of Joseph Groumly, who was scalded in a boiler-burst.

The canal, six miles long and at least four and a half feet deep, with three locks at the south end and one at the head end, opened

The Enfield covered bridge built in 1832.

November 11, 1829, the first boat through being Thomas Blanchard's newly invented stern wheeler. In 1845, when the railroad came through, the canal turned to manufacturing, granting 999-year leases to concerns that erected mills.

of bridges and trains

The first bridge from Enfield to Suffield, a fine covered structure, was built in 1808, financed by a lottery. This was replaced by another covered bridge in 1832 by Captain Rufus Granger. The flood of 1901 swept away most of the ancient structure, and with it went Hosea B. Keach, the railroad station agent, who was watching the bridge in the interest of the railroad, whose own bridge was further downstream. In the dramatic episode which followed, Keach, at first unconscious, revived and beat a hole through his imprisoning gable, then hoisted himself out with the aid of an old sign, "Horses must not be driven faster than a walk." Meanwhile, a southbound train dropped off a note at Warehouse Point Station so Arthur Blodgett and R.A. Abbe hastened to the railroad bridge just in time to pluck off Keach with a rope. He lost his agent's cap!

The second rail line, north through Scitico, was a more local affair. It started as the Connecticut Central Railroad, and stock subscriptions were made by East Windsor, Broad Brook Manufacturing Company, individuals in South Windsor, Hazard Powder Company, and the Enfield Shakers. Omar Pease of the Shakers' North family was a

Looking southwest on Commerce Street . . . now North River Street.

director, as were A.D. Bridge, George Wilcox of Enfield, and Francis Gowdy. The latter was also treasurer.[19] The line was leased to Connecticut Valley railroad, and trains were running in 1876.

electricity and
the telephone

Another industrial transition was about to take place. Faraday had invented an electric generator in 1831, and Weston and Edison raised its efficiency in 1878. Edison also made incandescent lamps in 1879; Stanley in Great Barrington produced a long-distance transmission by using transformers, and lighted his home town in 1886; and Tesla invented induction motors in 1888. The world's first commercial telephone exchange opened in New Haven in 1878.[9] The Hartford Railroad station had electric light on

R. R. Station, Thompsonville, Conn.

The railroad station from a postcard of the early 1900s.

April 7, 1883,[8] and in the same year Enfield had its first telephone service. Waterbury and Bristol undertook street lighting. Local companies sprang up, at first mainly for town lighting. Now power could be delivered wherever it was wanted, and the electric age had dawned.

The Enfield telephones in 1883 were serviced from Windsor Locks. The 1888 directory listed 45 customers in the area, including two in Enfield. By 1911 there were 502.[21] Equipment was primitive: the galvanized iron wires were strung over trees and along fences, and the wall-mounted instruments had to be cranked by hand to induce a ring. "Points within 50 miles can usually be heard without difficulty; however, owing to atmospheric disturbances along the line, long-distance talking is not always satisfactory." To cross the river, the company erected pylons 835 feet apart at the site of the old wrecked covered bridge and slung joisted cables between them. The lead-covered phone cables were supported by this narrow catwalk, and worked for several years. One Connecticut directory listed all of the subscribers in the state, by name only, but in 1888 numbers were assigned, and in 1889 their use became obligatory.

Southern New England Telephone Company opened the Thompsonville office in 1911 in Brainard block, with Miss Florence Calhoun as chief operator. Shortly afterward, Miss Bertha Varno held the position, and was succeeded by Miss Jessie Gourlie in 1915.

the years of growth / 219

Pylons and catwalk support telephone cables across the Connecticut.

Fire broke out in the exchange on High Street on April 29, 1916. It was quickly discovered by P.W. Miller, the test man, and Hardy Lohmes, district foreman, who marshalled all hands to action. Operators remained at the switchboard until it was too late to save coats and hats. Quick thinking of cable foreman Clark enabled him to cut the cables to the outside before they were ruined. Nine hundred lines were out, but by Herculean effort a temporary central was in action on Pearl Street in thirty hours. Workers toiled as neighboring stores and restaurants kept open, and Connecticut Light and Power furnished flood lights. Tony Markle, digging furiously in a new trench, on being told that sandwiches were ready, shouted up: "T'hell widda eat. Digga da trench first; then we eat!"

The new building at 895 Enfield Street (Mullen Road) went into service in 1938, dial phones were installed, and in 1970 the exchange officially became Enfield. Today there are almost 30,000 telephones in town, the reliability is superb, and the directory remains a marvel of accuracy. Realtus McCuin, manager since 1957, has found time not only to build and maintain the efficiency of his group but also to serve as town Councilman, a thankless, unpaid job, and as director of many public service groups.

Telephone company managers over the years were:

1882-1883   George H. Coe (Hartford Division)

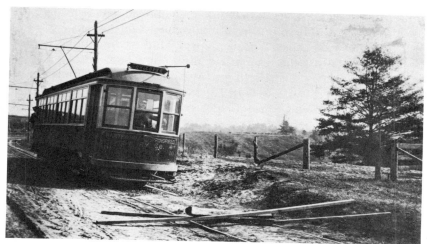
Somers to Chicopee Trolley . . . attempted sabotage at Scitico.

1883-1886	F.L. Mather
1886-1902	Miss Nettie E. Holcomb
1902-1939	George C. Rising
1939-1942	P.J. Ranney (including Manchester and Rockville)
1942-1947	D.L. Hobron ” ” ” ”
1947-1957	R.A. Mixson, Windsor Locks and Enfield
1957-1965	R.A. Mixson, Windsor Locks
	R.E. McCuin, Enfield
1965-	R.E. McCuin, Windsor Locks and Enfield.

electric power
and the trolley

Power supply in Enfield had its genesis in the 1890s[9][21] when the Enfield Gas Company furnished 600 Btu. gas from New Haven Coke Company and the Enfield Electric Light and Power Company began town lighting. Electric service was available nights only five days a week. By 1907, all service was much improved and the companies, together with Windsor Locks Electric Light Company, merged to become Northern Connecticut Light and Power Company. This organization prospered for many years (until 1947) under the able and professional guidance of Walter P. Schwabe, who also found time to help out in innumerable town projects.

The trolley came. L.S. Upson, George Mathewson, Judge Briscoe, and local capitalists built the Enfield and Longmeadow Street Railway in 1895 to connect Springfield and Warehouse Point, with a modest power station on Freshwater. In 1898 the company was incorporated into the Hartford and Springfield Street Railway Company, greatly improving service between the two cities and extending feeder lines to Somers (1902) and other towns. One could ride directly from Somers to the Scitico railroad bridge, along (present) Hazard Avenue through the woods, down South Pearl Street, north along Pearl Street to the central town station at the junction of Main, South Main, and North Main, thence back to Enfield Street, and north all the way to Chicopee.

Henry S. Newton, a skilled engineer, was general manager. By 1923 the competition from automobiles was severe, the company started operating buses from Suffield, revenues deteriorated and finally ceased, and in 1937 the rails were removed from Franklin, Pearl, and North Main Streets as a WPA project.

Northern Connecticut Light and Power Company, after many years, was again to merge. Electric companies in Waterbury, New Britain, and along the Housatonic had been acquired by the New York, New Haven and Hartford Railroad Company, then sold off in 1910 and 1911. With the strong backing of United Gas Improvement Company of Philadelphia, the entire group was launched August 9, 1917, as the Connecticut Light & Power Company.[8] In 1935, Northern Connecticut joined the group, and improvements in service continued: gas was enriched to 800 Btu. as it came through Hartford, steam plants came on line, and power networks provided flexibility in floods and winter ice storms. By 1950 C.L.&P. had capital of $160,000,000 against starting capital of $8,000,000, and with a reasonably stable dollar the domestic rate of 10 cents per Kwh in 1918 had dropped to 3.3 cents by 1949. Gas supply switched to much richer natural gas from Algonquin pipe lines, atomic power plants were added, and the Company considered the next obvious step of generating from municipal solid waste and from scrap paper available in excess of rework. Fair technology in both these fields is already available. Enfield division managers since Walter Schwabe have been:

Abner Bristol	January, 1947 - March, 1957
Robert Coleman	April, 1957 - February, 1963
W. Lindsey Booth	February, 1963 - July, 1968

George W. Russell   July, 1968 -

The Company is expected to participate in the use of the newer energy supplies from coal as oil dwindles, and the alternate, continuously received supplies—from sun, wind, and tide—as these develop.

CHAPTER 10

MILITARY HISTORY

IN ITS LONG AND INTEREST-ING HISTORY of nearly 300 years, the record shows that the men and women of Enfield have proven loyal to their country and have always answered the call to arms in defense of the nation. Many made the supreme sacrifice; many more returned home wounded during military action dating from the Revolutionary War to current times.

Much has been written from an Enfield standpoint about the Revolutionary War, the Civil War, and World War I, but unfortunately research discloses little or no information nor written local history concerning World War II, the Korean War, and the Vietnam War. Information on local aspects of the Spanish-American War is also scanty.

A Civil War monument in tribute to veterans of that war is located in downtown Thompsonville at the corner of North Main and Church Streets. A memorial to Captain Thomas Abbey (Revolutionary War) is located in front of the Enfield Congregational Church at the corner of South Road and Enfield Street. Details and contents of both the monument and memorial are included in the article that follows.

In appreciation of its veterans the State of Connecticut instituted a cash bonus payment system for military service during war years, starting with World War II. A sum of $10 per month is paid to qualified veterans serving during military conflicts, with a maximum payment of $300.

World War II veterans also qualified as recipients for a special program by the federal government, designed to assist during the transition period into civilian life from military service. Veterans who qualified for active military service during the war were paid a sum of $20 per week for one year. This was known to veterans as the 52-20 program.

The Enfield Veterans' Council was formed shortly after the end of World War II. There are eight recognized veterans' organizations in the community. Membership on the council is comprised of three delegates and one alternate from each of the veterans' posts plus a liaison member of the Town Council.

Principal aims and purposes of the Council are based on the assistance and furtherance of all veterans and their rights and benefits within the community, state, and nation. Other aims are: To act as liaison agent between all local veterans' groups and the community government; to help unify divergent groups in the interests of all veterans; to expedite and assist in the orderly return of all veterans to civilian life by protecting their rights during military service and to assist in the rehabilitation of all veterans by providing counsel concerning veterans' benefits and opportunities.

The Enfield Veterans' Council receives necessary funds annually from the town budget, approved by the Town Council, in order to carry out its aims and duties. The local veterans' unit is responsible for sponsoring annual parades on Memorial Day and Veterans' Day, in honor of all veterans and the dead of all wars. Graves of all veterans in town cemeteries are also decorated on both these occasions.

A special luncheon program is also held annually for Gold Star parents and their families.

early military service

In Enfield's long and glorious history of nearly three hundred years, its men and women have nobly responded to our country's call to defend the nation in its various wars and military conflicts. Our civilian population also did its share in other ways, such as buying war bonds and producing military supplies and other needs of the nation.

No wars disturbed the peace of Enfield for the first sixty-five years of its existence. During the mid 1700s, the country was harassed by frequent French and Indian Wars. Enfield youths fought in them, an estimated three hundred men serving in some way over a period from 1755 to 1762, according to muster payrolls in the State Library and listed in Allen's *History of Enfield*. Many of them made the supreme sacrifice.

There were nine of the town's original settlers who had seen service in King Philip's War, which had ended three years before Enfield was settled. Three of these men were Benjamin Jones, Isaac Morgan, and Thomas Abbey.

When the call came to take up arms for England against France in the Louisberg Expedition in 1745, Enfield's patriots caught the enthusiasm of the times. A large band of local men took part in the successful expedition to Cape Breton, along with others from New England.

A glorious and almost bloodless victory had been won—nothing less than the conquest of Louisberg, then the key to Canada and the strongest fortress in the Western World.

Later, this fine army which had achieved such a glorious victory began dying from famine and disease by the hundreds amidst the inhospitable climate of Cape Breton.

In all of the succeeding colonial conflicts, Enfield always rose nobly to England's defense. As noted earlier, the town was called upon to furnish recruits during the French and Indian Wars from 1755 to 1762. Although fulfilling her patriotic duty to the mother country, Enfield, in common with many other communities, was becoming restive under England's continuing acts of oppression.

the American Revolution

The climax of protests came later by the adoption in March, 1774, of the Boston Port Bill. Enfield was among the first towns to assemble her citizens in protest against this obnoxious measure. Although the people were torn between allegiance to their King and the feeling that they must proclaim their stand against the injustices of England, they met in Enfield on July 11, 1774, in a full meeting.

This session established a resolution of protest, resolving unanimously "That a firm and inviolable union of the Colonies is absolutely necessary for the defense and support of our Civil Rights, without which all our efforts will be likely to prove abortive."

The resolution continued, "That the most effective measure is to break off all commercial intercourse with Great Britain until all these oppressive acts are repealed."

A committee of correspondence was appointed to confer with com-

Memorial to Capt. Thomas Abbey, Revolutionary War soldier and patriot, was dedicated in November, 1916.

mittees of other towns to secure the best methods to be adopted in this crisis and to receive and forward contributions for the relief of those persons in Boston and Charlestown "who are distressed by the unhappy consequences of the Boston Port Bill." Members of this Enfield committee included Ephraim Terry, Peter Raynolds, Edward Collins, Nathaniel Terry, Ephraim Pease, Isaac Kibbe, and Thomas Parsons.

These and many similar actions elsewhere led to the Revolutionary War, which established the freedom and birth of a new nation after its break from the mother country, England.

Nearly a year later, with "the shot heard 'round the world," Enfield was prepared. When the news of the battle of Lexington was brought by a post rider to Enfield the next day, the famous incident of Captain Thomas Abbey and the drum was enacted.

The people had assembled in the church for the regular Thursday lecture. The Reverend Elam Potter, the minister, was in the midst of his discourse when suddenly the furious drum beat of the "long roll" was heard outside.

The congregation rushed out in excitement to hear the momentous message and the eagerness of the men to enlist immediately in the defense of the colonies. The next day, a company of about seventy-five men from Enfield marched to the relief of Boston, each with his flint-lock musket and powder horn.

They were led by Major Nathaniel Terry; Thomas Abbey was one of the men. The center of this dramatic episode, now the old Town Hall on Enfield Street, stood then on the opposite side of the road. Its site is marked by the monument commemorating the event and memorializing the Abbey family.

The "Memorial of Capt. Thomas Abbey, his ancestors and descendants of the Abbey Family" is located in front of the Enfield Congregational Church on Enfield Street at the corner of South Road. It was erected by his great-granddaughter, Frances Maria Abbey, wife of Joel F. Freeman, and family.

It records and honors Captain Abbey's accomplishments and participation in military conflicts of our country. He was born on April 11, 1731, and died on June 3, 1811.

Besides his active participation in the Revolutionary War and the famous drum incident in calling men of Enfield to arms, Captain Abbey also was a soldier in the French and Indian Wars, and took part in the capture of Fort Ticonderoga in 1758 and the conquest of Canada in 1761.

The old meeting house on Enfield Street is now "The Old Town Hall," still preserved for the posterity of Enfield. It was built in 1775 by Isaac Kibbe and succeeded the church which stood on the green, about one-third of a mile to the south. It was there that on July 8, 1741, Jonathan Edwards preached his famous sermon, "Sinners in the Hands of an Angry God."

Enfield's patriotism continued unabated throughout the Revolutionary War. Quotas for the town were always promptly filled; demands were met for support of the families of the soldiers for their clothing and tents, as well as for their wages when Congress found it difficult to raise money for the support of the Army.

Nearly two hundred Enfield men were in the Continental Forces, which seems a large proportion of the town population of 1,580 persons in 1783. The first census of the Town of Enfield was taken in 1756, with the record showing a total population at that time of 1,050 persons.

In 1841, Secretary of State records in Connecticut disclosed the fact that Connecticut furnished more soldiers in the Revolutionary War in proportion to population than any other of the original thirteen states.

In the town's cemeteries, sixty graves of Enfield's Revolutionary War heroes have received bronze markers, given by the Penelope Terry Abbey Chapter, Daughters of the American Revolution.

War of 1812

When war was declared against England in 1812, as a culmination of the difficulties with that country, Enfield was probably as bitterly opposed to the struggle as the rest of New England. Yet its patriotism stood the test and it contributed generously to the prosecution of the War.

Besides the men enlisted for the service, a company of seventy-four, under command of Captain Luther Parsons, marched to the defense of New London in 1813. Other detachments went there for the same purpose, and with them were Major Robert Morrison and Captain Jabez Collins.

the Mexican War

Very few Enfield names are found in the list of Connecticut men in the regular army during the Mexican War, but one of the town's most distinguished sons, while not an actual participant in the war, had a prominent part with General Sam Houston in one of the events that led to it, the Revolution that freed Texas from Mexico.

He was Elisha Marshall Pease, son of the Honorable Lorain T. Pease, and a direct descendant of the first settler of Enfield, John Pease. After the independence of Texas was secured, Mr. Pease drafted the constitution and by-laws for the new republic, and was one of the council to consider taking up arms against Mexico on account of the difficulty growing out of the annexation of Texas to the United States in 1845.

He was later elected Governor of the new state in 1853, serving four years, and from 1867 to 1870 he was provisional Governor.

No company was formed in Enfield for the Spanish-American War in 1898. However, twelve men enlisted from this town, some of them in the 1st Connecticut and 2nd Massachusetts Infantry Regiments, and some in the Navy.

The story of the military role of Enfield would not be complete without some reference to its connection with the militia. A parade ground was provided for training in 1680 on a tract on Enfield Street near the present Post Office. John Pease, Jr., served as the first captain of the first militia company.

Divisions and brigades were first constituted in Connecticut in 1776. The first division of the First Hartford County brigade included the Enfield 19th Regiment. Some notable military displays of this brigade took place on special occasions. One of these was when it escorted Lafayette on his visit to Hartford in September, 1824. The local unit was headed by Captain Jabez King and "attracted much attention for its soldierly bearing and fine drill."

Enfield's first rifle company was organized in 1838, with George C. Owen as captain. Scitico had a rifle company comprised of thirty-three men in 1847, headed by Captain Charles M. Collins. This company was the last in the county and later disbanded in 1851. A number of new companies were organized later, among them Rifle Company A of Enfield, headed by Captain Walter A. Luce in 1863 and later disbanded in 1871.

The term "militia" was dropped in 1865 and later became known as the Connecticut National Guard.

the Civil War

At the outbreak of the Civil War Enfield residents became aroused as they had not been since the Revolutionary War. A town meeting assembled in 1861 on April 29 and passed unanimous resolutions of loyalty to the general government. This spirit of loyalty never waned throughout the conflict, sometimes referred to as the war of rebellion.

The resolutions of loyalty to the general government "asserted that it was the duty of every citizen to assist in punishing treason, suppressing rebellion; maintaining the constitution and enforcing the laws."

A total of 421 Enfield men enlisted in the Army for military service during the Civil War. By July, 1864, there were fifty-eight more men in the service than had been called for. On account of its generosity in bounties and provisions for soldiers' families, Enfield incurred a debt of $40,000.

A descendant of Enfield Terrys became a noted figure in this war—General Alfred Howe Terry, grandson of General Nathaniel Terry—a native of the town; great-grandson of Colonel Nathaniel

Early postcard view of Soldiers' Monument, erected in 1885.

Terry of Revolutionary fame, and sixth in line from Samuel Terry, one of the founders of the settlement.

General Terry rose in rank in the Rebellion from colonel of the 7th Connecticut Infantry to major-general of volunteers. He was considered the ablest general next to General Miles, who had risen from the civilian ranks.

Another grandson of General Nathaniel Terry to achieve distinction in the Rebellion was Commander Edward Terry, U.S.N. He served under Admiral Farragut and was executive officer of the *Richmond* in the Battle of Mobile Bay in 1864. In 1878 he served as chief of staff to Admiral Rogers, commanding the Pacific Squadron.

State military records cite the fact that Company B of the 8th Infantry Regiment during the Civil War was comprised largely of Enfield men, listing nearly one hundred names of Enfield residents. Records note, "The men of Enfield showed unusual patriotism at the outbreak of the war. Volunteers for military service far exceeded the town's quota in numbers. In all their military records, they were distinguished for their patriotism and courage."

The Soldier's Monument located in downtown Thompsonville at the corner of Church and Main Streets was erected by the Town of Enfield in 1885, in tribute to the men of Enfield who served their country during the Civil War.

The monument portrays a Union soldier standing with his musket by his side. An inscription on one side of the monument reads, "In memory of the men of Enfield, who on land and sea periled their lives for union and liberty during the Civil War, 1861-65."

The Roll of Honor lists a total of twenty-nine Enfield men who were either killed in action or died from wounds received in the conflict. Fifteen other men died in service while they were prisoners of war at the Andersonville Prison in Georgia.

World War I

As in all past wars engaged in by our country, Enfield again contributed heavily in all demands of the nation during World War I against Germany and the Kaiser. This war was also known as "Making the World Safe For Democracy."

Records vary as to how many men and women of Enfield took part in this war. However, it was reliably documented in a town program on September 1, 1919, "A Reception and Celebration" in tribute and honor to all World War I Veterans, that a total of 517 men and women served our country actively during the conflict. A large percentage of these served overseas in France. The total includes twenty who served in the Polish Legion, seventeen were in the student Army Training Corps, nine were connected with the British-Canadian recruiting station, seven served as Red Cross nurses, one was in the Merchant Marine, and nine took part in United War Activities.

The war came to an end on November 11, 1918, when the Armistice was signed.

The war records also show that a total of eight men from Enfield were killed in action during the World War I conflict, and another five died in service including a Red Cross nurse.

The north side of the Soldier's Monument in downtown Thompsonville has an inscription, "In Memory of Those Who Gave Their Lives in the Great War for World-Wide Liberty—1917-19."

There were also about three hundred names of Enfield men who served during the war with the State Guard. Of course, hundreds of people also engaged in Red Cross work in the headquarters or in their homes.

According to reliable information submitted by William G. Thompson, one of the town's World War I veterans, Enfield contributed the most men serving in the military service, based on percentage of population, of any town in the State of Connecticut. Estimated population of the town in 1918 was about ten thousand persons.

During the war, the civilian population gave of their time and effort in many ways. A total of nearly $47,000 was contributed for the various drives; a donation of 350 volumes was made to the town library; a total of more than $1.4 million was raised in five "Liberty Loan" drives for the government—which was a lot of money in those years.

The *Thompsonville Press* (now known as the *Enfield Press*) published a complete list in alphabetical order of World War I veterans who served in the armed forces. The publication date was May 25, 1939, during the twentieth observance of Memorial Day. A similar list was reprinted in the same newspaper on November 11, 1965, probably from the same list which had appeared in a souvenir program for a reception held in honor of all World War I veterans on September 1, 1919, by the Town of Enfield.

The reception program held on that date included a special parade, a luncheon, and a clambake for all veterans, and a band concert. Another feature was a baseball game between "Overseas Men" and "Domestic Servicemen," for a purse of fifty dollars in gold.

Main Street, Thompsonville, could have been Main Street U.S.A. in 1912 with World War I still five years away.

Walter P. Schwabe served as chairman of the general committee for the program.

After the end of World War I, America enjoyed a generation of peace and prosperity in the 1920s, followed by the Great Depression of the 1930s.

Germany was preparing for war in the mid-1930s by building one of the most powerful military machines in world history. Germany invaded Poland on September 1, 1939, after which England and France declared war on Germany.

World War II

Although the sympathies of our country remained with the Allies, the United States did not enter World War II until the sneak attack on Pearl Harbor by the Japanese on December 7, 1941. Most of the Pacific Fleet that lay anchored there was destroyed by more than one hundred Japanese planes that took part in the attack on that fateful day. More than two thousand Americans, military and civilian, were killed in that bombing.

Thus began the greatest war in history, with more than sixteen million men and women of our country in the various military services during the war period that lasted almost four long years.

Our military forces were far-flung all over the globe, serving in many foreign countries as we battled for survival against Japan and Germany. Troops were stationed overseas in Europe, Africa, Asia, the Philippines, Hawaii, in many stronghold islands in the Pacific and in Alaska.

The great military invasion by the Allies of German-held France, known as "D-Day" on June 6, 1944, later led to the collapse of the German military machine in Europe. American forces were led by General George Patton, with General Dwight Eisenhower serving as supreme commander of the Allied Forces.

The Germans later made a desperate, last-ditch fight in the "Battle of the Bulge," but succumbed to the might and power of the Allied Forces. Germany finally ended the war in Europe with an unconditional surrender on "V-E Day" on May 8, 1945.

Shortly before Germany surrendered, President Franklin D. Roosevelt, who served for an unprecedented fourth term in the White House, died in Warm Springs, Georgia, on April 12, 1945.

Vice President Harry S. Truman then assumed the Presidency. He later made the agonizing decision to authorize the first use of the atomic bomb on two Japanese cities, on Hiroshima, August 6, 1945, and on Nagasaki, August 9, 1945, thus bringing World War II to a rapid end.

The Japanese surrendered on August 14, 1945, but the actual, official date of surrender was on September 2, 1945, later known as "V-J Day."

The exact number of men and women from Enfield who served our country in World War II is not known. A town honor roll listing in alphabetical order all men and women serving during the war through November, 1946, showed that more than 2,000 Enfield men and women served in all branches of the military services.

However, research statistics on Connecticut veterans, published in 1960 by the Veterans Administration, reported a total of 2,902 World War II Enfield veterans. This figure was tabulated, based on a twenty-five percent sampling of the U.S. population.

In many cases, there were two, three, or more men serving in the military forces from a single family.

A reliable report indicated that a total of fifty-two men from Enfield were killed in action during World War II. The number of men wounded in action is not known.

Charles Gatto, former director of Enfield Veterans Rehabilitation and Counseling Commission after World War II, claimed that Enfield had the most men and women in military service in the State of Connecticut, based on a percentage ratio of the town's population then estimated at 13,500.

It was also generally claimed after the end of the war that Enfield had the highest percentage ratio to population of men in military service in the entire country. However, this was never officially proven or substantiated as fact.

Mr. Gatto also reported that Enfield had one of the best programs in the state for assisting World War II veterans in rehabilitation and training during the post-war period.

Records show that more than 210,000 Connecticut men saw action in many parts of the world during the war. About 75,000 of these enlisted voluntarily for service. About 5,700 lost their lives and countless unknown thousands were wounded.

An estimated total of 3,308 Connecticut women entered the Wac (Women's Army Corps) during the same period.

The majority of men and women who served in the various branches of our military forces during the war were in the eighteen to thirty-five age bracket.

the Korean War

The United States became involved in the Korean War on June 27, 1950, when President Harry S. Truman ordered General Douglas MacArthur to aid South Korea and the 7th Fleet to protect Formosa. Despite the fact that no official declaration of war was made against North Korea by the Congress, our country became deeply involved in this conflict in Truman's efforts to stop the spread of Communism in that sector of the world.

The United Nations was titular leader in efforts to resist the Communist forces, although the United States played the leading role in assisting South Korea to fight the aggression.

President Truman termed the intervention in Korea as "a police action."

The war had three phases: (1) The North Korean drive, as checked by U.S. and allied troops, with the help of a brilliant landing by U.S. Marines at Inchon on September 15, 1950; (2) A counterattack by large numbers of Chinese Communist forces who crossed the Yalu River; this offensive later stopped by United Nations troops who pushed the Chinese back across the parallel; and (3) the removal of General MacArthur from command on April 11, 1951; and start of negotiations for truce along the 38th parallel on July 10, 1951.

Cease-fire and armistice talks began July, 1951, and dragged on with numerous breakdowns until July 27, 1953, when an armistice was signed.

Prisoner repatriation began in August, 1953. The United Nations then turned over nearly 76,000 prisoners, most of them from North Korea; and the Communists released nearly 13,000 prisoners, including 3,597 Americans.

The Korean War ended in a stalemate, with the country divided into two sectors at the 38th parallel, North Korea and South Korea, the parallel serving as a buffer zone. The United States has kept a military force in South Korea since the end of that war in order to restore the relative balance of military strength that the armistice was intended to preserve.

Unfortunately, little or no information is available on the extent of Enfield's participation in the Korean War. Research efforts proved disappointing, but it is estimated that a total of 1,782 local men and women served in the military forces during the conflict, including those who continued service from World War II. These figures were reliably estimated, based on a 25 percent sampling of the national population in 1960 by the Veterans Administration.

No known figures are available as to Enfield casualties in the war.

The *World Almanac* reports that more than 5.7 million men and women served in our military forces during the Korean War, with 33,629 battle deaths, plus an additional 20,617 who died from wounds or other reasons during service. More than 100,000 were wounded.

the Vietnam War

Like the Korean War, there is scant information available on the Vietnam War from an Enfield standpoint. It is not known how many Enfield men or women took part in that, or how many Enfield men and women were casualties.

American combat involvement for about twelve years made the Vietnam War the longest in United States history. Our country first showed an interest in the area when President Harry S. Truman on June 27, 1950, sent a small military advisory team of thirty-five to aid the French in their fight against Communist forces in North Vietnam.

The major American commitment in Vietnam began after the U.S. destroyers *Maddox* and *C. Turner Joy* were reportedly attacked on August 2, 1964, by North Vietnamese torpedo boats in the Gulf of Tonkin. Congress passed the "Gulf of Tonkin Resolution," giving the President power "to take all necessary measures to repel any armed attack against the U.S. forces, and to prevent further aggression."

Within the next year or two, U.S. forces in Vietnam increased to total of more than 400,000 men, including 60,000 men in the U.S. Fleet and some 33,000 men stationed in Thailand.

One of the major battles of the war was the "Tet Offensive" on January 30, 1968, when the Vietcong and North Vietnamese attacked thirty provincial capitals in South Vietnam. Record casualties were suffered on both sides.

The war was probably the most bitterly opposed by the civilian population in our country's history. Large-scale protests resulted in marches in many sections of the country and on the college campuses. Hundreds of arrests followed the protests.

The war continued as preliminary peace talks opened in Paris on

May 10, 1968, between the U.S. and North Vietnam. In Chicago, police and troops clashed with 10,000 to 15,000 demonstrators during the Democratic National Convention on August 26-29 that year.

American forces in South Vietnam reached a final peak of 543,400 in April, 1969. Withdrawal of our combat troops began on July 8, 1969, and on November 3 of that year President Richard Nixon announced a policy that would transfer the fighting to the South Vietnamese forces.

Protests in the country continued, however, as hundreds of thousands of Americans demonstrated in opposition to the Vietnam War on October 15, 1969, in a nation-wide "moratorium." Some 250,000 demonstrators gathered in Washington, D.C., on November 15, 1969, in the largest anti-war protest in United States history.

The war came to an end after peace pacts were formally signed in Paris on January 27, 1973, by the United States, North and South Vietnam, and the Vietcong. Some American prisoners of war were later released by North Vietnam, although it was reported at that time that some 1,359 Americans were missing in Indochina.

The last American troops left Vietnam on March 29, 1973, officially ending any direct U.S. military role.

More than 8.7 million men and women in the military forces of our country took part in this war. Battle deaths were reported at 46,397, with 10,346 other deaths due to other reasons during service. A total of 153,311 were wounded in action.

Special ceremonies were held in Enfield on May 20, 1973, upon return of the bodies of four local servicemen who were killed in action during the Vietnam War.

A total of 136,900 men in this country either evaded the draft into military service or became military deserters during the Vietnam War. President Gerald Ford in 1974 offered these men a conditional amnesty program, with up to two years in public service jobs. Organized groups of exiles in various countries condemned the program and few took advantage of it. President Ford later extended the deadline for amnesty to March 31, 1975, for draft evaders and military deserters to apply for clemency. Less than 10,000 of those eligible signed up for the program.

overview of the
last thirty years

One lesson that is strongly emphasized, resulting from the many wars and military conflicts engaged in by our country, is that the price of freedom is eternal vigilance. From the days of our forefathers until the present time, this is the watch word.

Ever since the end of World War II in 1945, we have been engaged in a continual "cold war" with Russia and the Communist World. Since the use of the first atomic bombs in World War II, both sides have been engaged in an arms race. Development of the atomic and nuclear weapons since that time has reached frightful proportions, with potential firepower of the hydrogen bomb and other similar weapons listed as several hundred times stronger than the first atomic bomb used in World War II.

The Chinese, in the United States' bicentennial year of 1976 exploded a nuclear blast in outdoor testing that was at least 200 times stronger than the original atomic bomb used in Japan to end the war in 1945.

An attitude of co-existence has developed in recent years between the Communist and the Free Worlds. Strong efforts are continually made in peace "offensives" in all parts of the world to avoid a nuclear war which could possibly lead to the end of our civilization, as we know it.

We can thank a kind Providence that despite the tremendous loss of life and property on both sides in the Korean and Vietnam Wars no nuclear or atomic weapons were used.

Strong diplomatic and peace efforts are the continual watchword between nations of the world to keep the many so-called brush fires from turning into a major conflagration that could lead to a nuclear world war.

The Enfield Veterans Council, as mentioned earlier, is a unit comprised of delegates of the eight recognized veterans' posts and organizations of the Town of Enfield. It is responsible for assisting all veterans in their rights, benefits, and welfare.

This article will conclude with a listing of all past commanders of the local veterans' posts. Most of the posts were named after Enfield residents who died in military action in the various wars. An asterisk denotes that the person is deceased.

The complete list follows:

TANGUAY-MAGILL POST, 80, AMERICAN LEGION
(Organized and chartered Jan. 20, 1920—the oldest post in Enfield)

Past Commanders:

1920 John L. Sullivan* (First Comdr.)	1948 Frank H. Morrison*
1921 Dr. Frank E. Simonton*	1949 Sidney C. Smith*
1922 Dr. Frank E. Simonton*	1950 Ivan O. Brodeur*
1923 Dr. Frank E. Simonton*	1951 Joseph F. Nadeau
1924 Harold Bromage*	1952 George Krom*
1925 Orin Beehler*	1953 George Krom*
1926 John Hutton*	1954 Harold Madsen
1927 Kenneth W. Stevens*	1955 Lawrence F. Strecker
1928 James E. Breslin*	1956 Herbert Varno, Jr.
1929 Samuel Sisisky*	1957 Robert Osenbach, Jr.
1930 David Beckman*	1958 Raymond Millett
1931 Abe Sisisky*	1959 Alfred Fritze
1932 Thomas A. Fahey*	1960 Francis Whalen
1933 Dr. William Fancher*	1961 Raymond Rookey
1934 Charles W. Blunden*	1962 Benjamin Gambino
1935 Edgar Gorman*	1963 Charles Damon
1936 Darius J. Bouchard	1964 John Bartley
1937 Lawton B. Needham*	1965 Francis Cormier
1938 Thomas H. Hillery*	1966 Irene Jennison
1939 Charles A. Furey*	1967 Ernest Jennison
1940 William G. Thompson	1968 Daniel Quinn
1941 Louis A. Haight*	1969 John Vesce
1942 Willard R. Young*	1970 Euclid Bishop
1943 Edmond G. Meagher*	1971 Armand Casarella
1944 Edward F. Ryan*	1972 Everett Downer
1945 Henry L. MacDonald*	1973 Nathan Hefferman
1946 John A. Dougan*	1974 Orville Heck
1947 Arthur B. Fitzgibbons	1975 Joseph L. Beninato
	1976 Joseph L. Beninato

JOHN MACIOLEK POST, 154, AMERICAN LEGION
(Post was organized in November, 1945, and chartered February 7, 1946)

Past Commanders:

1945-46 Joseph A. Rarus (First Comdr.)	1948-49 Theodore Misiaszek
1946-47 Clair Niemiec	1949-50 Theodore Misiaszek
1947-48 Stanley Yesukiewicz	1950-51 Stanley Bania
	1951-52 John Panek

1952-53 Matthew Salva
1953-54 Pat J. Lamagna
1954-55 Walter Piepul
1955-56 Stanley Swiatowski
1956-57 Mitchell Pabis
1957-58 Edward Buika
1958-59 Armand Casarella
1959-60 Ralph Wallace
1960-61 Joseph Turek
1961-62 Fred Mays
1962-63 Stanley Halgas
1963-64 Wilfred Jarvis
1964-65 Nelson F. Knight*

1965-66 Joseph Martin*
1966-67 Joseph Martin*
1967-68 Edward Buika
1968-69 Edward Buika
1969-70 Miss Sophia Podosek
1970-71 Joseph A. Rarus
1971-72 Joseph A. Rarus
1972-73 Albert Calsetta
1973-74 Albert Calsetta
1974-75 Edward Zukowski
1975-76 Edward Zukowski
1976-77 Edward Zukowski

PATRICK F. TRIGGS POST, 1501, VETERANS OF FOREIGN WARS
(Post was organized on June 10, 1930)

Past Commanders:

1930-31 Martin J. Tierney*
        (First Comdr.)
1931-32 Russell F. Maylott*
1932-33 Russell F. Maylott*
1933-34 Martin J. Watton*
1934-35 Joseph Larabee*
1935-36 William R. Salmon*
1936-37 Thomas Halpin*
1937-38 Thomas Halpin*
1938-39 Edward LaGrange
1939-40 Francis A. Burke
1940-41 Francis A. Burke
1941-42 L. Lawrence Sullivan*
1942-43 L. Lawrence Sullivan*
1943-44 Charles Martin*
1944-45 Charles Martin*
1945-46 Charles Martin*
1946-47 William Miltner*
1947-48 William Miltner*
1948-49 John Fitzgerald*
1949-50 Robert B. Watton
1950-51 Irving Piorek
1951-52 Martin J. Watton*
1952-53 Martin J. Watton*

1953-54 James McMahon*
1954-55 James McMahon*
1955-56 Edwin Wishart
1956-57 Edwin Wishart
1957-58 Leo Sullivan
1958-59 Leo Sullivan
1959-60 George Hensel
1960-61 Francis Lamagna*
1961-62 Francis Lamagna*
1962-63 Joseph Bielecki
1963-64 John Kowalchuck
1964-65 Lewis Wilby
1965-66 Roland Blanchard
1966-67 George H. Buckley
1967-68 John E. Welch
1968-69 Theodore J. Plamondon, Jr.
1969-70 John E. Welch
1970-71 Robert F. Kennedy
1971-72 Robert F. Kennedy
1972-73 Paul Skarzynski
1973-74 Arthur R. LaGrange
1974-75 Theodore J. Plamondon, Jr.
1975-76 Paul Skarzynski
1976-77 Paul Skarzynski

AMVETS POST, 18
(Post was organized in 1953)

Past Commanders:

1953-54 Michael Marinaccio (First Comdr.)	1965-66 Ronald Sullivan, Jr.
1954-55 Ernest Mankus	1966-67 Fred Weiss
1955-56 Anthony Porto	1967-68 Roy Smith
1956-57 Raymond Montagna	1968-69 Robert Rookey
1957-58 James Delore	1969-70 Gerald Archambault
1958-59 Earl Miller	1970-71 Robert Rookey
1959-60 Donald Jones	1971-72 Gerald Cote
1960-61 Cornelius Cowhey*	1972-73 Gerald Cote
1961-62 Roy Smith	1973-74 Robert Calsetta
1962-63 Salvatore Ragno	1974-75 William Edgar
1963-64 Salvatore Ragno	1975-76 William Edgar
1964-65 Roy Smith	1976-77 Richard Crane

ALBERT V. POOLE BARRACKS, 868, WORLD WAR I VETERANS
(Organized and Chartered on Feb. 10, 1966)

Past Commanders:

1966 James Brigada*	1972 Herbert Edes
1967 James Brigada*	1973 Herbert Edes
1968 James Brigada*	1974 Herbert Edes
1969 Charles Herbage	1975 Charles Herbage
1970 Byron Mohrbacher	1976 John D. Gallo
1971 Byron Mohrbacher	1977 John D. Gallo

JAMES RINALDI-ROY FEDE POST, 17, ITALIAN-AMERICAN WAR VETERANS
(Post was organized in 1945)

1945-46 Louis Ragno (First Comdr.)	1955-56 Francis J. Scalia
1946-47 Joseph Bonelli*	1956-57 Anthony F. Scavotto*
1947-48 Joseph Bonelli*	1957-58 Anthony F. Scavotto*
1948-49 Alphonse Vella*	1958-59 Carl S. Iacolino
1949-50 Samuel J. Fiore	1959-60 Patrick J. D'Amato
1950-51 Samuel J. Fiore	1960-61 Patrick J. D'Amato
1951-52 Harold C. Nuccio	1961-62 Anthony L. Scavotto
1952-53 Harold C. Nuccio	1962-63 Jasper M. Gambino
1953-54 Charles J. Brutto	1963-64 Carmen J. Brutto
1954-55 Charles J. Brutto	1964-65 Joseph P. Lauria
	1965-66 Joseph J. Cusimano

1966-67 James F. Porcello	1972-73 Joseph J. Fede
1967-68 Peter T. DiSalvo	1973-74 Joseph Santacroce
1968-69 Antonio Barbieri	1974-75 Salvatore A. Scrivano
1969-70 Antonio Barbieri	1975-76 Antonio Barbieri
1970-71 Joseph P. Tiroletto	1976-77 Dominic J. Verizzi
1971-72 Joseph P. Tiroletto	

ENFIELD DETACHMENT, MARINE CORPS LEAGUE
(Post was organized in 1966)

Past Commanders:

1966-67 Armand Casarella	1971-72 Gilman Soucie
(First Comdr.)	1972-73 Alex Bellefleur
1967-68 Armand Casarella	1973-74 Charles Armstrong
1968-69 Eugene Medeiros	1974-75 Charles Armstrong
1969-70 Joseph Cullen	1975-76 Daniel Clark, Jr.
1970-71 Joseph Cullen	1976-77 Daniel Clark, Jr.

HAZARDVILLE STATION POST, 10219,
VETERANS OF FOREIGN WARS
(Post was organized in February 1971)

Past Commanders:

1971 John Croll	1973-74 Loren Owens
(First Comdr.)	1974-75 Antonio Neves, Jr.
1971-72 Harry Young	1975-76 John Shlatz
1972-73 Stephen Shlatz	1976-77 Robert Behrendt

the
transition
years | **3**

Symbols of change . . . Hazard
Avenue cloverleaf and the sign of
an old business threatened by
urban renewal

CHAPTER 11

ENFIELD: ALL-AMERICA CITY

H AVE YOU HEARD What's Happened to Enfield?" So read a ques-
tion on the cover of the April, 1975, issue of *Country Journal*. Four short
years earlier, the same question was on the lips of Enfield's own citizens, asked with pride, with wonderment, even with overtones of
skepticism.

The skepticism came from the "old guard" die-hards who had been
"satisfied with things the way they've always been." Wonderment
sounded in the voices of some who had not cared too much one way or
the other what had been going on. But joy and pride filled the hearts
and voices of the citizens who had seen in Enfield a greater potential
than being the town "on the wrong side of the river."

The answer to the question, of course, was that Enfield had been
selected an All-America City for 1970. In an annual competition co-
sponsored by the National Municipal League and Look Magazine,
Enfield was one of eleven communities presented with the coveted
award.

The National Municipal League, a non-partisan organization founded in 1894 to promote good government, has sponsored the All-America Cities competition for twenty-three years. The competition has for its purpose the encouragement of communities to solve their problems and the recognition of citizen participation in which "representative groups of citizens and public officials work together to build more whole communities."

Indeed Enfield could qualify for the need to be made "more whole." It had mushroomed from a country town of 15,000 in the nineteen fifties to a burgeoning small city approaching 50,000 in 1970. The growth, chaotic because of lack of planning, brought with it the need for services not provided by a town government which had been acquainted only with small-town needs and small-town politics. As might be expected, the situation presented a crisis to the "new people" who had taken advantage of an unrestricted building boom to buy low-cost housing in the community which was a bedroom town for workers in nearby larger cities.

In the face of opposition from the established powers, it remained for Enfield's new residents to fight the apathy which left them without sewers for their new homes, with old and crowded schools for their children, with no social service programs, with no inducement for industrial or commercial development which would lower their tax rate. In a speech before the All-America Cities jury on August 2, 1970, the town manager aptly described the reaction of these citizens "Enfield's new young residents, bursting with the enthusiasm born of desperate need, overcame the lethargy and interrupted a course towards disaster."

Pride in the accomplishments of these Enfield citizens was the basis for Jaycee James Baum's nomination of the town in the All-America Cities competition.

The nomination stressed the significant progress in community projects which had been achieved in three general areas:

1. In the field of government reform, the outmoded selectmen town meeting form of government was replaced by a council manager form in 1963.
2. Social and health services were improved by establishment of the Department of Social Services and employment of a director. Some outgrowths of this action were the Mental Health Council, the Neighborhood Center, a Juvenile Review Board, a Drug Advisory Council, the Community Chest United Fund, and an organization of local doctors and citizens to promote health care

3. School building needs were met by construction of ten schools from 1960 to 1970. For the first time in twenty-five years, the town had no school on double sessions.

Sponsors of the All-America Cities Awards cite citizen action and citizen teamwork as the keynote to valid civic improvement, and indeed such action and teamwork have been the outstanding feature of Enfield's achievements since 1960. In 1963, the town's new progressive government made individual involvement a primary aim. Such involvement was made easier by the large number of organization-oriented community leaders willing to assist in developing and promoting programs for improvement.

Important ingredients for the accomplishments of Enfield's "re-makers" were the initiative which spurred action on a local level and the quest for professional advice to assist the efforts of citizens. All of this effort resulted in the transformation of a sleepy rural community set in the midst of tobacco fields into a huge retail center with two malls, two shopping centers, and an industrial park in the making.

Many problems are yet to be solved, some remaining from the "old days," some that are to be expected in any modern urban community. The town manager's speech before the All-America Cities jury characterized Enfield's experiences as "a story of civic accomplishment, an impressive victory in the battle against public apathy in twentieth century suburbia where people are not only proud to live but anxious to be involved."

Here, then, is the secret of the All-America Cities award to Enfield; here is also the assured promise for Enfield's future.

In August, 1970, Town Manager C. Samuel Kissinger presented the case for Enfield before the All-America Cities Awards Jury in Portland, Oregon.

CHAPTER 12

THE BICENTENNIAL CELEBRATION

ENFIELD CHOSE to celebrate the birth of our nation rather than commemorate a revolution. It was the desire to rededicate prayerfully the call to arms of those Enfield soldiers who marched off to fight in the Revolutionary War to help our nation become free and independent. It was also intended to celebrate joyfully the courage, strength, and vision of our forefathers as they formed a new nation based on the principles of self-determination, democracy, and freedom for all.

The ravages of war were not felt in Enfield, but the citizens contributed much to the formation of the new nation. During the Bicentennial the people of Enfield sincerely renewed the meanings of freedom and democracy as they rededicated themselves to the values, goals, and principles upon which this country was founded. It was the common wish to maintain the spirit of "The American Dream" for which ethnic, religious, and other groups came to these shores.

the beginning

Under the auspices of the Enfield Historical Society a meeting was held on October 22, 1973, at which Charles R. Clulee from the Bicentennial Commission of Connecticut spoke on "Planning for Our Nation's Bicentennial." Although the meeting was poorly attended, town officials were impressed with the importance of the forthcoming celebration and later requested the Enfield Historical Society to assume responsibility for the entire project. Subsequently the Town Council appointed Anthony S. Secondo as General Chairman and authorized him to select a committee to assist in planning a suitable celebration for the Town.

In order that the Town of Enfield be designated as a Bicentennial Community by the U.S. American Revolution Bicentennial Administration, it was necessary to prepare and file various applications with that agency. The proposed projects and activities listed were those planned by the Enfield Historical Society as well as anticipated projects and activities. It was planned that they would be available to and involve the schools and business community, as well as civic, ethnic, and religious organizations. It was also promised that:

1. The list of projects and activities would contain some permanent programs.

2. Periodic progress reports would be sent to State and National Bicentennial Commissions.

3. The National Bicentennial Symbol would be used in accordance with the prescribed guidelines, and

Enfield's Commemorative Bicentennial Medal

4. Congressmen and Representatives serving Enfield would be informed of the application.

On December 20, 1973, the application was approved by the Connecticut Bicentennial Commission and national approval was received on February 26, 1974. The official acceptance took place April 22, 1974, at ceremonies at the State Capitol in Hartford, which were attended by Barbara N. Mankus and Anthony S. Secondo. Later the Town of Enfield received a Certificate of Recognition and an official Bicentennial flag. Both items were subsequently displayed during the Bicentennial period at the Enfield Town Hall and at numerous pageants, fairs, shows, and parades.

organizing for
the celebration

Unfortunately, when the Commission was formed during 1974, the Town of Enfield was faced with many financial demands and there were no "starter" funds. It immediately became evident that financial support would be required if the commission hoped to prepare a suitable Calendar of Events, and that projects and activities would have to be financed through contributions from citizens and various groups.

Many organizations volunteered to assist with contributions and/or fund-raising activities. The first civic group to come forward was the Enfield Rotary Club which donated $500 to be used for funding the striking of a commemorative medal which would be sold to raise money for the Bicentennial Celebration.

Arlene K. Wilcox submitted several sketches for possible use on the medal. The final design was the result of ideas of and contributions of Bicentennial Commission members. The final artwork was completed by Thomas M. Parakilas. The obverse side of the medal depicts "Enfield's Call to Arms," by Captain Thomas Abbey. This event originally occurred on Wednesday, April 20, 1775, in the vicinity of the Old Town Hall. The reverse side of the medal relates Enfield's Bicentennial Celebration to that of Connecticut and the nation. In addition to the medals, the Committee also designed and marketed commemorative plates and glasses. Both items contained designs previously identified with the medal.

The Greater Enfield Chamber of Commerce sponsored "Auction

75" to which many merchants contributed merchandise or services. A portion of the proceeds was donated to the Commission. Many other individuals and organizations subsequently assisted the Commission financially. Unfortunately space limitations make it impossible to mention each.

Having formulated a financial plan, the Commission then drew up and adopted a number of guidelines which provided, among other things, that the celebration would span the period from 1975 through 1976, it would encompass all groups in town, it would not be commercialized, all funds remaining at the conclusion of the Celebration would be used toward the restoration of Enfield's Old Town Hall 1775, and that a special *Bicentennial News Letter* would be written and sent to all interested in following the activities of the celebration.

Once the Bicentennial Celebration was organized volunteers were sought to sponsor and undertake various projects and activities. A brief description of some of the more noteworthy events follows.

the bicentennial celebration events

APRIL 20, 1975, REENACTMENT

The "shot heard round the world" echoed here two hundred years later as Enfield inaugurated the first of its many major celebrations on April 20, 1975. Some five thousand people gathered to witness this spectacular event. The event was reenacted in the vicinity of the Old Town Hall and the Enfield Congregational Church, as it initially occurred in 1775.

The historic area resembled a colonial village of 1775 complete with authentically dressed minutemen, townspeople, horses and horse-drawn carriages. All participants dressed much as they did two hundred years ago. Women wore long cotton dresses and white caps, while men walked around dressed in knickers, muslin shirts, and tricornered hats.

The event included excerpts from an original colonial sermon of 1777. The service, filled to capacity, featured music of that period played on an original cello used in the church in 1875. Before and after the simple church service the 6th Massachusetts Minutemen and the Spirit of '76 Fife and Drums entertained with music and volleys of musket-fire.

Enfield's "Call to Arms" following the battles of

As onlookers cheered, a post rider rode by, depicting the post rider of 1775 who alerted the citizens of the attack on Boston. Thanks to him Enfield's own company of minutemen gathered to depart for Boston to join the Revolutionary War. During the day's events, the recently reconstructed Abbey Memorial was rededicated. The program also included a colonial dinner and demonstration of colonial style dancing. (See also Enfield Company of Minutemen)

COLONIAL PARADE, MUSTER, BATTLE

The Redcoats came to Enfield on June 27, 1976, met the local militia unit and were defeated before a crowd at the Enfield High School. The ceremonial mock battle followed a brief parade to the school athletic fields. The event included the Enfield Company of Minutemen and similar colorful units from throughout the area.

Lexington and Concord was reenacted on April 20, 1975.

The event followed a five mile marathon which had taken place in the morning. Months of preparation went into this effort. The audience included twenty Europeans who visited Enfield for firsthand accounts of our nation's celebration. Muskets and cannon roared as the Colonists defeated the British. (See also Enfield Company of Minutemen)

ENFIELD COMPANY OF MINUTEMEN

Perhaps no other Enfield group involved with the Bicentennial was as active as the Enfield Company of Minutemen. This group was organized on March 19, 1975, its immediate purpose being the Bicentennial Reenactment of "Enfield's Call To Arms" which took place on April 20, 1975. The long range objective was for the group to appear at various functions in commemoration of the Bicentennial.

Enfield Company of Minutemen was reorganized on March 19, 1975 and officially reactivated for the Bicentennial on July 31 by Governor Ella T. Grasso.

The unit appeared dressed and accoutered as colonial civilian farmers and shopkeepers of 1775. They were equipped with various arms commonly used by the local militia of colonial times.

In an effort to be as authentic as their 1775 counterparts, a subcommittee was formed to research and design a colonial drum as conceivably used by Captain Thomas Abbey in 1775. The drum committee chaired by Harold A. Staples arranged to have the drum custom-made by Mr. Robert Atwell, a respected craftsman from Durham, Connecticut. Artist Robert A. Smith of Enfield, was commissioned to decorate the drum complete with a unicorn. The drum was made possible by the financial assistance of the Patrick F. Triggs Post 1501 V.F.W. Drum Corp. Association. The attractive drum became an important part of the stirring music played by the fife and drum section of the militia unit. After the Bicentennial celebrations, the drum will become part of the special Historical Society Bicentennial Display being planned for the Old Town Hall Museum.

On April 20, 1975, and on many subsequent appearances, the group created an amazingly accurate portrayal of Enfield's own Militia of 1775. Enfield's Company of Minutemen was officially reactivated for

Bicentennial purposes on July 31, 1975, by her Excellency the Governor of Connecticut, Ella T. Grasso. During the 1975-1976 period the unit appeared in approximately fifty parades, musters, mock battles, scout and civic programs throughout the New England area. Of particular importance was the singular honor of being invited to participate as an honor guard unit for the visit of Queen Elizabeth II during her visit to Boston, Massachusetts, in July, 1976.

Although Bicentennial activity has somewhat subsided, the Enfield Militia Unit has voted to continue indefinitely with the goal of participating in Enfield's 300th Anniversary in 1980.

FERMI "76" COMMITTEE

Spearheaded by Social Studies teacher Dr. Franklin S. Gross, a multifaceted program called "Fermi 76" was developed at the Enrico Fermi High School. Perhaps the earliest school to develop Bicentennial programs in the country, it achieved state and national recognition for the extent and content of its observance.

In the planning stages since 1972, the program included the planting of a heritage garden, pageants, fairs, trips to historic points of interest, fashion shows, and studies of Enfield's past. A number of interested teacher advisors and students assisted Dr. Gross. Unfortunately, space does not permit the listing of all names.

GRAND BICENTENNIAL PARADE

Perhaps the most impressive event of the Bicentennial period was the parade held on April 24, 1976. People began lining Enfield Street as early as 9:00 A.M. in order to assure themselves a good view of the parade which was scheduled to start at 1:00 P.M. Enfield's parade was

Enfield Minuteman drum was based on this artist's sketch derived from drum at base of Captain Thomas Abbey Memorial.

Enfield Students painted Bicentennial murals.

the first Bicentennial parade in Connecticut and attracted so much attention that thousands of people arrived early equipped with lawn chairs. As parade time drew nearer it appeared that all roads led to Enfield.

Stirring music was provided by twenty-two drum and bugle and fife and drum units. Included were all of the local school bands, the Centurians, and the Enfield Sabers Drum and Bugle Corps. Many out-of-town musical units were also invited, including the well-known McGuire Air Force Band from New Jersey. A highlight of the parade was the appearance and performance by the Enfield Company of Minutemen. It was during this parade that the unit's flintlocks were fired for the first time in public as they marched to the shrill sound of their fife and drum unit.

Providing much color and beauty were the forty-one floats which were spaced throughout the parade. The first float to appear was the Bicentennial Commission float with an oversized drum depicting the drum used by Captain Abbey to alert local citizens in 1775. Many organizations, schools, and businesses entered floats.

Approximately 4,500 participants paraded on Enfield Street, starting in front of the Old Town Hall and terminating at the modern day Town Hall, a distance of slightly less than two miles. It was difficult to estimate the number of people who witnessed the parade, it being reliably estimated that approximately fifty thousand to sixty thousand came to the parade in about twelve thousand vehicles. In spite of these numbers, the police were able to prevent confusion and disperse the crowd in smooth continuity.

Awards were made for excellence of floats. The Grand Prize for the Best Float in the parade was awarded Lego Systems.

RESTORATION OF OLD TOWN HALL 1775 MEETING HOUSE

A challenging project of the Bicentennial planning involved the restoration of Enfield's Old Meeting House, commonly referred to as the Old Town Hall 1775. This venerable former church played an important part in "Enfield's Call To Arms" in 1775. Captain Thomas Abbey, a veteran of the French and Indian Wars, had received the post rider's message concerning the skirmishes at Lexington and Concord. He marched around the local meeting house with his drum, thus alerting the congregation of the news. In response to this alert, seventy-four Enfield militiamen, led by Captain Abbey, marched to the defense of Boston.

From 1849 through the early 1950s the Meeting House was used continuously as the seat of Enfield's Town Government and more recently as a community center. The building was declared unsafe in the 1950s and it was most appropriate that this important part of our past be spared from demolition. Sparked by a revived interest in our historic past, in 1973 the Enfield Historical Society formed the present Restoration Committee with Chairman Robert L. Tanguay and Vice Chairman, Anthony S. Secondo. One of the first steps taken by the committee was to file an application to have the building included in

the National Register of Historic Places. The request was granted in September, 1974, and the almost impossible task of restoring the Old Meeting House for eventual use as a historical museum and meeting hall was begun.

Although not available for public occupancy, the building was restored sufficiently to be the scene of several events during the Bicentennial period. Perhaps most noteworthy of these events was the April 20, 1975, reenactment of "Enfield's Call To Arms." Other Bicentennial events which occurred in the vicinity of the Old Town Hall were the Colonial Parade and Mock Battle on June 27, 1976, and the Time Capsule Ceremony of July 3, 1976. The Grand Bicentennial Parade of April 24, 1976, began in front of the Old Town Hall.

Much credit for the restoration progress to date is due many Enfield citizens and organizations for their contributions to the Restoration Fund. To date, the foundation, first floor, and windows have been replaced. In addition the front of the building was completely painted. Hopefully, the building will be completed and in use for Enfield's 300th Anniversary in 1980.

TIME CAPSULE CEREMONY

How will Enfield residents celebrate in the year 2076? What will they think of our 1976 celebration?

During the spring of 1976 Enfield residents were given an opportunity to donate items to place in a capsule which will be opened during our nation's 300th anniversary. Items donated included many articles in daily use today such as telephones, plastic items, newspapers, Enfield Bicentennial commemorative items, and many other articles.

The capsule measured 3' x 6' and was donated by the Greater Enfield Chamber of Commerce. A suitable ceremony took place on July 3, 1976, which climaxed a Student Fund Drive for the Old Town Hall and served to highlight the interment of the time capsule. The capsule now rests at the immediate front of the Old Town Hall with instructions to our Town Fathers that it be opened during the year 2076.

· OTHER IMPORTANT EVENTS

The memorial honoring Captain Thomas Abbey, Enfield's Revolutionary War hero, received much attention during the 1975-1976 period. The weather beaten marble pedestal that supported Captain Abbey's statue, erected in 1916, was replaced and made ready for a rededication ceremony on April 20, 1975.

Aerial view of the Grand
Bicentennial Parade with Town
Hall in foreground.

Float sponsored by Lego Systems won "Best of Parade" award.

A project undertaken by Raymond C. Abbe was the publication of a book *Extracts from the Memorial of Captain Thomas Abbey.* The book contains interesting historical information concerning Captain Abbey, the Memorial, and Enfield families.

Oldsters recalled the good old days and youngsters tried to figure out what made these contraptions run during the Antique Auto Tour and Show staged on August 15, 1976. Antique car owners toured the Martha A. Parsons Home prior to a trip to the Weymouth Road Fire Station Training Grounds. At the field, about seventy antique cars were on display while owners enjoyed a buffet lunch in the picnic area.

Members of the Somers Antique Bottle Club sponsored an Antique Bottle Show on February 23, 1975, and February 24, 1976. Both shows featured glass and related items from our historical past. Antique bottles, electrical insulators, and special Beam and Avon bottles were available in abundance.

Members of the Artists Guild painted beautiful tour markers used to denote each of the homes and buildings included in the Historic Home Tour of May 9, 1976. The Guild was also responsible for painting a large sign which was attached to the rooftop of the Daniel Libby barn on South Road. The sign depicted the Abbey drum with the theme Enfield: 1776-1976.

On March 26 and 27, 1976, the Enfield Square Shopping Complex was the scene of the Bicentennial Art Exhibit sponsored by the Tobacco Valley Artists Association. Works of art were displayed in an attractive colonial setting and exhibited in the center court were scenes of historical significance.

A concert was presented May 22, 1976, at the J.F. Kennedy Jr. High School. The program was narrated by former Enfield resident Brad Davis of WFSB TV. The concert included musical selections of the past two hundred years. Approximately 100 participants from ages eighteen to eighty took the audience back in time to the tunes that recalled our American heritage and historic events.

One of the earliest groups to support the Commission was the Enfield Jaycee Wives. This group enthusiastically and expeditiously published a Bicentennial Cookbook containing recipes contributed by local citizens. Approximately one thousand books were published, released for sale in April, 1975, and sold out by December, 1975. All proceeds from the sale of the books were donated to the Commission for general use.

In an effort to inform and involve people and organizations with the Bicentennial, special newsletters were mailed approximately every six weeks starting in January, 1975. Included in the

Time Capsule Ceremony on July 3, 1976 took place at Old Meeting House.

newsletters was information concerning scheduled activities and projects, participating and contributing organizations, and activities available for interested groups.

An interesting example of colonial type handiwork was the preparation of a Bicentennial Quilt made by a group known as the Quilting Bees of Enfield. Members of the group prepared detailed symbols and pictures associated with American history. The quilt was displayed at various events during the celebration. On April 26, 1976, the Quilt was presented to the Enfield Historical Society for display at the Society's museum expected to be completed in the near future.

With renewed interest in Enfield's past history, many citizens recognized the lack of historical books and manuscripts pertaining to Enfield. James Johnston, an employee of the Enfield Public Library System, assumed responsibility for the collection of rare books, letters, manuscripts, and photographs of Enfield's past. Many citizens loaned or donated material which will be housed in a special display case. All printed material was added to a book catalog which serves as the collection's index.

The Enfield Historic Marker was made available to the town by the Connecticut Historic Commission. Made of heavy cast aluminum and mounted between two posts, the marker describes the circumstances of the founding and significant events of early Enfield History.

Recognizing the plight of the fundless Bicentennial Commission, the Junior Woman's Club raised funds in April, 1975, for general use by the Commission. Another challenging endeavor was the community improvement project involving the beautification of Powder Hollow Park. Other projects involved the beautification of a Vietnam War Memorial erected by their group in the recreation area, located at the intersection of School Street and Hazard Avenue, and purchase of Bicentennial Series History Books for all town libraries. In addition about fifty members assisted in preparing a float entry for the Grand Bicentennial Parade.

The Enfield Lions Club rate high for their total involvement with the Bicentennial. On November 16, 1975, the Lions staged a Pancake Festival for the benefit of the Commission. On June 27, 1976, a massive Colonial Parade, Muster, Battle and Five Mile Marathon was staged in cooperation with the Enfield Congregational Church, Enfield Company of Minutemen and the Bicentennial Commission.

Perhaps the most significant affair sponsored by the Lions Club was the Grand Bicentennial Ball. This event took place at the Enfield Armory on October 30, 1976. More than two hundred persons attended the event. Many of those attending wore colonial costumes, complete with long haired white wigs.

Chairman Lou Wry with painting of Congregational Church at Bicentennial Art Exhibit.

On behalf of local business, the Chamber of Commerce assisted with several activities during the celebration. Auction "75" was a project to raise funds for the town's Bicentennial effort. The Auction featured new merchandise and services donated by area businessmen to be auctioned off on November 14, 1975, at the Red Coach Inn in Windsor Locks. The Chamber of Commerce also assisted the Commission with organization and awards for the Grand Bicentennial Parade of April 24, 1976. In March, 1977, an announcement was made of a substantial contribution by the Chamber to the Old Town Hall Restoration Committee for the purchase of display cases.

Early 19th century homes and buildings were included in a Historical Tour, conducted by the Women's Club of Enfield on May 11, 1976. Homes and buildings were identified by a specially prepared drum emblem painted by the Artists Guild. A special luncheon was served at the St. Joseph's Residence.

In addition to the Historical Tour, the Woman's Club of Enfield has also assisted by underwriting the publication of this book, agreeing to purchase approximately 285 books for use by the Enfield Public School System.

Asnuntuck Community College was the scene of a Folk Festival co-sponsored by the Enfield Jewish League and the YWCA Suburban Women's Club. The event took place on October 23, 1976. Various ethnic singers and dancers performed in a festival atmosphere surrounded by tables of ethnic foods.

The Order of DeMolay, under the direction of Advisor Leroy A. Strout, and Master Councillors David Hallis and Richard Marks, assisted by sponsoring two activities.

"One Flag from Many" a story about the evolution of the flag was presented on June 14, 1976, at the St. Joseph's Residence by members of DeMolay. The 1976 DeMolay Decathlon took place on September 25, 1976, at Kosciuszko Junior High School. The event, open to DeMolay Chapters in the area, was won by the local Pinemeadow Chapter, Order of DeMolay.

Economic conditions and the ravages of time had affected the downtown Thompsonville area. During the 1970s most of the area buildings were scheduled for demolition and redevelopment. It was in this area that Enfield's early commercial development was concentrated. In an effort to record this segment of Enfield's history, Bruce Oliver, assisted by his mother, Elizabeth W. Oliver, undertook the project of extensively photographing all of the redevelopment area prior to demolition of the buildings. This effort will insure the availability of material for future scholars.

The Martha A. Parsons House was built by John Meacham in 1782. The home has particularly good paneling and distinctive decoration. In 1800 the home was purchased by a Captain John Ingraham of Saybrook. Captain Ingraham showed his patriotism by having Washington memorial wallpaper placed on the walls of the main hall. It is believed this wallpaper remains on only one other home in Bennington, Vermont.

The home was willed to the Enfield Historical Society in 1963. During the Bicentennial period, the home underwent sufficient restoration to be included in the Bicentennial Historical Tour on May 11, 1976, and also the Antique Auto Tour of August 15, 1976. When completely restored the home is expected to be opened to the public on a continual basis.

In a progam sponsored by the Bicentennial Commission of Connecticut local town commissions were asked to submit names of citizens who met the ideals established. At an appropriate ceremony held on June 25, 1976, at the State Capitol, former Enfield Mayor Frank Mancuso was one of the ninety-six foreign-born honored as a "20th Century Pilgrim." During the town's Community Celebration on July 4, 1976, Enfield's Commission presented Frank and his wife Eunice awards on behalf of the citizens of Enfield.

in conclusion

Space limitations have prevented the naming of each person and group who worked in the name of the Enfield Bicentennial Commission. Participants were recognized in a variety of ways and energies expended were sincerely appreciated. Hopefully, the reward was the joy of serving Enfield during our nation's time of festivity and celebration.

Enfield prepared for and was ready for the celebration. The curtains were parted to show a full display of all the wonders of personal interchange and human warmth, of all the feelings of rededication and patriotism, of all the appreciation for freedom, responsibility, and democracy that are ours today as we have rejoiced and honored this great land of ours.

Peter Russell taps out a
Revolutionary rhythm on the
lawn of the 1763 Field House
to the delight of Lauree and
Sherree Nuccio.

Traveling "Indians" from Huntington, Long Island, visited Enfield "natives" on June 26, 1976.

ENFIELD BICENTENNIAL CELEBRATION

Executive Board

Anthony S. Secondo, Chairman
Edward C. Allen, Vice Chairman
Mona O. Piotrowski, Secretary
William L. Hunt, Treasurer

Andler L. Alexander
Michael C. Blaney
Ruth E. Bridge
Joseph Cimino
James G. Johnston
John C. Kinnear
F. Russell Meyer

Elizabeth W. Oliver
Mary B. O'Neil
Marie E. Ravenola
James F. Reveruzzi
Eileen J. Russell
Rose G. Sokol
Robert L. Tanguay
Robert B. Watton

Bicentennial Events
1974-1976

DATE	EVENT	SPONSOR
1974		
May 19	Fermi "76" Heritage Fair	
June 1	Flag Display	St. Martha's Church
November 25	Fermi "76" School Workshop	
December 14-15	Pancake Feast	Kiwanis Club
1975		
February 23	Bottle Show	Somers Bottle Club
February 24	Songs of the Revolution	Historical Society
April 20	Reenactment "Enfield's Call to Arms"	
May 4	Fermi "76" Heritage Fair	
June 7	Flag Display	St. Martha's Church
June 13	Fermi High School Band	Washington D.C. Performance
June 14	Strawberry Festival	Calvary Presbyterian Church
July 4	Community Celebration	Jaycees
October 8	Kodak Movie "Profiles '76"	
November 14	Auction '75 Dinner Dance	Chamber of Commerce
November 16	Pancake Festival	Lions Club
1976		
February 12	Bottle Show	Somers Bottle Club
March 26-27	Art Exhibit	Tobacco Valley Artists
April 3	Jonathan Edwards Sermon	First Baptist Church
April 24	Bicentennial Parade	Veterans Council/ Chamber of Commerce
April 26	Bicentennial Quilt Presentation	Quilting Bees
May 8	Combined Schools Heritage Fair	
May 11	Historical Tour	Womens Club
May 22	Bicentennial Concert	
June 14	Evolution of the Flag	Order of DeMolay
June 16	Charter Oak Seedling Planting	Martha A. Parsons Home
June 22- July 7	International Visitors	
June 25	20th Century Award to Frank Mancuso	
June 26	Visit from Huntington, N.Y. Indians	
June 26	Community Fireworks	Enfield Square
June 27	Marathon	Lions Club
	Colonial Parade and Muster	Enfield Minutemen
July 3	Time Capsule Ceremony	Historical Society
July 4	Jonathan Edwards Sermon	Living Waters
	Community Celebration	Jaycees
July 11	Minutemen reviewed by the Queen of England at Boston	
August 15	Antique Auto Tour	
September 25	Decathlon	Order of DeMolay

October 23	Folk Festival	Jewish League/
		Suburban Women
October 30	Bicentennial Ball	Lions Club
1977		
May	Historic Marker Dedication	
June	Publication of history:	
	Challenge of Change	

BICENTENNIAL COMMITTEES

The Commemorative Committee
John C. Kinnear, *Chairman;* Andler L. Alexander, Edward C. Allen, Lawrence W. Blanchard, Lucy Caracoglia, William L. Hunt, Robert W. King, Dr. Gus J. Pappas, Thomas M. Parakilas, Mona O. Piotrowski, Anthony S. Secondo, Rose G. Sokol, Alan K. Tracy, Robert L. Tanguay, Arlene K. Wilcox

April 20, 1975 Reenactment

Enfield Congregational Church Service
Rev. Robert C. Lane, Deacon William Harmon, David Wilber, *Cello Player;* F. Russell Meyer, *Coordinator*

Abbey Memorial Rededication
Rev. Robert C. Lane, Raymond C. Abbe

"Enfield's Call to Arms"
Frank Gawle, *Director;* Gerald J. Mon, *Narrator;* Dale H. Hewey, *Post Rider;* Steven Wilcox, *Capt. Abbey;* Andler L. Alexander, Edward C. Allen, Anthony S. Secondo

Enfield Company of Minutemen
Andler L. Alexander, *Chairman*

Fermi "76" Committee
Dr. Franklin S. Gross, *Chairman*

Grand Bicentennial Parade
Robert B. Watton, *Grand Marshall;* Marcel St. Saveur and Anthony S. Secondo *Co-Chairmen*

Restoration of the Old Town Hall 1775 Meeting House
Robert L. Tanguay, *Chairman;* Anthony S. Secondo, *Vice Chairman;* William Budlong, Thomas V. Hines, James W. Sherman, Robert J. Tanguay, Henry Turbak

Time Capsule Ceremony
Robert L. Tanguay, *Chairman;* Virginia D'Agostino, Phyllis L. Tanguay, Barbara Landry

Abbey Memorial
Raymond C. Abbe, *Chairman*

Antique Bottle Show
Ted Koneski and Robert Sokol, *Co-Chairman*

Artists Guild of Enfield
Grace M. Dignam, *Advisor;* Steve Blanchard, Linda Buvarsky, Richard Hickson, Richard Lynes, James Sacheli

Bicentennial Art Exhibit
Mrs. Lou Wry, *Chairman*

Bicentennial Concert
Mrs. Alice Allen, *Chairman;* Joyce Young, *Vice Chairman*

Bicentennial Cookbook
Mrs. Sylvia H. Foster, *Chairman;* Mrs. William Bolinder, Mrs. William Carlson, Mrs. David Cheney, Mrs. Joel DeNigris, Mrs. Gary Gibson, Mrs. Donald Leis, Mrs. Jack Lindgren, Mrs. Robert Moores, Mrs. Thomas Olyneiw, Mrs. Anthony Rezoski, Mrs. Charles Sharp, Mrs. Nancy Thompson, Mrs. Alfred Walker, Miss Lucy Caracoglia

Bicentennial Newsletter, Publicity, Photography
Rose G. Sokol, *Chairman*

Bicentennial Quilt
Ann Smyth, *Chairman;* Margaret Aidukonis, Nellie Bernier, Thelma Derochick, Jo Fergerson, Isabelle Furey, Eleanor Hayden, Doris LaJoie, Anna Peitier, Mae Pelkey, Catherine Peters, Mildred Washer

Enfield Centennial Library Collection
Jay Johnston, *Chairman*

Enfield Historic Marker
Anthony S. Secondo, *Chairman;* Gail Sanford Abbe, *Author of text*

Enfield Junior Women's Club
Mrs. Betty Ann Reilly, *Co-Chairman;* Mrs. Joann Tait, *Co-Chairman;* Mrs. Pat Caputo, Mrs. Pat Nelson, Mrs. Marie Ravenola

Enfield Lions Club
Committee Chairmen: John Carey, Joseph Cimino, Harold Daigneau, Joseph Dreyer, Ralph C. Fiore, Francis Lutwinas, Joseph Morris, Ben Pallota, John A. Reveruzzi, David Rochan, Robert Vezina

Greater Enfield Chamber of Commerce
Auction "75" Committee
Dexter S. Burnham, *Co-Chairman;* Robert E. Kemp, *Co-Chairman;* Marcel St. Sauveur, *Executive Director;* Francis A. Burke, Jr., *Master of Ceremonies;* Emmet Gemme, *Auctioneer*

Lasting Gifts Committee
Richard Stevens, Jr., *Chairman;* Charles Alaimo, Francis Burke, Jr., Teri Leonaitis

Historical Tour

Mrs. Peter J. Russell and Mrs. Thomas R. Smyth, *Co-Chairmen;* Mrs. Charles Boudreau, Mrs. Ralph Cerrato, Mrs. Wallace A. Faber, Mrs. Francis Gaudet, Mrs. John Haznar, Mrs. Henry Julian, Mrs. Arthur Keller, Mrs. John Koseian, Mrs. Michael Panella, Mrs. Leo Porcello, Mrs. William Rasmussen, Mrs. John Reveruzzi, Mrs. James A. Tatoian, Mrs. John A. Trappe, Mrs. Anthony Troiano, Jr., Mrs. James Viola

International Folk Festival

Lester H. Kahn and Susan Cihocki, *Co-Chairmen*

Order of DeMolay

Leroy A. Strout, *Chairman;* David Hallis, Richard Marks

Research of Freshwater Pond Redevelopment Area

Elizabeth W. Oliver and Bruce Oliver, *Co-Chairmen*

Restoration of Martha A. Parsons Home

Arlene K. Wilcox, *Chairman;* Ruth E. Bridge, Barbara N. Mankus, Normand Prior, James W. Sherman, Alice Simpson, Henry Turbak

Enfield
Today

. . .a
photographic
portfolio

"Enfield today is truly a city
. . . but a city of many faces."

I-91 and the Regional Shopping Complex.

The Hallmark Cards complex and Wallace Manufacturing on Manning Road.

"From I-91 it is the Regional Shopping Complex with G. Fox dominant and all the implied linear sprawl of shopping centers, industrial parks, and inevitable signs of the growth which begets more growth . . ."

Enfield Square from within.

Eli Lilly and Co. on Freshwater Boulevard.

Proposed housing in Thompsonville Redevelopment Area.

The people speak as the Town Council listens.

Interior of Central Library, Middle Road.

"But it is also a city of homes and people . . . and of people's concern with decisions that govern their community's future and the needs of their neighbors."

Simon Road homes . . . typical of Enfield's newer houses.

Cardio-alert unit . . . a first.

Enfield senior citizens follow the geese on local park trip.

Community improvement project . . . Junior Woman's Club.

" . . . a city in which personal interests follow many paths . . . at work, at play, and in the patterns of daily living."

Bread for Enfield . . . from brick ovens.

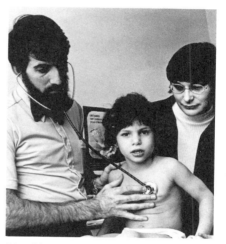

Monthly clinic . . . Visiting Nurse Association.

Rehearsal time for local thespians.

" . . . from the joy of youth on an autumn afternoon . . . to a senior citizen's new found skill . . . or a peaceful interlude with pipe and rod where the shad still run at the Enfield Rapids."

epilogue

*the
challenge
of
change*

CHAPTER 13

THE CHALLENGE OF CHANGE

CHANGE IS perhaps the dominant characteristic of Enfield. Its history spans three centuries of change, adjustment, and growth from a typical frontier colonial settlement to a sprawling melange of farms, businesses, shopping malls, and interstate cloverleafs. Enfield today is truly a city—but a city of many faces.

From I-91 it is the Regional Shopping Complex with G. Fox dominant and all the implied linear sprawl of shopping centers, industrial parks and inevitable signs of the growth which beget more growth. It is also a city of homes and people and of people's concern with the decisions that govern their community's future and the needs of their neighbors. It is a city in which personal interests follow many paths—at work, at play, and in the patterns of daily living—from the joy of youth on an autumn afternoon . . . to a senior citizen's newfound skill . . . or a peaceful interlude with pipe and rod where the shad still run at the Enfield Rapids.

Looking at Enfield today it is difficult to realize the changes which have taken place over the years but they are recorded in the prior sections of this book. Change does not stop, however. It is a continuous process and those who are concerned with what may be in store and how future change can be controlled, must also look to the past. History is wasted unless its lessons are heeded.

To bring this record of Enfield to its logical conclusion—a look at the Enfield of tomorrow—some of the authors who were so deeply involved with writing about the past agreed to tell what changes they foresaw between now and the year 2,000. The observations speak for themselves even when they are in conflict.

Enfield today

"When I was a child in Enfield, then Thompsonville, all the families in each section of the town knew each other well. When we hailed the advent of electricity, what a thrill that was! At that time you never feared being on the streets. We had three or four policemen (whom we knew) and the Chief, but crime was unknown. However, as Enfield grew so suddenly after being in a static state for so long, we no longer knew our townspeople. Crime infiltrated our streets, journals and newspapers changed from chatty town news to reporting delinquency and vandalism. With growth, here as elsewhere, respect for authority of any kind grew less and less."

"Enfield is no longer a small town. I feel that there is a neighborliness within the different community areas but the former feeling of knowing everyone in town is gone. It is primarily a bedroom town and the majority of people commute to Hartford to earn their living. In many cases husbands and wives both work to meet the increasing needs and desires of their families so there is little time for fraternizing. It is not that people are unfriendly but each tends to his own business. However, in times of need the neighborhood is always there ready to help."

"The town is not without its problems. Traffic congestion, burglarizing, destruction of property, ecological problems, high living costs, increasing tax loads, and other difficulties complicate life here, just as they do elsewhere."

"Perhaps a more appropriate name for Enfield than the 'All America City' would be the 'Mall City.' Malls have taken over and the patronage of Massachusetts and local Connecticut residents helps them to prosper. Although the individual businesses carried on in the malls have not always been successful and there is a constant change of tenants, they do help the town treasury. This is important because many small stores have failed and agriculture no longer thrives as in the old days, hence many new and varied businesses are needed to help provide services and support the tax needs of the city."

"In spite of the fact that Enfield is a bedroom town, there seems to be quite a bit of civic pride here which I think will increase with time as the inhabitants become more involved in local functions and as the town becomes more a part of their life. In fact, it has been my observation that many of the newcomers show more enthusiasm for, and are involved in more of the town functions than some of the old-timers who have lived here all their lives and view any and all changes in the town as bad. It is these newcomers who have changed the face of the town in recent years and who will influence its future to a great extent."

Enfield in the year 2000

"In the year 2000 I see Enfield becoming more aware of its human resources. I believe a change in government is inevitable. Enfield will finally be recognized as a *city* that does contribute significantly to Connecticut's economy. Enfield has been pushed into the background for too many years by the state government in Hartford. No longer will we be the "hick" town up there to the north, to be used by state government for their social misfits."

further development

"The town grew so fast during the last thirty-five years that the momentum will continue. The basic needs will remain the same but enlargement of facilities and expansion will continue until most of the open space is filled. Farms will be a rarity."

"I cannot conceive of an Enfield that is completely built up by the year 2000. Certainly the face of it will change and with good planning, hopefully for the better. There will be more re-development giving opportunity for changes which will improve the town, and with more time for leisure and recreation, there appears to be more interest in preserving land for open space."

open space

"With shorter working hours giving added time for leisure and recreation, there appears to be more interest in preserving land for open space. Land used for agriculture provides open space more economically than any other method and will continue to supply land for this purpose as long as the economic climate is right for profitable farming."

"There has been interest in developing the Powder Hollow and adjoining Scantic River lands into a state park. While this project has been shelved for the present because of current state fiscal austerity, I would expect that if the economy improves the development would be reconsidered. Another possibility is that the town could develop this land on its own."

population growth

"The end of the baby boom has already closed some schools and a continuation of this trend will probably slow the city's growth. Housing starts have diminished during the last few years and a lower birth rate will probably discourage home building."

"I look to a tapering off to a much slower rate of growth for Enfield. When the city planners first began their work they projected the ultimate population of the town at about eighty thousand and I would predict that by the year 2000 we might reach that figure, but I doubt if we shall top it."

shopping malls

"I do not envision Enfield as becoming the 'Shopping Center of the East.' I realize that situated as we are between Hartford and Springfield and beside I-91, we enjoy a most fortunate situation for drawing trade from a large area. However, the market is not limitless as recent events have shown. The Enfield Mall has already declared bankruptcy and there are still many empty shops there. The First National store moved out, the A and P supermarket in Scitico closed and still has not been replaced. As population increases the market situation will improve but it has been amply shown that the market can easily become saturated to the detriment of all concerned. As always, the law of the survival of the fittest will prevail and the most efficient businesses will win out. I doubt that there will be any great additional expansion of shopping centers here in the future. I would expect, instead, that the area of greatest development in Enfield in the next twenty-five years would be in the area of industry, mostly light— and of all types."

"The next five years will see the continued growth and diversification of Enfield's industrial base, making substantial progress in the cycle of a community dominated by one industry to one with a broad spectrum of growing industrial firms."*

planning objectives

"The main thrust of our efforts will be in two areas where we have inherent natural advantages for industrial development. First would be the continued development of the industrial area along Interstate Route 91 which would obviously include the Enfield Memorial Industrial Park. The second area would be in the eastern section of town along the Highland Spur Line. The first offers immediate access to the interstate highway network, and, in many cases, offers interstate visibility. In the latter case, there seems to be a general resurgence of rail use.

"If we continue to work with and be cognizant of the needs of our existing industry, plus continue our efforts to make Enfield attractive to new firms, 1982 should show a marked change from our prior image of a bedroom community."*

* Source: Town Planners

cultural and
recreational concerns

"I foresee that as our new developments become old ones and the families become more settled and a part of the city, we shall see more genuine interest in cultural activities such as music, theater, and the arts, with the result that Enfield will develop cultural facilities of its own and be less dependent on Hartford or Springfield."

"I hope we will have top technical and cultural educational facilities. My great hope is that just a small portion of the Shaker community can be preserved. We have made fabulous headway in making local people aware of our heritage and I hope to see our Old Town Hall as a fine museum."

"By the year 2000 a four-year college may be using one of the vacated high school buildings. The schools in outlying sections which inevitably will be closed could become neighborhood centers run by local groups of citizens."

"A few small parks could be provided for the benefit of small children in areas where the population is greatest and the houses close together. These would be the responsibility of local residents."

Throughout the prophecies runs a strong current of optimism and belief in the potential of Enfield and its fine people. "In the end the future of Enfield lies in the hopes and dreams of its citizens. Whatever they want it to become—and are willing to work for—it will be."

This, then, is the real meaning of the Challenge of Change.

appendices

BIBLIOGRAPHY

CHAPTER 1

Bulletin of the Archeological Society of Connecticut #18, December, 1945, pp. 1-12.
Howe, Henry F., *Prologue to New England*. New York, Farrar & Rinehart, 1943.
Perry, Charles E., *Founders and Leaders of Connecticut*. Boston, D.C. Heath & Co., 1934.
Stiles, Henry R., *History of Ancient Windsor*. New York, Charles B. Norton, 1859.
Personal Interviews

CHAPTER 2

Allen, Francis Olcott, *History of Enfield, Connecticut*. Lancaster, Penn., Wickersham Printing Co., 1900.
Bauer, Frank, *At the Crossroads - Springfield, Mass. 1636-1975*. Bicentennial Commission of Springfield, 1975.
Earle, Alice Morse, *Home Life in Colonial Days*. New York, Macmillan Co., 1899.
Fennelly, Catherine, *Life in an Old New England Country Village*. New York, Thomas Y. Crowell, 1969.
——————————— *Town Schooling in Early New England*. Sturbridge, Mass., Old Sturbridge, Inc., 1962.
Fletcher, Henry, *Studies in the History of Enfield, Conn*. Litchfield, Conn., Enquirer Press, 1934.
Green, Mason A., *Memorial History of Springfield*. Springfield, Mass., C.A. Nichols & Co., 1888.
Humphrey, Zephine, *A Book of New England*. New York, Howell, Soskin, 1947.
Morison, Samuel Eliot, *The Intellectual Life of Colonial New England*. New York, N.Y. University Press, 1965.
Parsons, Martha A., *Early Architecture and Some Early Homes in Enfield*. Unpublished D.A.R. Papers, 1925.
Peck, Ellen Brainard, *Connecticut's Early Textbooks*. Hartford, Conn., *Connecticut Quarterly*, January, 1898, pp. 61-72.
Sheldon, Franklin, *Nonsense, Common Sense, Incense*. 1926.
Stiles, Henry R., *History of Ancient Windsor*. New York, Charles B. Norton, 1859.
Trumbull, J. Hammond, *Memorial History of Hartford County*. Boston, Edward L. Osgood, 1886.
Tunis, Edwin, *Colonial Living*. New York, World Publishing Co., 1957.
Van Dusen, Albert E., *Connecticut*. New York, Random House, 1961.

CHAPTER 3

Andrews, Edward Deming, *The People Called Shakers*. New York, Dover Publications, Inc., 1953.

Brainard, Jessie Miriam, *Mother Ann's Children in Connecticut*. Connecticut, *Connecticut Quarterly*, October-December, 1897, pp. 461-474.
Melcher, Marguerite Fellows, *The Shaker Adventure*. Cleveland, Ohio, The Press of Case Western Reserve University, 1968.
Case Western Reserve Historical Library, Shaker Collection, Cleveland, Ohio.

CHAPTER 4
Allen, Francis Olcott, *History of Enfield, Connecticut*. Lancaster, Penn., Wickersham Printing Co., 1900.
Connecticut and Tobacco. Washington, D.C., The Tobacco Institute, 1972.
Fletcher, Henry F., *Studies in the History of Enfield, Connecticut*. Litchfield, Conn., Enquirer Press, 1934.
Pease, Isaac. His personal journal and farm account book, 1823-1832.
Trumbull, J. Hammond, Editor, *History of Hartford County*. Boston, Edward L. Osgood, 1886.
Van Dusen, Albert E., *Connecticut*. New York, Random House, 1961.
Various newspaper clippings.
Land Records, Town of Enfield, Conn.
Personal interviews and recollections of the author.

CHAPTER 5
Allen, Francis Olcott, *History of Enfield, Connecticut*. Lancaster, Penn., Wickersham Printing Co., 1900.
Buckley, Helen, *The Polish National Catholic Church*. National Council of Churches of Christ in the U.S., *Outlook*, May, 1958.
Personal interviews.

CHAPTER 6
Allen, Francis Olcott, *History of Enfield, Connecticut*. Lancaster, Penn., Wickersham Printing Co., 1900.
Burpee, Charles W., *History of Connecticut*. New York, American Historical Co., 1939.
Hoyt, Joseph, *The Connecticut Story*. Connecticut, Reader's Press, 1961.
Lee, W. Storrs, *The Yankees of Connecticut*. New York, Holt, Rinehart and Winston, 1957.
Purcell, Richard J., *Connecticut in Transition 1775-1818*. Middletown, Conn., Wesleyan University Press, 1963.
Sanford, Elias, *History of Connecticut*. Hartford, S.S. Scranton & Co., 1889.
Annual Reports, Town of Enfield, Conn.
Tercentenary Commission of the State of Connecticut, Committee on Historical Publications, #17

CHAPTER 7
Allen, Francis Olcott, *History of Enfield, Connecticut*. Lancaster, Penn., Wickersham Printing Co., 1900.
Brainard, Mrs. A.S., *Early Connecticut Schools*. D.A.R. Papers, 1923.
Dennehy, Rev. Thomas J., *Centennial Jottings*, St. Patrick's Church Bulletins during Centennial Year, 1963.
Felician Sisters, *Response*, Felician Centenary Chronicles, pp. 90-96, undated manuscript in bound book form.
Fennelly, Catherine, *Town Schooling in Early New England*. Sturbridge, Mass., Old Sturbridge, Inc., 1962.
Fletcher, Henry, *Sketch of History of Eastern Enfield*. Litchfield, Conn., Enquirer Press, 1934.

Olschafskie, Rev. Frederick H., *Essay on St. Patrick's Parish*, (undated).
Sheldon, Franklin, *Nonsense, Common Sense, Incense*. 1926.
Thompsonville Press, issues: June 26, 1930; November 21, 1895.
Trumbull, J. Hammond, *Memorial History of Hartford County*. Boston, Edward L. Osgood, 1886, p. 155.
Van Dusen, Albert, *Connecticut*. New York, Random House, 1961.
Warner, Anne S., "The Town That Wanted to Grow". *Country Journal*, April, 1975.
Wright, Lewis, *The Cultural Life of the American Colonies*. New York, Harper Bros., 1957.
Annual Reports, Town of Enfield, Conn.

CHAPTERS 8 AND 9

1. Allen, *History of Enfield, Connecticut*. Lancaster, Penn., Wickersham Printing Co., 1900.
2. Andrews, *The Community Industries of the Shakers*. Charlestown, Mass., Emporium Pubs., 1971 (from N.Y. State Museum Handbook No. 15, 1933).
3. Anon, *A Brief History of the Windsor Locks Canal and the Connecticut River*, courtesy of G.W. Russell.
4. Archives, Greater Enfield Chamber of Commerce.
5. Bishop, *History of American Manufacturers*, 1868.
6. Bridge, Dr. John L., Unpublished notes (1943).
7. Bridge, Rockwell, communication.
8. Campbell, C.L., *A Brief History of Connecticut's Largest Electric and Gas Utility*. Newcomen Society, 1950.
9. Communication from the company described.
10. DeBell, Goggin & Gloor, *German Plastics Practice*, 1946.
11. Dutton, du Pont, *One Hundred and Forty Years*. New York, Charles Scribner's Sons, 1942.
12. Ewing and Norton, *Broadloom and Businessmen*. Cambridge, Mass., Harvard University Press, 1955.
13. Fletcher, *Studies in the History of Enfield, Connecticut*. Litchfield, Conn., Enquirer Press, 1934.
14. Grant, *Yankee Dreamers and Doers*. Pequot Press, 1974.
15. Hazard, George, *Save Your Lives and Property*. Enfield, September, 1853. (Pamphlet probably privately printed.)
16. Jellison, *The Hazard Powder Company and Its Place in the Gunpowder Industry from 1835 to 1913*. Thesis, Bates College, March, 1961.
17. Johnson, Booth, and Pease, *Historical Sketch of the Town of Enfield*. Hartford, Conn., Case, Lockwood and Brainard Company, 1876.
18. Pease, Dr. John Chauncey, *An Historical Sketch of the Town of Enfield*, 1829 (in Allen History).
19. *Springfield Daily News*, December 21, 1875.
20. Stevens, William S., *The Powder Trust, 1872-1912*. Quarterly Journal of Economics, Harvard University Press, November, 1911.
21. Thompsonville Press, February 3, 1938: Special Historical Edition, July, 1911.
22. VanGelder and Schlatter, *History of the Explosives Industry in America*. New York, Columbia University Press, 1927.
23. Encyclopedia Britannica, Volume 21 (1941).

A host of friends have contributed to this record: practically every living person whose name appears in the text. Help has been especially received from Mr. Edward Allen, Mrs. Milo Wilcox, Mr. and Mrs. Raymond Abbe—all noted historians in their own right; town officials, including Town Manager C. Samuel Kissinger, Town Clerk Philip Clarkin, and Town Planner Paul Fox; Mr. John Roddy and Mr. Richard Berozsky, who with Mr. Fox provided or produced photographs; Messrs. Kalk and Johnston of the

Enfield Library; Mr. Dexter Burnham of the Enfield Press; Mr. Walter Wieler and Mr. John Blomquist, now or formerly of Bigelow-Sanford (with Mr. Roddy); Mr. Herman Billings, Mr. Albert Merrill, Mr. C. Rockwell Bridge, Mr. R. Dudley Bridge; the Chester Brainards, Senior and Junior; Mr. George Russell of Connecticut Light & Power Company; Mr. Marcel St. Sauveur of the Chamber of Commerce and Mr. Realtus McCuin of Southern New England Telephone Company. DeBell & Richardson, Inc., kindly furnished secretarial time. The final draft was prepared by my former business associate, Mrs. Mavis Hartung.

Readers will confer a favor by calling attention to the inevitable errors and omissions, that these may not be perpetuated.

Finally, the trust of Miss Ruth Bridge in commissioning this effort is appreciated.

John M. DeBell

CHAPTER 10

Abbe, Jessie Brainard, *Historical Sketch of Enfield* (250th Anniversary of Enfield, 1680-1930). Enfield, Conn., Town of Enfield. June 26, 1930.

Abbey Memorial, Enfield, Conn. East Orange, N.J., The Abbey Printshop, undated.

Alphabetical Listing of Enfield World War I Veterans. Enfield, Conn., Thompsonville Press, May 25, 1939 (Same list reprinted November 11, 1965).

Connecticut Adjutant General's Office, *Record of Connecticut Men in the War of Rebellion, 1861-1865.* Hartford, Conn., The Case, Lockwood & Brainard Co., 1889.

Connecticut Adjutant General's Office, *Record of Service of Connecticut Men in the (1) War of the Revolution; (2) War of 1812; and (3) Mexican War.* Hartford, Conn., The Case, Lockwood & Brainard Co., undated.

Connecticut Adjutant General's Office, *Service Records, Connecticut Men & Women in the Armed Forces During World War I, 1917-20, Vol. I.* New Haven, Conn., United Printing Services, Inc., undated.

Enfield, 250 Years Ago. Enfield, Conn., Thompsonville Press, April 17, 1930.

Reception Honoring World War I Veterans of Enfield, 1917-19. Enfield, Conn., The Town of Enfield, September 1, 1919.

U.S. Veterans Administration, Research Statistics Services, *Veterans in State of Connecticut, 1960.* Washington, D.C., January, 1963.

Van Dusen, Albert E., *Connecticut.* New York, Random House, 1961.

Veterans Honor Roll—Alphabetical Listing of Enfield World War II Veterans. Enfield, Conn., The Town of Enfield, November, 1946.

World Almanac & Book of Facts. New York, Newspaper Enterprise Association, 1976.

Personal interviews of residents of Enfield, Conn.

Many thanks are extended to all persons who assisted the writer in the lengthy and difficult research work that made this article possible—especially to Miss Ruth Bridge of Somers for her guidance; to the staff of the Enfield Central Library, especially to James G. Johnston, assistant director, and Mrs. Alice Wilkerson, reference assistant; to Chairman Robert B. Watton and secretary Anthony Porto, both of the Enfield Veterans' Council; to Dexter S. Burnham, managing editor of the Enfield Press for his kind assistance and cooperation; to Charles Gatto, former director of Enfield Veterans' Services; to William G. Thompson and Mrs. James Brigada for research on World War I; to all post commanders and members of various town Veterans' Posts, who also assisted in many ways.

All information included in the chapter is based on careful research. The writer apologizes for any possible inaccuracies that may have resulted inadvertently from the preparation of this text.

Joseph A. Rarus

CHAPTER 11

All-America City–1970 Citizen Participation Award, National Municipal League and *Look Magazine*.

All-America Cities Competition, National Municipal League and *Look Magazine.*

All-America City, Enfield, Conn. Award Presentation, March 20, 1971.

"All-America Cities 1970," *Look Magazine*, March 23, 1971, p. 74.

"Enfield, All-America City," supplement, *The Hartford Courant*, March 21, 1971.

"Enfield, All-America City," supplement, *The Hartford Times*, May 9, 1971.

Warner, Anne S., "The Town That Wanted To Grow," *Country Journal*, April, 1975, p. 28+.

"A Bedroom Town Awakens to the Urban Crisis," speech before the All-America Jury, August 23, 1970.

ILLUSTRATIONS

The Editor and those directly concerned with the development and production of *The Challenge of Change* are deeply indebted to the many individuals and organizations who so generously loaned photographs, maps, and memorabilia for consideration and possible inclusion in this volume. Final selection was difficult and, inevitably, space limitations precluded the use of many which were of genuine historic interest. A list of those providing material ultimately included appears below.

ORGANIZATIONS

Bigelow-Sanford Carpet Company
Town of Enfield
Enfield Central Library

Enfield Congregational Church
Enfield Historical Society
Enfield Press and Bazaar

INDIVIDUALS

Raymond C. Abbe
Edward C. Allen
Ruth E. Bridge
C. Rockwell Bridge
Edwin H. Collins
John M. DeBell
Raymond S. Epstein
Paul Fox
John C. Kinnear
F. Russell Meyer

Ernest Mokus
Stella P. Olmsted
Howard E. Pierce
Norman C. Roy
Anthony S. Secondo
Robert D. Smyth
Clarissa H. Stow
Robert L. Tanguay
Henry Turbak
Arlene B. Wilcox

C. John Zirolli

Special thanks are due Mr. Zirolli whose fine photography of the local scene over the past several years adds greatly to the quality of the book, particularly in the last section.

The photographs of Enfield Shaker furniture appearing on pages 52 through 55 were furnished through the courtesy of the Women's Auxiliary of the United Cerebral Palsy Association of Greater Hartford, and originally appeared in a special brochure prepared for the Enfield Shaker Antique Show, held in November of 1975.

LIST OF ILLUSTRATIONS

INDEX—NAMES

C

E

D

F

House, Arthur W., 210
Houston, John, 151
Houston, John L., 179, 207
Houston, Sam, 230
Howarth, John, 195
Howe, Edmund G., 178
Howson, John, 101
Hoyt, Joseph B., 123
Hunt, William L., 272, 274
Hunting, Henry, 77
Hunting, William, 77
Hutton, John, 241

I

Iacolino, Carl S., 243
Ingraham, John, 271

J

Jackson, Andrew, 129
Jackson, James, 183
Jarvis, Wilfred, 242
Jefferson, Thomas, 128
Jefferson, 173
Jennison, Ernest, 241
Jennison, Irene, 241
Jezek, 210
Jones, Benjamin, 18, 171, 226
Jones, Donald, 243
Jones, Elija, 33
Johnson, Aholiab, 159
Johnson, L.A., 197
Johnson, S.M., 212
Johnston, Jay, 275
Johnston, James G., 267, 272
Julian, Mrs. Henry, 276

K

Kahn, Lester H., 276
Kaleda, Joe, 80
Karszes, Arthur, 202
Keach, Hosea B., 217
Keller, Mrs. Arthur, 276
Kelly, Father Michael, 166
Kemp, Robert E., 275

Kendall, Hugh, 176
Kennedy, Robert F., 242
Keshan, John, 196
Kibbe, Elisha, 61
Kibbe, Isaac, 27, 66, 97, 228, 229
Kibbee, Charles, 33
Kilcoyne, Father William, 167
Killam, Lot, 26, 174
Killam, Timothy, 174
King, Bert, 212
King, Jabez, 230
King, John, 174, 203
King, Robert W., 274
Kingsbury, Henry, 174
Kinnear, John C., 272, 274
Kissinger, C. Samuel, 213, 251
Knight, Nelson F., 242
Knight, Thomas, 174
Knight, William H., 176
Knowland, Richard G., 182, 183
Koneski, Ted, 275
Koselan, Mrs. John, 276
Kowalchuck, John, 242
Krom, George, 241
Kweder, William, 142

L

Laffargue, Richard, 213
LaGrange, Arthur, 242
LaGrange, Edward, 242
LaJoie, Doris, 275
Lamagna, Francis, 242
Lamagna, Pat J., 242
LaMere, John, 196
Landry, Barbara, 274
Lane, Rev. Robert C., 274
Larabee, Joseph, 242
Larson, Wesley S., 201, 202
Lathrop, F.S. & D., 207
Lauria, Joseph P., 243
Law, Alexander, 203
Law, James B., 203
Law, John, 203
Leanard, James, 196
Leanard, William, 195
Leary, Francis P., 191
Lee, Ann, 31, 32, 33, 43, 172
Lee, Karl D., 154
Lee, Nancy, 31
Lee, William, 31

Murphey, James, 195
Murry, William, 195

N

Nadeau, Joseph F., 241
Needham, Lawton B., 241
Neelands, James, 196
Nelson, Mrs. Pat, 275
Neves, Antonio, Jr., 244
Newcomen, 172
Newhall, W.H., 161
Newton, Henry S., 222
Nickerson, M.H., 201
Niemiec, Clair, 241
Nixon, Richard, 239
Norman, John F., 181
Norris, Lyman, 89
Nottatuck (Notatuck), 17, 171
Nuccio, Harold, 243
Nuccio, Lauree, 271
Nuccio, Sherree, 271

O

O'Connell, Father John B., 168
Offord, Miriam, 38
Oliver, Bruce, 269, 276
Oliver, Elizabeth W., 269, 272, 276
Olko, Tadeus, 213
Olmstead, Albert, 198
Olmstead, John, 203
Olmsted, Mr., 87
Olmsted, John, 174
Olmsted, Joseph, 174
Olmsted, Olin, 86
Olmsted, Simon, 174
Olyneiw, Mrs. Thomas, 275
O'Neil, Mary B., 272
Osenbach, Robert, Jr., 241
Owen, George C., 230
Owens, Loren, 244

P

Pabis, Mitchell, 242
Pace, Stephen, 189, 195
Pallota, Ben, 275

Panek, John, 241
Panella, Mrs. Michael, 276
Pappas, Gus T., 274
Parakilas, Thomas M., 254, 274
Parkman, Edgar H., 154, 163
Parsons, Benjamin, 171
Parsons, Christopher, 63
Parsons, Elisha, 174
Parsons, Luther, 229
Parsons, Philip, 16
Parsons, Sam, 65
Parsons, Samuel, 207
Parsons, Thomas, 228
Partington, Mary, 31
Pasini, Joseph, 90
Patrick, Marion, 38
Patton, George, 235
Payne, Robert D., 209
Pease, Capt., 26
Pease, Enoch, 38
Pease, Elisha Marshall, 230
Pease, Ephraim, 228
Pease, Ezekiel, 146
Pease, Heber, 174
Pease, Horace, 174
Pease, Isaac, 71
Pease, Isaac, Sr., 65
Pease, Isaac T., 207
Pease, Jane, 98
Pease, John, 66, 171, 230
Pease, John Jr., 13, 17, 61, 125, 230
Pease, John Sr., 9, 17, 61
Pease, Joseph, 64
Pease, L.H., 208
Pease, L.T., 174
Pease, Lorain T., 230
Pease, Omar, 37, 69
Pease, Robert, 13, 61, 171
Pease, Ruben, 174
Pears, Jonathan, 146
Peitier, Anna, 275
Pelkey, Mae, 275
Perkins, Robert, 179, 181
Peters, Catherine, 275
Peterson, Elliot, 183
Phillips, John, 44
Pickering, F.A., 206
Piepul, Walter, 242
Pierce, Hiram, 195
Pierce, Howard, 83
Pierce, James, 195
Pierce, Mat, 196
Pilches, the, 90
Pilch, brothers, 91

Shacknow, Julius, 116
Sharapan, Mr., 90
Sharp, Mrs. Charles, 275
Shaw, Frank A., 208
Shea, Bernard, 87
Sheldon, Franklin, 148
Shepherd, James, 31
Sherman, James W., 274, 276
Shlatz, John, 244
Shlatz, Stephen, 244
Simonton, Frank E., 241
Simpson, Alice, 276
Sisisky, Abe, 241
Sisisky, Samuel, 241
Skarzynski, Paul, 242
Slate, James, 38
Slater, Samuel, 173
Smith, Franklin, 198
Smith, George W., Jr., 114
Smith, James E., 207
Smith, James Elnathan, 174
Smith, Maurice, 154
Smith, Miss, 196
Smith, Robert, 258
Smith, Roy, 243
Smith, Sidney C., 241
Smyth, Ann, 275
Smyth, George, 87
Smyth, Richard, 87
Smyth, Mrs. Thomas R., 276
Sokol, Robert, 275
Sokol, Rose G., 272, 274, 275
Soucie, Gilman, 244
Spaulding, A.L., 157, 159
Spencer, John, 198
Spencer, Leroy, 197
Spencer, Wells, 197
Springborn, Robert, 201
Stanley, 218
Stanley, Abraham, 31, 32
Staples, Harold A., 258
Starr, S. Leger, 212
Steele, Treat, 197
Stevens, Richard, Jr., 275
Stevens, Kenneth W., 241
Steward, Rev. Melville, 112
Stillman, Samuel A., 174
Stocker, Jacob, 196
Stone, E. Wadsworth, 183
Stone, F.M., 98
Stowe, J.D., 197, 198
Stratton, B., 196
Strecker, Laurence F., 241

Stroud, Thomas, 38
Strout, Leroy A., 269, 276
Sullivan, John L., 241
Sullivan, L. Lawrence, 242
Sullivan, Leo, 242
Sullivan, Ronald, Jr., 243
Sunderland, Richard, 85
Sweetser, John A., 182, 183
Swiatowski, Stanley, 242
Syberla, Charles, 154

T

Tait, Joann, 275
Tanguay, Phyllis L., 274
Tanguay, Robert J., 274
Tanguay, Robert L., 261, 272, 274
Tansley, George, 203
Tansley, William, 197
Tarnowicz, Alexander, 208
Tart, Mrs., 26
Tatoian, Mrs. James, 276
Taylor, O., 196
Tedesco, Francis, 142
Terry, Alfred Howe, 231, 232
Terry, Captain, 65
Terry, Christopher H., 174
Terry, Ebenezer, Jr., 66
Terry, Edward, 232
Terry, Ephraim, 64, 228
Terry, Geer, 174
Terry, Henry, 174
Terry, Nathaniel, 228, 231, 232
Terry, Samuel, 125, 171, 232
Terry, Selah, 174
Terry, Solomon, 174
Tesla, 218
Thompson, 174, 177
Thompson, Edward N., 6, 7
Thompson, Henry, 174
Thompson, H.G., 207
Thompson, Henry G., 178
Thompson, Martin E., 6, 7
Thompson, Matthew, 174
Thompson, Nancy, 275
Thompson, Orrin, 99, 100, 101, 105, 130, 174, 175, 176, 178
Thompson, Robert, 175
Thompson, W.G., 207
Thompson, William G., 233, 241
Tierney, Martin J., 242

SUBJECT INDEX

Long Hollow Road, 191
Longmeadow, 11, 211
Longmeadow Brook, 17, 125
Look Magazine, 249
Loomis, Denslow and Co., 186
Lord, A.T., 207
Louisberg, 226
Louisberg Expedition, 226
Lowell, 181
Lowell Manufacturing Co., 176
Lowell Textile Complex, 181
Lozier Bicycle Works, 180
Ludlow, 11
Lutheran Church of Our Redeemer, 110

M

Main Street, Thompsonville, 222
Manchester (CT), 112, 221
Manchester, England, 31
Manning Road, 209, 210
Manufacturing Service Co., 212
Marshall Field, 178
Massachusetts, 124, 125, 211
Massachusetts Bay Colony, 11, 144
Massachusetts Institute of Technology, 163
6th Massachusetts Minutemen, 255
McGuire Air Force Band, 260
McLane Report of 1932, 176
Mechanic's Hall, 102
Memorial Day, 225
Memorial Hall, 116
Men's Dart League, 119
Mental Health Clinic Opened, 143
Merchant Marine, 233
Methodists, 30, 128
Methodist Church, 7
Mexico, 230
Mexican War, 230
Middletown, 22
Militia, the, 230
Miller, Carl E., 207
Milton, Kent, England, 203
Missouri, Synod, 110
Mohawks, 8
Mohegan Indians, 6
Moody Road, 205
Mount of Olives (Holy Hill), 42
Mount Tom, 8
Mullen Road, 220

N

Nagasaki, 236
National Bicentennial Symbol, 253
National Council of Churches, 109
National Municipal League, 249, 250
National Printing Co., 202, 207
National Register of Historic Places, 263
Negroes, 25, 26
Neighborhood Youth Center, 160
New Britain, 222
New England, 33, 202, 226, 229
New England Association of Colleges and Secondary Schools, 168
New England Entrance Certificate Board, 163
New England Milk Producers Association, 85
New Haven, 186, 218
New Haven Coke Co., 221
New Haven, Hartford and Springfield Railroad, 207
New High School (1925), 163
New Jersey, 260
New King Street, 163
New Lebanon, 32, 34
New Light Baptists, 32
New London, defense of, 229
New York, 31, 32, 186, 189
New York, New Haven and Hartford Railroad Co., 222
New York State, 186
Niskeyuna, 31, 32
Norfolk, Nebraska, 209
North Congregational Church, 97
North Main Street, 160, 225
North Maple Street, 206
North River Street, 209
North School, 149, 159
North Vietnam, 238
Northern Connecticut Light and Power Co., 208, 221, 222
Nutmeg Building Supply, 208

O

Oak Street, 197, 203
Odd Fellows' Hall, 102
Oliver Road, 18
Old King Street, 100

15⁰⁰ SIGNED
Presentation
Copy